A Guide to the Crim Investigations

CL Ryan LLB, LLM
Barrister and Solicitor (NZ)
Reader in Law, City University
S Savla, BA, LLM, Barrister
Lecturer in Law, City University
G Scanlan, LLB, Solicitor
Senior Lecturer in Law, City University

Butterworths
London, Edinburgh, Dublin
1996

United Kingdom	Butterworths a Division of Reed Elsevier (UK) Ltd, Halsbury House, 35 Chancery Lane, LONDON WC2A 1EL and 4 Hill Street, EDINBURGH EH2 3JZ
Australia	Butterworths, SYDNEY, MELBOURNE, BRISBANE, ADELAIDE, PERTH, CANBERRA and HOBART
Canada	Butterworth Canada Ltd, TORONTO and VANCOUVER
Ireland	Butterworth (Ireland) Ltd, DUBLIN
Malaysia	Malayan Law Journal Sdn Bhd, KUALA LUMPUR
New Zealand	Butterworths of New Zealand Ltd, WELLINGTON and AUCKLAND
Singapore	Reed Elsevier (Singapore) Pte Ltd, SINGAPORE
South Africa	Butterworths Publishers Pty Ltd, DURBAN
USA	Michie, CHARLOTTESVILLE, Virginia

All rights reserved. No part of this publication may be reproduced in any material form (including photocopying or storing it in any medium by electronic means and whether or not transiently or incidentally to some other use of this publication) without the written permission of the copyright owner except in accordance with the provisions of the Copyright, Designs and Patents Act 1988 or under the terms of a licence issued by the Copyright Licensing Agency Ltd, 90 Tottenham Court Road, London, England, W1P 9HE. Application for the copyright owner's written permission to reproduce any part of this publication should be addressed to the publisher.

Warning: The doing of an unauthorised act in relation to a copyright work may result in both a civil claim for damages and criminal prosecution.

© Reed Elsevier (UK) Ltd 1996

Crown copyright material is reproduced by permission of the Controller of HMSO.

Chris Ryan, Sandeep Savla and Gary Scanlan have asserted their rights under the Copyright, Designs and Patents Act 1988 to be identified as the authors of this work

A CIP catalogue record for this book is available from the British Library.

ISBN 0 406 99249 5

Printed and bound in Great Britain by Clays Ltd, St Ives plc

Preface

The general public's perception of the criminal justice system is that it is unwieldy, inefficient and in need of reform. The recommendations of the Royal Commission on Criminal Justice (the Runciman Report) were rational steps towards meeting these concerns. The Criminal Procedure and Investigations Act 1996 is an enactment whose genesis was, at least in part, inspired by the Commission's report. It is to be hoped that the Act reflects a commitment by Government and the Home Office to a continuous process of active reform in this area of the law.

This book is intended to provide practitioners and others involved in the operation of the criminal justice system with a clear, straightforward analysis and explanation of this new legislation. Cross-referencing to the statute itself, the full text of which is included, should make this book useful for legal practitioners, court officers, the police and other investigative and prosecuting authorities and lay people alike.

The authors enjoy an efficient and congenial relationship with the publishers and are grateful, in particular, to the Statutory Materials department. Thanks must also go to Mrs Christine Trinder and Mrs Lynn Childs of the Law Department, City University, who managed to provide invaluable secretarial assistance amongst a busy schedule.

One of the authors would like to give special thanks to "Elliott" whose first birthday corresponded with the commissioning of this work.

C L Ryan
S Savla
G Scanlan
September 1996

Contents

		Page
Preface		v
Table of Statutes		ix
Table of Cases		xv
1	Introduction	1
2	The disclosure provisions	4
3	Criminal investigations	16
4	Preparatory hearings	28
5	Rulings	35
6	Committal and transfer	39
7	Magistrates' courts	49
8	Miscellaneous and general provisions	56

Appendix

Criminal Procedure and Investigations Act 1996
(with annotations)   67

Index   155

Table of Statutes

References in this Table to *Statutes* are to Halsbury's Statutes of England (Fourth Edition) showing the volume and page at which the annotated text of the Act may be found.

	PARA
Administration of Justice (Miscellaneous Provisions) Act 1933	
s 2(2)	6.30
(b)	2.15; 8.21
Attachment of Earnings Act 1971	
s 3(3B), (3C)	7.22
Bankers' Books Evidence Act 1879	
s 4, 5	6.29
Children and Young Persons Act 1969	
Sch 5	6.33
Contempt of Court Act 1981	2.32; 8.7
s 4(2)	8.7
Sch 1	
paras 4, 4A	8.7
Criminal Justice Act 1948	
s 41	6.31
Criminal Justice Act 1967	
s 9	8.27
11	2.14
Criminal Justice Act 1972	
s 46	6.34
Criminal Justice Act 1982	
s 71(1)	6.17
Criminal Justice Act 1987	1.8; 4.1, 4.9, 4.24; 5.15, 5.16; 6.3, 6.8; 8.31
s 4	2.3, 2.15
7	4.6, 4.9
(1)	4.25
8	4.9
9	4.9
(3)	4.25
(6)	8.33
(11), (12)	4.24
10	4.9
11	4.30; 8.33
Criminal Justice Act 1988	
s 11(3A)	6.45
13(7)	6.46
16(6A)	6.47
20(8A)	6.47
23(5)	6.40
24(5)	6.40
26, 27	6.41
30(4A)	6.42
32	8.14
(3C)–(3E), (6A)–(6D)	8.14
32A	6.43
40	6.44
159	8.13

	PARA
Criminal Justice Act 1991	1.8; 6.8
s 53	2.3, 2.15
Criminal Justice and Public Order Act 1994	1.8; 4.19; 6.3
s 34, 36, 37	6.7
44	6.3, 6.7; 7.4
(3)	6.9
51	1.12
(1)	8.3
56	8.16
80	7.4
Sch 4	6.7; 7.4
Pt II	
para 72	6.9
Sch 5	
Pt I	7.4
Sch 11	6.7
Criminal Justice (Scotland) Act 1995	8.32
Criminal Law Amendment Act 1867	
s 6, 7	6.28
Criminal Procedure and Investigations Act 1996	3.14
Pt I (ss 1–21)	1.2; 2.1, 2.2, 2.4, 2.5, 2.6, 2.7, 2.8, 2.11, 2.13, 2.31, 2.33; 3.1, 3.6, 3.13, 3.15, 3.20, 3.25, 3.26, 3.37; 4.20; 5.18; 8.37
s 1	2.2
(1)(a)–(c)	2.2
(2)	2.3
(a)–(e)	2.3
(3)	2.4
(4)	2.6
(5)	2.4
2(2), (3)	2.7
3	2.8, 2.9, 2.15, 2.18, 2.24
(1)	2.8
(a)	1.2; 2.8
(b)	2.8
(2)	2.8
(3)	2.9, 2.19, 2.23
(4), (5)	2.9, 2.16, 2.19, 2.23
(6)	2.8, 2.10; 3.13
(7)	2.11
(8)	2.12
4	2.13
5	2.14, 2.15, 2.16, 2.19, 2.23, 2.24
(1)	2.15
(b)	2.15

Table of Statutes

	PARA
Criminal Procedure and Investigations Act 1966—*contd*	
s 5(2)–(4)	2.15
(6)	2.15, 2.18
(a)–(c)	2.15
(7)	2.17, 2.18; 8.33
(8)	2.17, 2.18
6	2.18, 2.19, 2.23, 2.24
(1)(a), (b)	2.18
(3)	2.18
7	2.24
(1)	4.25
(2)(b)	2.20
(3), (4)	2.19
(5)	3.13
(6), (7)	2.20
8	2.22
(1)–(4)	2.21
(5), (6)	2.22
9	2.15, 2.23; 3.1, 3.37
(1)–(5), (7)	2.23
(8)	2.23; 3.13
(9)	2.23
10	2.24
(2), (3)	2.24
11(1)	2.25
(2)	2.26
(3)	2.25
(4)	2.26
(5)	2.25
12	2.17, 2.18
(1), (2)	2.12
(3)(a)–(g)	2.12
(5)	2.12
(a), (b)	2.12
13(1), (2)	2.12
14	2.28, 2.30
(3), (4)	2.28
15	2.29, 2.30
(4)	2.29
(5)(b)	2.29
16	2.30
17	2.31, 2.32
18	2.31, 2.32
(1), (2)	2.32
19(1)	2.33
20(3), (4)	2.34
21(1)	2.4
(2)	2.5; 3.13, 3.20
(3)	2.4
Pt II (ss 22–27)	1.3; 2.8, 2.13; 3.1, 3.3; 8.37
s 22	3.3
(1)–(3)	3.3
23	3.41

	PARA
Criminal Procedure and Investigations Act 1966—*contd*	
s 23(1)–(5)	3.4
(6)	3.5
(8)	3.4
24(3)	2.13
25	3.2, 3.41; 8.36
(1)–(4)	3.2
26(1)	3.38
(2)–(4)	3.40
Pt III (ss 28–38)	1.5, 1.6, 1.7; 2.16; 4.1, 4.2, 4.4, 4.15; 5.1, 5.8, 5.15, 5.16; 8.31
s 29	4.7, 4.9
(1)	4.7
(2)	4.6, 4.25
(3)	4.9
(4)	4.7
31	4.11
(2), (3)	4.11
(4)(a)	4.11
(5)	4.11
(6), (7)	4.12, 4.18
(8)	4.18
(9)	4.12
(11)	4.21
32	4.13
34	4.19; 8.31
35(1)–(3)	4.22
36	4.19, 4.23
37	4.19; 8.31
(1), (2)	4.27
(3), (4), (6)	4.28
(9)	4.27
38	8.31
(1)–(3)	4.29
Pt IV (ss 39–43)	1.5, 1.6, 1.7; 4.1, 4.2, 4.14; 5.1, 5.8
s 39	5.8
(3)	5.11
40	5.8
(1)–(3)	5.11
(4)	5.12
(6)	5.10, 5.12
41(1)–(6)	5.13
42	5.13
Pt V (ss 44–47)	1.8; 4.2; 6.3; 8.16
s 44(2)	6.7
46	6.9
47	6.10
Pt VI (ss 48–53)	1.9, 1.10; 7.1, 7.2
s 48	7.2, 7.3
49	7.1
(2)	7.4, 7.14

Table of Statutes

	PARA
Criminal Procedure and Investigations Act 1966—*contd*	
s 49(4)	7.7
50	7.2, 7.15
51	7.2, 7.17
52	7.1
(1), (2)	7.20
(3)	8.34
53	7.2, 7.22
Pt VII (ss 54–81)	1.11, 1.12, 1.13; 8.1
s 54	8.1, 8.2, 8.3, 8.5, 8.7
(1)	8.3
(2)	8.5
(3)	8.6
(4)	8.5, 8.7
(5)	8.5
(6)	8.3
55	8.1, 8.2, 8.5
(1)–(3)	8.5, 8.7
(4)	8.5, 8.6, 8.7
(5), (6)	8.6
(7)	8.34
56	8.1, 8.2, 8.5
(1), (2)	8.6
57	8.1, 8.2, 8.5, 8.7
(1), (2)	8.7
58	8.8, 8.9, 8.13
(3), (4)	8.9
(5)	8.10
(7), (8)	8.8, 8.9
(9)	8.8
59	8.13
(1)–(3)	8.11
60	8.13
(1)–(5)	8.12
61	8.13
(3)	8.13, 8.15
(6)	8.13
62	8.14
(1), (2)	8.14
63(2)	8.15
64	8.16, 8.18
65	8.19
66	8.20
(3)	8.25
67	8.25
68	6.49; 8.26
69	8.27
70	8.28
71	4.17; 8.29, 8.30
(1)–(3)	5.16
72	8.31
73	8.32
74	2.14; 8.33
75	8.34

	PARA
Criminal Procedure and Investigations Act 1966—*contd*	
s 76	8.35
77	8.36
(5)	8.36
78	8.37
(2)	8.37
79	8.38
(1)	4.30
Sch 1	6.3, 6.10
Pt I (paras 1–13)	6.48
para 3	6.11
4	6.12, 6.17
5	6.19
6	6.20
7	6.21
8	6.22
9	6.18, 6.23, 6.26
10	6.24
11	6.25, 6.28
12	6.26
13	6.27
Pt II (paras 14–38)	6.10, 6.48
para 14	6.28
15, 16	6.29
17	6.30
18	6.31
20	6.32
21	6.33
22	6.34
23	6.35
24	6.36
25	6.37
26	6.38
27	6.39
28, 29	6.40
30, 31	6.41
32	6.42
33	6.43
34	6.44
35	6.45
36	6.46
37, 38	6.47
Pt III (para 39)	6.10, 6.48
Sch 2	6.49
Sch 3	8.31
Sch 4	8.38
Sch 5	6.18
Criminal Procedure (Attendance of Witnesses) Act 1965	8.19
s 2	8.20
(1)–(3)	8.20
(4)–(7)	8.21
2A	8.20, 8.22, 8.25
2B	8.20

Table of Statutes

	PARA
Criminal Procedure (Attendance of Witnesses) Act 1965—*contd*	
s 2B(1)	8.22
2C(1), (2)	8.23
(4)	8.20, 8.23
(6), (7)	8.23
(9)	8.24
2D, 2E	8.25
3(1A)	8.25
4(1)	8.25
Criminal Procedure (Scotland) Act 1995	8.32
s 65(1)	8.32
Sch 9	8.32
Insolvency Act 1986	
s 235, 236	3.29
Interception of Communications Act 1985	
s 2	2.11, 2.20, 2.22, 2.23; 3.5, 3.26
6	2.11
Justices of the Peace Act 1979	
s 53 (1A)	8.28
Law of Libel Amendment Act 1888	
s 3, 8	8.13
Magistrates' Courts Act 1980	6.3, 6.10; 8.19, 8.35
s 5	7.1, 7.20, 7.21
5A	6.11, 6.18, 6.34
(3)	6.26
5B	6.11, 6.12, 6.14, 6.26, 6.33, 6.34
(2)–(5)	6.12
(6)	6.12, 6.13
5C	6.11, 6.13, 6.14
(3)–(6)	6.13
5D	6.11, 6.14, 6.40
5E	6.11, 6.15
5F	6.11, 6.16, 6.41
6(1)	6.12, 6.17
(2)	6.17, 6.18
9	7.9
(1)	7.7
10(1)	7.1, 7.20, 7.21
13(2), (2A), (2B)	7.3
17A	7.4, 7.6, 7.7, 7.9, 7.10, 7.13, 7.14
(2)	7.6
(3)	7.7
(4)	7.7
(b)	7.8
(5)–(8)	7.7
17B	7.4, 7.6, 7.7, 7.9, 7.10, 7.13, 7.14
(1)(b)–(d)	7.6
(2)(a)–(d)	7.7

	PARA
Magistrates Court Act 1980—*contd*	
s 17B(3)	7.7
17C	7.1, 7.4, 7.14, 7.20, 7.21
(3)	7.7
18	7.13
(1)	7.7
(4)	7.1, 7.20, 7.21
19	7.7, 7.12
(2)(a)	7.7
(3)	7.10
20	7.7
(3)(b)	7.4
21	7.4, 7.7
22, 23	7.7
25	6.19
28	6.20
38	7.9, 7.11
(2)	7.8, 7.12
82	7.16
87	7.15
(1), (3)	7.15, 7.16
97(1)	7.17, 7.18, 7.19
(2)	7.18, 7.19
(2B), (2C)	7.17, 7.19
97A	6.21
(7)	6.22
102	6.12, 6.18, 6.23, 6.26, 6.33, 6.34
103	6.24
105	6.25, 6.28
106	6.26
127(1)	8.6
128(1A)	7.14
(c)	7.20
(3A)	7.14, 7.20, 7.21
(c)	7.20
(3C), (3E)	7.14
128A	7.20, 7.21
(1)	7.20
130(1)	7.14
144(1)	2.33, 2.34
Sch 3	6.27
Offences Against the Person Act 1861	
s 44, 45	8.7
Perjury Act 1911	
s 1	8.3
Police and Criminal Evidence Act 1984	
s 63A	8.17
(1), (1A)	8.16
66	3.9
67	3.40
(9)	3.38
71	6.36
76(9)	6.37
78(3)	6.38
Sch 3	6.39

Table of Statutes

	PARA
Powers of Criminal Courts Act 1973	
s 35	7.22
Prosecution of Offences Act 1985	
s 22	5.16; 8.29
(11)	8.30
Road Traffic Act 1988	
s 7(3)	8.15
(bb)	8.15
Sexual Offences (Amendment) Act 1976	
s 3	6.35
Supreme Court Act 1981	
s 84(1)	2.33
Theft Act 1968	
s 27	6.31
28	6.32
Transport and Works Act 1992	
s 31(4)	8.15
War Crimes Act 1991	6.9

Table of Cases

A

Arrows Ltd (No 4), Re [1993] Ch 452, [1993] 3 All ER 861, [1993] 3 WLR 513, [1993] BCLC 1222, [1993] BCC 473, [1993] 22 LS Gaz R 37, [1993] NLJR 688, CA; affd sub nom Hamilton v Naviede [1995] 2 AC 75, [1994] 3 All ER 814, [1994] 3 WLR 656, [1994] 2 BCLC 738, [1994] BCC 641, [1994] NLJR 1203, HL...   3.29
A-G's Guidelines (1981) 74 Cr App Rep 302, CA 2.1, 3.13, 3.31

D

D (Infants), Re [1970] 1 All ER 1088, [1970] 1 WLR 599, 68 LGR 183, 134 JP 387, 114 Sol Jo 188, CA 3.30

E

Evans v Chief Constable of Surrey [1988] QB 588, [1988] 3 WLR 127, 132 Sol Jo 898, [1988] 28 LS Gaz R 45, sub nom Evans v Chief Constable of Surrey Constabulary (A-G intervening) [1989] 2 All ER 594 ....   3.27

G

G (a minor) (social worker: disclosure), Re [1996] 2 All ER 65, [1996] 1 FLR 276, [1996] Fam Law 143, [1995] 44 LS Gaz R 30, [1996] NLJR 85, [1995] TLR 588, 140 Sol Jo LB 10, CA 3.30
Goodwin v Chief Constable of Lancashire [1992] 44 LS Gaz R 35, CA 3.26

M

Makanjuola v Metropolitan Police Comr [1992] 3 All ER 617, [1989] NLJR 468, CA: 3.32
Marcel v Metropolitan Police Comr [1992] Ch 225, [1991] 1 All ER 845, [1991] 2 WLR 1118; on appeal [1992] Ch 225, [1992] 1 All ER 72, [1992] 2 WLR 50, CA ...   3.23
Marks v Beyfus (1890) 25 QBD 494, 55 JP 182, 59 LJQB 479, 17 Cox CC 196, 38 WR 705, 63 LT 733, 6 TLR 406, CA 3.24

O

O'Sullivan v Metropolitan Police Comr (1995) 139 Sol Jo LB 164 ....   3.27

P

Practice Direction (plea and direction hearings) [1995] 4 All ER 379, [1995] 1 WLR 1318, [1995] 2 Cr App Rep 600 ....   5.6
Practice Note (crown court: defendant's evidence) [1995] 2 All ER 499, sub nom Practice Direction [1995] 1 WLR 657, [1995] 2 Cr App Rep 192, CA 4.19

Table of Cases

R

R v Bayliss (1993) 98 Cr App Rep 235, 157 JP 1062, [1994] Crim LR 687, CA	3.38
R v Brown (1987) 87 Cr App Rep 52, [1987] Crim LR 239, CA	3.26
R v Brown [1994] 1 WLR 1599, [1994] 31 LS Gaz R 36, 138 Sol Jo LB 146, CA: .	3.15, 3.31
R v Chief Constable of West Midlands Police, ex p Wiley [1995] 1 AC 274, [1994] 3 All ER 420, [1994] 3 WLR 433, 159 LG Rev 181, [1994] 40 LS Gaz R 35, [1994] NLJR 1008, 138 Sol Jo LB 156, HL...	3.18
R v Daley (1987) 87 Cr App Rep 52, [1988] Crim LR 239, CA................	3.26
R v Davis [1993] 2 All ER 643, sub nom R v Johnson [1993] 1 WLR 613, 97 Cr App Rep 110, [1993] Crim LR 689, [1993] 10 LS Gaz R 35, 137 Sol Jo LB 19, CA:	2.1, 3.35
R v Director of Serious Fraud Office, ex p Saunders [1988] Crim LR 837, [1988] NLJR 243..	3.38
R v Gunawardena [1990] 2 All ER 477, sub nom Re Gunawardena, Harbutt and Banks [1990] 1 WLR 703, 91 Cr App Rep 55, 154 JP 396, 134 Sol Jo 517, [1990] 10 LS Gaz R 35, CA...	4.24, 4.25
R v Horseferry Road Magistrates' Court, ex p Bennett (No 2) [1994] 1 All ER 289, 99 Cr App Rep 123, [1994] Crim LR 370	3.33
R v Hunt [1994] STC 819, [1994] Crim LR 747, CA........................	4.24
R v Jennings (1993) 98 Cr App Rep 308, CA..............................	4.24
R v Johnson [1989] 1 All ER 121, [1988] 1 WLR 1377, 88 Cr App Rep 131, [1988] Crim LR 831, 132 Sol Jo 1430, CA..	3.25
R v Keane [1994] 2 All ER 478, [1994] 1 WLR 746, 99 Cr App Rep 1, [1995] Crim LR 225, 138 Sol Jo LB 76, CA..	2.1, 2.10
R v Lindley (23 September 1992, unreported), CA.........................	4.24
R v McCay [1991] 1 All ER 232, [1990] 1 WLR 645, 91 Cr App Rep 84, 154 JP 621, [1990] Crim LR 338, 134 Sol Jo 606, [1990] 19 LS Gaz R 39, CA	3.15
R v Maxwell (21 December 1994, unreported).............................	4.24
R v Maxwell (9 February 1995, unreported)	4.24, 4.25
R v Moore (5 February 1991, unreported), CA...........................	4.24
R v Preston [1994] 2 AC 130, [1993] 4 All ER 638, [1993] 3 WLR 891, 98 Cr App Rep 405, [1994] Crim LR 676, [1994] 3 LS Gaz R 46, [1993] NLJR 1601, 137 Sol Jo LB 256, HL..	2.11, 3.4
R v Rankine [1986] QB 861, [1986] 2 All ER 566, [1986] 2 WLR 1075, 83 Cr App Rep 18, [1986] Crim LR 464, 130 Sol Jo 315, [1986] LS Gaz R 1225, CA	3.25
R v Sanusi [1992] Crim LR 43, CA.....................................	3.38
R v Saunders (5 February 1990, unreported); affd [1990] Crim LR 597, CA	4.24
R v Smith (Gerald) (18 August 1993, unreported), CA	4.24
R v Smith (Wallace) [1994] 1 WLR 1396, 99 Cr App Rep 233, CA	4.24
R v Smithson [1994] 1 WLR 1052, [1994] Crim LR 913, CA...............	4.24, 4.25
R v Turner [1995] 3 All ER 432, [1995] 1 WLR 264, [1995] 2 Cr App Rep 94, CA .	3.24
R v Virani (22 September 1993, unreported), CA..........................	4.24
R v W(E) [1996] 28 LS Gaz R 29, 140 Sol Jo LB 168, CA	3.17
R v W(G) [1996] 28 LS Gaz R 29, 140 Sol Jo LB 168, CA...................	3.17
R v Ward [1993] 2 All ER 577, [1993] 1 WLR 619, 96 Cr App Rep 1, [1993] Crim LR 312, [1992] 27 LS Gaz R 34, [1992] NLJR 859, 136 Sol Jo LB 191, CA	2.1, 3.22
RSPCA v Eager [1995] Crim LR 59	3.38

T

Taylor v Anderton (1986) Times, 21 October.............................	3.28

1 Introduction

BACKGROUND

1.1 In moving the Criminal Procedure and Investigations Bill in the House of Lords,[1] the Minister of State for the Home Office, Baroness Blatch, outlined the general purpose of the Bill. This was to implement proposals contained in three consultation papers issued by the Government, namely—'Disclosure' (May 1995) (Cm 2864); 'Improving the Effectiveness of Pre-Trial Hearings in the Crown Court' (July 1995) (Cm 2924); and 'Mode of Trial' (July 1995) (Cm 2908). In particular, the Bill represented the Government's response to the Report of the Royal Commission on Criminal Justice (1993) (Cm 2263) (the Runciman Commission).

---

1   HL 2R, 27 November 1995, col 462.

OUTLINE OF THE ACT

1.2 Part I of the Act provides for a statutory scheme imposing a duty upon both the prosecution and the defence to make disclosure. The Act provides for a 'staged approach' to disclosure which it is hoped will prevent abuse either by the Crown or the defence, which was a feature of the common law rules of disclosure (see para 2.1). The structure of Pt I is as follows. Under a staged process, the prosecution must disclose material which the Crown did not intend to adduce at the trial, but which might undermine the case for the prosecution ('primary' disclosure); this may be described as 'unused material' (see s 3(1)(a)). The defence in response must adduce the general nature of its case ('compulsory' disclosure). Following this disclosure by the defence, the prosecution must then disclose any additional 'unused material' which may be of assistance to the defence ('secondary' disclosure).

1.3 Part II of the Act, inter alia, imposes a duty upon the Home Secretary to prepare a code of practice to regulate the conduct of the police in relation to unused material which is to be disclosed by the prosecution. This Part determines the general content of the code of practice, and the matters with which the code may deal.

1.4 The effect of the code of practice will be to require the police to make available to the prosecution all material which may be relevant to an investigation. It is, however, the prosecution which will make decisions as to which material must be disclosed to the defence. Although the code of practice is principally for the guidance of the police, other parties or organisations involved in the investigation of crime must have regard to the code. The code of practice must be laid before Parliament by the Home Secretary before it can come into effect.

1.5 Parts III and IV make significant improvements to pre-trial procedures. Part III of the Act empowers a judge of the Crown Court to order a preparatory hearing in a prosecution where it is anticipated that the substantive trial may be of some length or complexity. In these cases the judge must be of the opinion that such a procedure will

1.5 *Introduction*

produce substantial benefits as regards the substantive trial. The preparatory hearing in these cases will be similar in nature to those held in respect of trials involving issues of serious or complex fraud. The scheme of preparatory hearings is as follows—

(a) A Crown Court judge may order either the prosecution or the defence to provide a statement of its case.
(b) The judge may seek by a range of orders to narrow the issues of dispute between the prosecution and defence.
(c) The judge may make rulings on the admissibility of evidence at the substantive trial, or on any point of law.
(d) Any such rulings are subject to a right of appeal.

If either the prosecution or the defence fails to comply with any requirement imposed by the judge at a preparatory hearing the recalcitrant party will be subject to sanctions prescribed under the authority of Pt III.

1.6 Part IV empowers a Crown Court judge to make a binding ruling on the admissibility of evidence at the substantive trial, or a ruling on any other point of law in any case at a pre-trial hearing. This judicial power is distinct from the power of a Crown Court judge to make orders at a preparatory hearing under Pt III of the Act. The principal difference between the two judicial powers is that the judge may vary any ruling made under Pt IV of the Act, although there is no appeal against any such ruling.

1.7 The Government's intention is that the provisions contained in Pts III and IV will encourage more thorough preparation of cases, and make trials more efficient and less time-consuming for jurors and witnesses.

1.8 Part V principally amends provisions in the Criminal Justice and Public Order Act 1994, the Criminal Justice Act 1987, and the Criminal Justice Act 1991 which relate to committal proceedings and transfer for trial.

1.9 Part VI of the Act initiates reforms with regard to procedure in magistrates' courts. This Part of the Act deals with a number of recommendations for reform espoused during the review of magistrates' courts procedures in 1992. It provides inter alia for an accused to indicate his intention as to plea before a decision is taken as to whether his case, if it is triable either way, is to be tried in a magistrates' court, or in the Crown Court.

1.10 Part VI also effects reforms in the law in respect of juveniles who are on remand awaiting summary trial or transfer. Remand procedures for juveniles and adults are more closely assimilated.

1.11 Part VII contains a number of disparate, miscellaneous and general provisions. This Part provides inter alia for the possibility of the re-trial of a case which resulted in the acquittal of the defendant if the acquittal has been tainted by a subsequent conviction of persons for interfering with the witnesses or jurors in the original trial. The court which has convicted must certify that there is a real possibility that the acquittal of the defendant in the original trial would not have happened but for the interference with witnesses or jurors. The High Court must, following the certification, make an order quashing the acquittal in the original trial in order that the re-trial can take place. In addition, the court which made the certification and the High Court must be satisfied that a re-trial would not in any way be contrary to the interests of justice.

1.12 Part VII implements a recommendation of the Runciman Commission,[1] although the provisions in the Act are wider than the recommendation in that the new statutory provisions empower the courts to certify and to order a re-trial following an acquittal where witnesses in the original trial have been intimidated. The Runciman Commission's recommendations were restricted to empowering judicial ordering of a re-trial to cases where jurors in the original trial had been intimidated or bribed (so-called jury nobbling). In this respect, Pt VII of the Act supplements the offence of witness intimidation introduced by the Criminal Justice and Public Order Act 1994, s 51.

1   Royal Commission on Criminal Justice (Cm 2263), Ch 8, para 36.

1.13 Part VII of the Act also enables a judge to impose reporting restrictions on false or irrelevant allegations made in a speech or in mitigation. Finally this Part provides that custody time limits are to operate up to the start of the substantive trial, and not merely up to arraignment, as was the case prior to the Act.

2 The disclosure provisions

BACKGROUND

2.1 Prior to the 1996 Act the system of pre-trial disclosure in criminal trials was subject to considerable difficulties. Notwithstanding the judicial recognition of the duty of the prosecution to make disclosure, the law required the prosecution to disclose to the defence any material which might be relevant to an issue at the trial, whether or not such material had any bearing on the nature of the defence which the accused adduced at the trial.[1] Furthermore it was possible for the defence to seek the disclosure of vast quantities of material which could be invoked as a tactic inter alia to delay the onset of the trial, or to provide an opportunity for the defence to uncover sensitive material which the prosecution could not have disclosed without the necessity of abandoning any proceedings. The Runciman Commission recommended the creation of a statutory scheme for disclosure in stages, to be supported by subordinate legislation or a code of practice. Part I of the Act follows in essence the recommendations of the Commission, but differs in detail in two important respects as follows—

(a) Where the Commission proposed a test for disclosure which was more wide-ranging than the previous requirements for disclosure, the scheme in Pt I of the Act operates in respect of material not previously disclosed which in the prosecutor's opinion might undermine the case for the prosecution.

(b) The Commission's recommendations for disclosure by the defence would have imposed upon the defence the obligation to give only the most general indication of the nature of the defence case. The provisions of Pt I of the Act, however, require the defence to provide detailed information so as to clarify in advance the essential issues between the prosecution and the defence which are to be determined at the trial.[2]

---

1 For the disclosure of 'unused material' to the defence in cases to be tried on indictment, see the *A-G's Guidelines (1) on the Disclosure of Information to the Defence in Cases to be Tried on Indictment* (1981) 74 Cr App Rep 302, CA; *R v Ward* [1993] 1 WLR 619, CA; *R v Davis* [1993] 2 All ER 643; *R v Keane* [1994] 1 WLR 746. For a full consideration of disclosure in criminal trials prior to the Act, see the Report of the Royal Commission on Criminal Justice (Cm 2263), Ch 6, paras 33–73.
2 Royal Commission on Criminal Justice (Cm 2263), Ch 6, paras 33–73.

APPLICATION OF PART I

2.2 Section 1 of the 1996 Act defines the circumstances in which the disclosure procedures prescribed by Pt I of the Act will operate. Disclosure will apply to both summary trials and to trials on indictment. Where a person is charged with a summary offence, and the court proceeds to summary trial, the prosecution will be obliged to make primary disclosure in respect of any charge to which the accused pleads not guilty (s 1(1)(a)). It should be noted that proceeding to trial is a requirement for disclosure by the prosecution in such cases, and not merely the entering of a not guilty plea by the defendant. Disclosure will also take place where a person who has attained the age of 18 is charged with an offence which is triable either way, and which proceeds to trial in a magistrates' court (s 1(1)(b)). Provision for disclosure in the trial of persons under the age of 18 is made in cases where the defendant is charged with an indictable offence which proceeds to summary trial, and to which the defendant pleads not guilty (s 1(1)(c)).

2.3 The relative paucity of trials on indictment and the general recognition of the greater gravity of offences tried on indictment ensures that the rules for disclosure in such cases differ from those applicable to summary trial. In cases where the defendant is to be tried in the Crown Court, disclosure will take place whenever the defendant is committed for trial (s 1(2)(a)). Accordingly a defendant will not be expected to decide on a plea without being informed of the nature of the case against him. Section 1(2) also provides for special cases involving trial on indictment where disclosure will operate. Disclosure will operate in cases where a person is charged with an indictable offence and the relevant proceedings are transferred to the Crown Court under a notice of transfer given under the Criminal Justice Act 1987, s 4, ie a case involving serious or complex fraud (s 1(2)(b)). Disclosure will also take place where proceedings are transferred to the Crown Court by virtue of a notice served on a magistrates' court under the Criminal Justice Act 1991, s 53 (cases which involve children) (s 1(2)(c)).[1]

1   See also s 1(2)(d), (e).

2.4 The provisions of Pt I of the Act are not retrospective, and will only apply where the investigation of the relevant offence has started on or after the appointed day (s 1(3)). The Act also provides for the general disapplication of the common law rules of disclosure once the Act is in force (s 21(1)). Therefore where Pt I does apply to the trial of an alleged offence, the common law rules of disclosure, with one exception noted below, will not apply. Accordingly the rules of common law disclosure which were effective before the appointed day and which related to the disclosure of material by the prosecutor will not apply as regards things falling to be done by the prosecution after the relevant time in relation to an alleged offence, that is, when the accused pleads guilty in a summary trial, or the accused is committed for trial, or proceedings are transferred to the Crown Court.[1] The appointed day for the purposes of the above is the day appointed for the coming into force of Pt I of the Act by the Secretary of State by order made by statutory instrument (s 1(5)).

1   Relevant time for the purposes of both summary trials and trials on indictment is defined by reference to s 21(3).

2.5 However, the common law rule as to whether disclosure is in the public interest is specifically preserved by Pt I of the Act (s 21(2)). This rule relates to the consideration by the courts of different aspects of the public interest in relation to the disclosure of certain kinds of information (see para 2.10). The courts may therefore, for example, continue to balance the public interest in not disclosing the identity of a police informer against the public interest of ensuring that the defendant receives a fair trial by the disclosure of such information.

2.6 Section 1(4) of the Act defines the role of the police or any other body involved in the investigation of crime with respect to Pt I of the Act. Such investigative bodies are under a duty to collect material which will enable the courts to decide whether an accused is guilty or not, and not simply to collect material which would indicate the guilt of an accused.

2.7 The disclosure provisions

2.7 Where there is more than one accused in any proceedings, Pt I of the Act applies to each accused independently of the other(s) (s 2(2)). It also applies to any body or individual who undertakes a prosecution, and is not restricted to prosecutions undertaken by the Crown Prosecution Service (the CPS) (s 2(3)).

PRIMARY DISCLOSURE BY PROSECUTOR

2.8 Where the duty of primary disclosure is imposed upon a prosecutor, the prosecutor must disclose to the defence certain prosecution material either in the possession of the prosecutor or any investigative body, usually the police, or must by a written statement certify that there is no such material in existence (s 3(1), (2)). The material which must be disclosed by the prosecutor is restricted to material not previously disclosed to the defence,[1] and which in the opinion of the prosecutor might undermine the case for the prosecution (s 3(1)(a)). This material must be in the possession of the prosecutor, the police, or other investigating body or have been inspected by the prosecutor under the code of practice operative under Pt II of the Act (s 3(2)). This criterion for the disclosure of material is narrower than the common law criteria for disclosure (which is superseded by Pt I of the Act), which imposed a duty upon the prosecution to disclose any material which may have been of relevance to the trial. Furthermore the statutory test for 'primary' disclosure created by Pt I of the Act is subjective; the prosecutor must apply his own judgment in determining whether the criterion for disclosure is satisfied in a particular case. The prosecutor must, subject to the above, disclose all such material falling within the statutory test, subject to considerations of the public interest (see para 2.10), or provide a written statement that there is no such material in existence (s 3(1)(b)). At the time of this 'primary' disclosure the prosecutor must also supply the accused with a schedule listing all material which the prosecution has retained and which is not subject to public interest considerations (s 3(6)). Furthermore the investigative body, usually the police, will have to certify to the prosecutor that they have complied with the requirements imposed upon them under the code of practice issued under the authority of Pt II of the Act.[2]

---

1 For example, material which may have been disclosed to a defendant in summary proceedings under the Magistrates' Courts (Advance Information) Rules 1985, SI 1985/601, which will consist of inter alia copies of the statements of intended prosecution witnesses.
2 See Ch 3 for a consideration of Pt II of the Act.

2.9 Section 3 also determines how material may be disclosed to the accused under the 'primary' disclosure rules. Material may, where it has been recorded in any form, simply be copied and the copy supplied to the accused. Any such copy may be in any form which the prosecutor deems fit. Where the provision of a copy of material to the accused is, in the opinion of the prosecutor, impracticable or undesirable, the accused must be given an effective opportunity to inspect such material (s 3(3)). Where material which is to be disclosed to the accused is not in a recorded form, but could be so rendered, the prosecutor may either render it into a recordable form and supply a copy of the same to the accused, or alternatively, where in the opinion of the prosecutor such a course of action is impracticable or undesirable, provide the accused with an opportunity to inspect the same (s 3(4)). Where the material does not consist of information then inspection of material by the accused or the taking of steps by the prosecutor to secure the opportunity for inspection is to be regarded as constituting disclosure (s 3(5)).

PUBLIC INTEREST

2.10 The prosecutor may apply to the court under s 3(6) in order to prevent the disclosure of material which the court concludes should not be disclosed to the defence on the ground that it is not in the public interest and orders accordingly. Under s 3(6), the court must weigh the competing public interests between disclosure and non-disclosure. Whatever the competing interests are in a given case, it is apparent from the case of *R v Keane*[1] that if the material may establish the innocence of the accused, or prevent a miscarriage of justice, then the balance is overwhelmingly in favour of disclosure. Nevertheless the court is obliged to consider each application by a prosecutor on its own individual merits and in the light of the particular circumstances.

1 [1994] 1 WLR 746.

2.11 Section 3(7) provides that material need not be disclosed by a prosecutor if it has been intercepted in obedience to a warrant issued under the Interception of Communications Act 1985, s 2, or if it indicates that such a warrant has been issued or such material has been intercepted. The rationale behind this provision is to disapply the requirement to make disclosure with respect to intercepted material or material indicating that a warrant had been issued or interception had taken place. By virtue of the Interception of Communications Act 1985, s 6, the Secretary of State is obliged when issuing a warrant to make arrangements to secure that the dissemination of intercepted material is kept to a minimum, and that such material is destroyed as soon as it is no longer necessary to retain it with regard to the purposes for which the relevant warrant was issued. In the case of *R v Preston*,[1] the House of Lords determined that the destruction of intercepted material was not only a permissible act under the aegis of the 1985 Act, but was an action which those persons responsible for interception were bound to perform under s 6 of the 1985 Act. Section 3(7) accordingly ensures that the operation of Pt I is consistent with the terms of the 1985 Act, by providing that the prosecutor must not disclose intercepted material.

1 [1994] 2 AC 130, [1993] 4 All ER 638, HL.

TIME LIMITS

2.12 The prosecutor must carry out the various aspects of the duty of primary disclosure within a prescribed time limit known as the relevant period (s 3(8)). This period is defined by s 12(1) as a period beginning and ending with such days as the Secretary of State prescribes by regulations (s 12(2)). The regulations may also provide that the relevant period may be extended by court order, although any such extension may be dependent on the satisfying of conditions prescribed in the relevant regulations (s 12(3)(a)–(c)). The regulations may provide that any extension to the relevant period may be at the court's discretion, or alternatively that any extension granted shall not exceed a prescribed number of days (s 12(3)(d), (e)). The regulations may in addition provide that there shall be no limit on the number of applications for extension of the relevant period, or they may limit the number of such applications (s 12(3)(f), (g)). In drafting the regulations the Secretary of State may take into account any factors that he sees fit (s 12(4)). Nevertheless without prejudice to this

2.12 The disclosure provisions

open-ended discretion, any conditions prescribed in any regulations prescribed by the Secretary of State with regard to the relevant period may be framed within the context and by reference to the nature or volume of the material concerned (s 12(5)(a)). Furthermore, the Secretary of State may have regard to the fact that material may in the opinion of the prosecutor be subject to non-disclosure on the grounds that issues of public interest may arise (s 12(5)(b)). In any case where regulations made under s 12 have yet to be brought into force, the prosecutor must act and make primary or secondary disclosure (see paras 2.8, 2.19) as soon as is reasonably practicable after the occurrence of any event prescribed, in the case of primary disclosure in s 13(1), and in the case of secondary disclosure, after the accused gives a defence statement (s 13(2)).

2.13 By virtue of s 4 of the Act, the prosecutor is obliged to supply the defendant with a copy of any schedule prepared by the police or any investigative body under s 24(3) of the Act while primary disclosure is being made. Such a schedule prepared in pursuance of provisions contained in a code of practice promulgated under the authority of Pt II of the Act[1] sets out material which is regarded as being non-sensitive material. Non-sensitive material is, within this context, material the disclosure of which would not be contrary to the public interest.[2]

1 See Ch 3 for a full consideration of Pt II of the Act and the relevant code of practice, which is, at the time of writing, in draft form.
2 See s 24(8), which defines sensitive material as material the disclosure of which under Pt I of the Act would be contrary to the public interest.

COMPULSORY DISCLOSURE BY THE ACCUSED

Crown Court

2.14 Section 5 imposes an obligation upon the accused in a Crown Court trial, subject to certain conditions, to make advance disclosure to the prosecutor. This is a new development in criminal procedure, although it has existed in a tenuous and rather restricted form in the case of the advance disclosure of an alibi defence.[1] The rationale behind this development was expressed by the Runciman Commission in the following vein—

> 'If all the parties had in advance an indication of what the defence would be, this would not only encourage earlier and better preparation of cases but might well result in the prosecution being dropped in the light of the defence disclosure, an earlier resolution through a plea of guilty, or the fixing of an earlier trial date. The length of the trial could also be more readily estimated, leading to a better use of the time both of the court and of those involved in the trial; and there would be kept to a minimum those cases where the defendant withholds his or her defence until the last possible moment in the hope of confusing the jury or evading investigation of a fabricated defence.'[2]

1 See the Criminal Justice Act 1967, s 11; see also s 74 of the 1996 Act (see para 8.33) and para 2.17.
2 Royal Commission on Criminal Justice (Cm 2263), Ch 6, para 59.

2.15 In general terms, s 5 gives effect to the Commission's proposals. Under s 5 where an accused has either—
- (a) been committed for trial to the Crown Court (s 5(1)), or
- (b) been charged with an indictable offence and proceedings have been transferred by virtue of a notice served under the Criminal Justice Act 1987, s 4, and a copy of the notice of transfer together with copies of the documents containing the evidence which forms the subject of the charge have been supplied to the accused (s 5(2)), or
- (c) been charged with an indictable offence and proceedings have been transferred by virtue of a notice served under of the Criminal Justice Act 1991, s 53, and a copy of the notice of transfer together with copies of the documents containing the evidence which forms the subject of the charge have been supplied to the accused (s 5(3)), or
- (d) where a bill of indictment has been preferred under the Administration of Justice (Miscellaneous Provisions) Act 1933, s 2(2)(b), and the prosecutor has served on the accused a copy of the indictment together with a copy of the set of documents containing the evidence which forms the subject of the charge (s 5(4)),

then the accused is obliged to supply to the court and to the prosecutor a defence statement under the terms of s 5, but only after the prosecutor has complied with, or purported to have complied with, the terms of s 3 of the Act (s 5(1)(b)).

Section 3 imposes upon the prosecutor the obligation to disclose to the accused any material which in the opinion of the prosecutor undermines the prosecution case. Until this requirement has been satisfied there is no obligation on a defendant to supply a defence statement under s 5. It should be noted that the prosecutor will be regarded as having satisfied the terms of s 3 for these purposes if he purports to have complied with the terms of s 3. This means that if the prosecutor has inadvertently failed to disclose all unused materials which undermine the prosecution case, but genuinely believes he has made full disclosure, he will be regarded as having complied with the terms of s 3 for the purposes of imposing an obligation upon the accused to supply a defence statement under s 5. This provision must be considered in the light of the continuing obligation of the prosecutor to make and to keep under review disclosure under s 9 of the Act (see para 2.23). The nature and contents of the defence statement are prescribed by s 5(6). The accused must provide the court and the prosecution with a written statement which sets out in general terms the nature of the defence (s 5(6)(a)). This provision follows closely the views of the Royal Commission which stated that—

> 'In most cases disclosure of the defence should be a matter capable of being handled by the defendant's solicitor (in the same way that alibi notices are usually dealt with at present). Standard forms could be drawn up to cover the most common offences, with the solicitor having only to tick one or more of a list of possibilities, such as "accident", "self defence", "consent", "no dishonest intent", "no appropriation", "abandoned goods", "claim of right", "mistaken identification" and so on. There will be complex cases which may require the assistance of counsel in formulating the defence'.[1]

However, the section goes on to provide that the defence statement should also indicate the matters on which the accused takes issue with the prosecution, and should set out in the case of each such matter the reason why the accused takes issue with the prosecution (s 5(6)(b), (c)).

---
1 Royal Commission on Criminal Justice (Cm 2263), Ch 6, para 68.

2.16 *The disclosure provisions*

2.16 The provisions of s 5 constitute a considerable extension of the proposals of the Runciman Commission for defence disclosure. The provisions assimilate this aspect of criminal procedure to civil procedure. Nevertheless, there is no obligation on the prosecution to provide a statement of its case to the defence, although the court may make an order to this effect within the context of a preparatory hearing under Pt III of the Act.[1]

---

1 See s 31(4), (5) and Ch 4. The statutory requirement to supply information by the prosecution to the defence in respect of, for example, either way offences under the Magistrates' Courts (Advance Information) Rules 1985, SI 1985/601, should also be noted.

2.17 Where the defence statement discloses an alibi, the accused must give particulars of the alibi defence in the statement, the details of which are prescribed in s 5(7). In particular, the accused must, if known to him, supply details of persons able to give evidence in support of the alibi. What constitutes such evidence is defined in s 5(8). The accused is obliged to supply the defence statement during the period specified by regulations made by the Secretary of State under s 12 of the Act, defined as the relevant period. This requirement, which also applies to the obligation of the prosecution to make primary disclosure, is discussed at para 2.12 within the context of primary disclosure.

VOLUNTARY DISCLOSURE BY THE ACCUSED

Summary trial

2.18 Section 6 provides that the accused in a summary trial may make a voluntary disclosure of his defence to the court and the prosecution. However, this section only operates when an accused has either—
  (a) been charged with a summary offence which proceeds to trial and in respect of which he pleads not guilty;
  (b) attained the age of 18 and is charged with an offence which is triable either way, in respect of which the court proceeds to summary trial, and to which the accused pleads not guilty; or
  (c) been charged with an indictable offence in respect of which the court proceeds to summary trial and in respect of which the accused pleads not guilty, and the accused is under the age of 18 (s 6(1)(a)).

Furthermore, the prosecutor must have complied or purported to have complied with s 3 of the Act with regard to the making of primary disclosure to the accused (s 6(1)(b)). This requirement has already been considered at para 2.15 in the context of primary disclosure by the prosecution and compulsory disclosure by the accused in Crown Court trials.[1] The accused having chosen to make voluntary disclosure of his defence must do so within time limits prescribed by the Secretary of State under s 12, that is within the relevant time.[2] The defence statement made by an accused in the case of a summary trial must comply with s 5(6)–(8) (s 6(3); see para 2.15).

---

1 See further para 2.8 et seq for a consideration of the nature of primary disclosure under s 3 of the Act by the prosecution.
2 Section 6(4). For a consideration of this concept within the context of primary disclosure of the prosecution case see para 2.12.

SECONDARY DISCLOSURE BY PROSECUTOR

2.19 Once the accused has made compulsory or voluntary disclosure under either ss 5 or 6, the prosecution is, under certain circumstances, obliged to make further disclosure of materials to the accused. Such disclosure must relate to materials either in the possession of the prosecutor or of any investigative body, usually the police (s 7(3)). The prosecutor is obliged to disclose materials which have not previously been disclosed to the accused and which might reasonably be expected to assist the accused's defence as disclosed by the defence statement given to the prosecution and the court. This requirement (secondary disclosure) would appear to impose upon the prosecution an objective standard of compliance. This should be contrasted with the subjective nature of the prosecutor's obligation to make primary disclosure. Disclosure of materials under the above provisions is satisfied if the prosecutor complies with the methods of disclosure prescribed by s 3(3)–(5) (s 7(4); see para 2.9).

2.20 The prosecution, as in the case of primary disclosure, is under the same restrictions not to disclose material which it is not in the public interest to disclose, or which is subject to the issue of a warrant or has been intercepted in obedience to a warrant issued under the Interception of Communications Act 1985, s 2.[1] The prosecutor must make such secondary disclosure within the relevant time (s 7(7)).[2] Where there is no such material either in the possession of the prosecutor or the police, or any investigative body, the prosecutor must give the accused a written statement to that effect (s 7(2)(b)).

1 Section 7(6). See para 2.11 for a consideration of these restrictions upon disclosure within the context of primary disclosure.
2 See para 2.12 for a discussion of the concept of the relevant time.

APPLICATION BY ACCUSED FOR DISCLOSURE

2.21 Notwithstanding the making of both primary and secondary disclosure by the prosecution, the accused may after disclosure of the defence case still be of the opinion that the prosecution has access to undisclosed material which may aid the accused in the presentation of his defence. Section 8 accordingly provides for the accused to make an application to the court for an order for the disclosure of undisclosed material which is in the possession either of the prosecution or the police, or other investigative body, and which has been inspected by the prosecutor, or which he was entitled to, but did not, inspect (s 8(3), (4)). The basis for the application is that the accused has reasonable cause to believe that the undisclosed material might reasonably be expected to assist the defence (s 8(1), (2)).

2.22 The court will not make an order under s 8 in respect of any material which it concludes, on the application of the prosecutor, is not in the public interest to disclose (s 8(5)). Neither will the court make an order for disclosure of material which has been intercepted in obedience to a warrant issued under the Interception of Communications Act 1985, s 2, or where there is an indication that such a warrant has been issued in respect of such material (s 8(6)).

2.23   *The disclosure provisions*

CONTINUING DUTY OF PROSECUTOR TO DISCLOSE

2.23   Section 9 imposes a continuing duty upon the prosecution to keep prosecution material under review, and to disclose to the defence under circumstances prescribed in s 9(2) any material not previously disclosed. By s 9(2) of the Act, the prosecution must keep under review the possible disclosure of undisclosed material which in its opinion might undermine the case for the prosecution; the prosecution must disclose any such material to the accused as soon as is reasonably practicable. In keeping under review the question of such further disclosure, the prosecution must have regard to the state of affairs pertaining at the time, including the standing of the case for the prosecution (s 9(3)). This obligation commences when the prosecutor makes primary disclosure, and ends when the accused is acquitted or convicted, or the prosecution decide not to proceed with the case (s 9(1)). There is also a continuing obligation for the prosecution to keep under review the question of further disclosure of material, and to disclose any such material which might reasonably be expected to assist the accused's defence as disclosed by the defence statement given under the authority of either s 5 or 6 of the Act (s 9(5)). This obligation arises from the time when the prosecution makes secondary disclosure until the proceedings are concluded, either by the acquittal or conviction of the accused, or by the decision of the prosecutor not to proceed with the case (s 9(4)). Disclosure by the prosecution under this section is satisfied by recourse to any methods of disclosure prescribed by s 3(3)–(5) of the Act (s 9(7)).[1] The prosecution may seek by court order the non-disclosure of material notwithstanding s 9 where the court on the application of the prosecutor determines that the disclosure of material would not be in the public interest (s 9(8)). Furthermore, the prosecution must not disclose material which has been intercepted in obedience to a warrant issued under the Interception of Communications Act 1985, s 2, or where there is an indication that such a warrant has been issued or material intercepted in obedience to such a warrant (s 9(9)).

1   See also para 2.9 for a consideration of the methods of disclosure prescribed by s 3(3)–(5).

PROSECUTOR'S FAILURE TO OBSERVE TIME LIMITS

2.24   It has already been noted[1] that where the prosecutor fails to make primary disclosure within the relevant period the defence is not obliged to make disclosure of its case under either ss 5 or 6 of the Act. Failure of the prosecution to make disclosure within the relevant period does not, however, impose upon the prosecution any particular sanction otherwise than that provided for by s 10 of the Act. Under s 10, where the prosecution fail to make either primary or secondary disclosure within the respective relevant periods, then the omission so to act may constitute grounds for staying the proceedings for abuse of process. For a court to make such a finding, the delay on the part of the prosecutor to make disclosure must be such that the accused is thereby denied a fair trial (s 10(2), (3)). Failure of the prosecutor to make disclosure would however, constitute breaches of the Bar's code of conduct, and the code of conduct for the CPS. A deliberate suppression of material by the prosecutor would render him liable to criminal sanctions such as the common law offence of perverting the course of justice.

1   See paras 2.15, 2.18.

FAULTS IN DISCLOSURE BY ACCUSED

2.25 The Runciman Commission recommended that an accused should be required to disclose information concerning his case. In order to prevent the evasion of this obligation the Commission also recommended that an accused who fails to do so be subject to sanctions in the form of the drawing of inferences in certain circumstances.[1] Accordingly where the prosecution in a Crown Court trial has made disclosure, and the defence either—

(a) fails to give a defence statement, or
(b) fails to give a defence statement within the relevant period, or
(c) sets out inconsistent defences in his defence statement, or
(d) puts forward a defence which is different from any defence set out in the defence statement at the trial, or
(e) adduces an alibi defence without disclosure of the same in the defence statement at the trial, or
(f) calls a witness at the trial in support of an alibi defence without having made reference to that witness in the defence statement,

then the court or, with the leave of the court, any other party may at the trial make any comment on the conduct of the defence as appears appropriate; this will include for example, a co-defendant. Furthermore, the court or jury may draw inferences as to the accused's guilt as appear proper in the circumstances of the case (s 11(1), (3)). The accused may not, however, be convicted solely on an inference drawn under s 11(5). There is a requirement for supportive evidence.

---

[1] Royal Commission on Criminal Justice (Cm 2263), Ch 6, paras 57–73.

2.26 Where the accused has put forward a defence which differs from any defence set out in the defence statement, the court, in deciding whether to make any comment or inferences as to guilt, will have regard to the extent to which the defence differs from that set out in the defence statement, and to whether there is any justification for the extent of the difference (s 11(4)).

2.27 The same inferences may be drawn in the same circumstances in the case of a summary trial, except where the accused elects not to make a defence statement, since the accused is not obliged to make a defence statement in any event (s 11(2)).

PUBLIC INTEREST

Review for summary trials

2.28 There is provision for a magistrates' court to keep under review whether it is at any time not in the public interest to disclose material in respect of which it has previously made an order for non-disclosure on the grounds of public interest. Section 14 requires that a magistrates' court should review a non-disclosure ruling on application by the accused. If the court concludes that the material to which the ruling applied should now be disclosed, the court must so order, and take reasonable steps to inform the prosecutor accordingly (s 14(3)). The prosecutor on being so informed must act in accordance with the order, or alternatively decide not to proceed with the case (s 14(4)).

2.29 *The disclosure provisions*

Review in other cases

2.29 In the case of trials commenced on indictment, there is similar provision for the court to keep under review whether it is at any time not in the public interest to disclose material affected by an order for non-disclosure. Section 15 provides that the court is obliged to keep this question under continuous review, without the need for an application by an interested party, although the accused may apply to the court for a review of that question (s 15(4)). Where the court makes an order for disclosure the prosecutor is informed, and as in the case of an equivalent order made in the magistrates' court, the prosecutor is obliged to comply with the terms of the order, or to decide not to proceed with the case (s 15(5)(b)).

2.30 Section 16 of the Act was added to the Bill during its passage through Standing Committee B in the House of Commons.[1] It provides that where an application is made by a party either for non-disclosure of material on the grounds of public interest, or for review of such an order under ss 14 or 15, and a person claims an interest in the relevant material, if that party applies to the court, and can show that he was involved solely or jointly with others, either directly or indirectly, in bringing the material to the attention of the prosecutor, the court cannot make any order either for non-disclosure or for disclosure of the relevant material unless that party has first been given an opportunity to be heard. The section recognises that sensitive material, ie, material which it is claimed is not in the public interest to disclose, may have originated from a third party such as a local authority social services department. In such cases, although the prosecutor can make representations to the court in relation to the material, the third party might be more knowledgeable about it and be better placed to argue on the issue of disclosure. In these circumstances the third party would be able to instruct separate counsel to make representations to the court.

1 HC Standing Committee B, 16 May 1996, col 84.

CONFIDENTIALITY OF DISCLOSED INFORMATION

2.31 The provisions relating to the confidentiality of disclosed information were also introduced into the Bill during its Committee Stage in the House of Commons.[1] The aims of ss 17 and 18 are to ensure the confidentiality of unused material containing information that has been disclosed to the accused by the prosecutor under Pt I of the Act. Section 17 requires the information disclosed to the accused to be treated confidentially, because it is recognised that the only reason that the accused has access to the information is that the prosecution has disclosed it. It may contain sensitive or even potentially embarrassing information about other persons that could be used to harass witnesses, or to blackmail individuals. Such material could be used for financial gain, or could be published without authorisation. The accused will be able to use disclosed unused material containing such information only to prepare his defence, or any appeal, but cannot use it for other purposes unless the court permits. The protection of confidentiality applies only to disclosed unused information. It does not apply to any material containing such information in the prosecution case which is served on the defence and which will form part of the court proceedings, or to anything which is read out in open court. Section 17 recognises that court proceedings are, in most instances, open to the press and to the public, and that the imposition of a duty of confidentiality on the accused in respect of the latter kinds of material would not be appropriate.

1   HC Standing Committee B, 16 May 1996, col 84; HL Consideration of Commons Amendments, 26 June 1996, col 960.

Contravention of confidentiality requirement

2.32 Any contravention by a party of the confidentiality requirement established by s 17 is punishable as a contempt of court (s 18). The penalties available to the courts in such cases are similar to those prescribed in the Contempt of Court Act 1981. The court which heard the case for which the material containing the information was disclosed will be the court which considers whether any contempt has arisen from misuse of the disclosed information (s 18(1), (2)). In addition the court will also have the power to confiscate or order the forfeiture of any such material containing the information in the possession of the party found to be in contempt of court.

RULES OF COURT—STATUTORY RULES OF DISCLOSURE

2.33 The Magistrates' Courts Act 1980, s 144(1) and the Supreme Court Act 1981, s 84(1) are modified so as to permit rules of court to be made under the authority of the above provisions which will enable the courts to administer and to give effect to Pt I of the Act (s 19(1)).

2.34 Section 20, inter alia, preserves other statutory rules which may create or preserve a duty of disclosure of material in a criminal trial. In particular s 20 reserves a power of a magistrates' court through rules of court made under the Magistrates' Courts Act 1980, s 144(1), so as to require a party to disclose expert evidence before trial, and to prohibit a party from adducing such evidence if he fails to make such prior disclosure (s 20(3), (4)).

3 Criminal investigations

INTRODUCTION

3.1 The provisions in Pt II of the Act deal with the first stage of the criminal process, namely the criminal investigation, and form the basis for the disclosure provisions in Pt I of the Act. Part II of the Act requires that the Secretary of State prepare a code of practice and sets out the parameters as to the contents of the code. At the time of writing, the code has been published in draft form, so that the remainder of the discussion must be seen against this background. The draft code contains provisions dealing with the procedure to be followed by the investigator, the officer in charge of an investigation, and the disclosure officer from the very inception of the investigation. As such, it contains provisions as to the information obtained by police officers in a criminal investigation, its recording and preservation, and its disclosure to the prosecutor. For the first time there is a statutory duty on the prosecutor under Pt I of the Act to disclose to the accused unused material that might undermine the prosecution case ('primary prosecution disclosure'),[1] or might reasonably be expected to assist the defence which the accused has disclosed ('secondary prosecution disclosure').[2] This is supplemented by the continuing duty of the prosecutor to disclose under s 9. The detailed provisions in the code provide the backdrop for disclosure under the Act.

1   See para 2.8 et seq.
2   See para 2.19 et seq.

3.2 Given that the precise substantive content of the code is not stated in the Act itself, s 25(1) of the Act provides that when the Secretary of State has prepared the code he shall publish it in the form of a draft and consider any representations made to him about the draft, which he may modify accordingly. When the Secretary of State has so acted, s 25(2) requires that he lay the code before each House of Parliament, and when he has done so he may bring it into operation on such day as he may appoint. The code is given prospective effect only in so far as it shall not apply to criminal investigations begun before the appointed day (s 25(3)). Where the Secretary of State, pursuant to a power under s 25(4), revises a code previously brought into operation, the provisions of s 25 mentioned above apply to the revised code as they apply to the code as first prepared.

3.3 Section 22 is an interpretation section for the purposes of Pt II. A criminal investigation is defined as an investigation conducted by police officers with a view to it being ascertained whether a person should be charged with an offence or whether a person charged with an offence is guilty of it (s 22(1)). References to material are to material of all kinds, and in particular include references to information and objects of all descriptions (s 22(2)). References to recording information are to putting it in durable and retrievable form (such as writing or tape) (s 22(3)). An amendment was sought at the Committee Stage to make it explicit that s 22 applied to samples, in order to ensure that blood samples are classified as material, but was withdrawn after clarification that such samples were considered to be material.[1]

1   HC Standing Committee B, 21 May 1996, col 103.

Draft code of practice 3.6

REQUIREMENT TO PREPARE CODE OF PRACTICE

Contents

3.4 Section 23(1) requires the Secretary of State to prepare a code of practice 'designed to secure' a number of aims, and sub-ss (2)–(5) set the broad parameters of the content of the code in permissive terms. Section 23(5) provides that the code may include provision about the time when, the form in which, the way in which, and the extent to which, information or any other material is to be revealed to a person who is involved in the prosecution of criminal proceedings arising out of or relating to the investigation and who is identified in accordance with 'prescribed' provisions. Section 23(8) defines 'prescribed' as meaning as prescribed by the code. Section 24 proceeds to give examples of the kinds of provision that may be included in the code by virtue of s 23(5).

3.5 The only negative limitation as to the content of the code, contained in s 23(6), is that it must be so framed so as not to apply to material intercepted pursuant to a warrant issued under the Interception of Communications Act 1985, s 2. By s 2(2) of the 1985 Act, the Secretary of State shall not issue such a warrant unless he considers that the warrant is necessary—
- (a) in the interests of national security;
- (b) for the purpose of preventing or detecting serious crime; or
- (c) for the purpose of safeguarding the economic well-being of the United Kingdom.

In *R v Preston*[1] the House of Lords held that the power of the Secretary of State under (b) above did not extend to the collection of evidence for the purpose of prosecuting offenders and that there was no duty to retain the material until trial for disclosure to the defence.[2] Section 23(6) therefore imposes an important limitation to prevent such material falling within the retention and disclosure provisions of the Act.

---

1 [1994] 2 AC 130.
2 See also para 2.9.

DRAFT CODE OF PRACTICE

Overview of contents

3.6 Paragraph 2.1 defines the meanings inter alia of disclosure officer, investigator, and officer in charge of the investigation. Separate duties are given to the investigator, the officer in charge of the investigation, and the disclosure officer (para 3.1). Paragraph 4 contains provisions as to the recording of information. Paragraph 5 deals with the retention of material, and para 6.1 proceeds to provide for the preparation by the disclosure officer of a schedule listing material which has been retained and which does not form part of the case against the accused so that the prosecutor can make informed decisions as to disclosure under Pt I of the Act. Paragraph 6.8 provides that the disclosure officer must list on a 'sensitive schedule' material which it is believed not to be in the public interest to disclose and the reasons for that belief (or in exceptional circumstances the disclosure officer may reveal the material separately to the prosecutor under para 6.9) and affords guidance by giving examples of material

3.6 *Criminal investigations*

which it may not be in the public interest to disclose. Paragraph 7 deals with the revelation of material to the prosecutor and para 8 provides for disclosure after the primary disclosure stage in the appropriate circumstances

3.7 The code, therefore, goes some way towards implementing the recommendations of the Runciman Commission, which had stated that job descriptions should be drawn up for the supervising ranks. Sergeants should work as supervisors as well as having their own caseloads, and detective sergeants should be given responsibility for a specified group of detective constables. The precise degree of supervision expected should be spelt out, and detective constables held accountable within reason for the performance of the group under their supervision.[1] Implicit in these recommendations is that there should be separation between the persons who undertake investigations and the persons who supervise those investigations. However, while the code provides in para 3.1 that the functions of the investigator, the officer in charge of the investigation, and the disclosure officer are separate, it states that whether they are undertaken by one, two or more persons will depend on the complexity of the case and the administrative arrangements within each police force.

1 Royal Commission on Criminal Justice (Cm 2263), Ch 2, para 59.

Recording of information

3.8 Paragraph 4 deals with the recording of information. If material which may be relevant to the investigation consists of information which is not recorded in any form, the officer in charge of an investigation must ensure that it is recorded in a durable or retrievable form (whether in writing, on video or audio tape, or on computer disk) (para 4.1). Relevant information should be recorded at the time it is obtained or as soon as practicable after that time (para 4.4).

3.9 The provisions as to the recording of information must be read in conjunction with Code of Practice C, issued under s 66 of the 1984 Act by the Secretary of State, which contains provisions as to the interviewing of suspected persons.[1] Paragraph 11.5(a) already requires that an accurate record must be made of each interview with a person suspected of an offence, whether or not the interview takes place at a police station, and para 11.5(c) provides that the record must be made during the course of the interview, unless in the investigating officer's view this would not be practicable or would interfere with the conduct of the interview, and must constitute either a verbatim record of what has been said, or failing this, an account of the interview which adequately and accurately summarises it. Paragraph 11.7 provides that if an interview record is not made during the course of the interview it must be made as soon as practicable after its completion.

1 Code of Practice for the detention, treatment and questioning of persons by police officers; see *Butterworths Rules of Court—Criminal Court Practice.*

3.10 Paragraph 4 of the draft code goes further in that it applies to information which may be relevant to the investigation, unlike the provisions of Code of Practice C which are limited to the questioning of a person regarding his involvement or suspected involvement in a criminal offence. In addition, para 4 applies to negative information when relevant to the investigation (para 4.3) and information obtained in house-to-house enquiries provided it does not require an investigator to take a statement from a witness where it would not otherwise be taken (para 4.4).

Retention of material

3.11 The procedures and duties in relation to the retention of material are contained in para 5 of the draft code. The investigator must retain material obtained in a criminal investigation which may be relevant to the investigation, including not only material coming into the possession of the investigator but also material generated by him (para 5.1). The duty to retain it under the code is subject to the provisions of s 22 of 1984 Act as to the retention of material seized under that Act (para 5.2). Paragraph 5.4 lists categories of material that in particular fall within the duty to retain, and by para 5.5 the duty to retain material falling into those categories does not extend to items which are purely ancillary to such material and possess no independent significance.

Preparation of material for prosecutor

3.12 The disclosure officer must ensure that a schedule listing material which has been retained and which does not form part of the prosecution case against the accused is prepared in circumstances where the accused is charged with—
    (a) an offence triable only on indictment;
    (b) an offence which is triable either way, and it is considered either that the case is likely to be tried on indictment or that the accused is likely to plead not guilty at a summary trial; or
    (c) a summary offence, and it is considered that he is likely to plead not guilty (para 6.1).

The disclosure officer must state on the schedule that he does not believe that the material listed on it is sensitive (para 6.4). The fact that the schedule will be sufficiently detailed to enable the prosecutor to make an informed decision on disclosure means that the defence will also be able to determine whether they have sufficient disclosure, and to make an application for disclosure under s 8, if necessary.

Sensitive schedule

3.13 Any material believed to be sensitive must either be listed on a sensitive schedule (para 6.8) or, in exceptional circumstances, be revealed to the prosecutor separately (para 6.9). The disclosure officer must list on a sensitive schedule any material which he, the officer in charge of an investigation, or an investigator believes it is not in the public interest to disclose, and the reason for that belief (para 6.8). Under Pt I of the Act, material inspected in pursuance of the code must not be disclosed by the prosecutor to the extent that the court, on application by the prosecutor, concludes it is not in the public interest to disclose it and orders accordingly,[1] and s 21(2) preserves the common law rules as to whether disclosure is in the public interest. Although the *A-G's Guidelines: Disclosure of Information to the Defence in cases to be tried on Indictment*[2] provides that 'sensitive' material, as distinct from material subject to public interest immunity, may be exempted from disclosure even where it satisfies the test of materiality because it is not in the public interest to disclose it, it has subsequently been held by the Court of Appeal in *R v Brown*[3] that only material subject to public interest immunity may be exempted from disclosure.

---

1 See ss 3(6), 7(5) and 9(8).
2 (1981) 74 Cr App Rep 302.
3 [1994] 1 WLR 1599.

3.14 Criminal investigations

3.14 It is instructive to consider the previous procedure as to the preparation of material for the prosecutor, in order to understand the effect of the provisions contained in the 1996 Act. Previously, the police would fill out a Disclosure Schedule in relation to Unused Material (Form MG 6C) and this would be reviewed by a CPS lawyer, who would state the reasons for non-disclosure of any material. The police would also fill out a Sensitive Material Schedule (Form MG 6D), which is not to be disclosed to the defence, describing the material and giving reasons for the sensitivity, and this would be reviewed by the CPS lawyer, who would state the review decision or the reason for non-disclosure. As such, it would appear that the code makes little difference to the procedure that existed before.

3.15 However, it would seem that the code places previous police practice as to unused material on a more formalised basis because, as stated above, the draft of the code will be laid before both Houses of Parliament;[1] although it may probably not be regarded as statutory authority[2] it is not subordinate legislation. The code states what constitutes 'material', and what is 'relevant to the investigation' (para 2.1). It provides guidance as to which material must be listed on the sensitive and non-sensitive schedules, and in what manner it must be so listed (para 6). With regard to the sensitive schedule, para 6.8 of the code structures but does not confine the decision of the police as to what may constitute sensitive material, so that the police may flag the material listed in para 6.8 and give reasons why such material is considered sensitive.[3] In effect, this will mean that there is better preparation of schedules under the code than was the previous practice, and this will in turn facilitate the making of an informed decision as to disclosure by the reviewing lawyer under Pt I of the Act.

---

1 See para 3.2.
2 Although *R v McCay* [1990] 1 WLR 645 seems to suggest that such a code would have statutory authority, see the commentary at [1990] Crim LR 340 for cogent reasons to the contrary.
3 It is interesting to note *R v Brown* [1994] 1 WLR 1599 at 1609, where the Court of Appeal recommended a statutory statement of the duties of the Crown regarding disclosure of relevant information. Although this was aimed towards Crown prosecutors and prosecuting counsel, para 6.8 of the code goes some way towards this since it provides an important statement as to non-disclosure for the disclosure officer from which the prosecutor subsequently makes the assessment under Pt I of the Act.

Public interest immunity

3.16 Material listed in para 6.8 of the code may be placed on a sensitive schedule by the disclosure officer, the officer in charge of an investigation, or an investigator, if he believes it is not in the public interest to disclose. In the House of Lords an amendment was moved by Lord McIntosh of Haringey giving the prosecutor, who has the responsibility of deciding what is to be disclosed to the defence, the responsibility of deciding what material is sensitive, except where an issue of national security arises. The amendment was withdrawn, having been resisted by Lord Mackay of Drumadoon. Lord Mackay pointed out that the structure of the Bill ensured that the police are responsible for the investigation and collection of material and for making it available to the prosecutors with the relevant schedules. The prosecutor is then under a duty to consider what falls to be disclosed to the accused. The duties were separate, whereas the amendment would have lead to duplication in that the police would examine the material, and then the same task would be undertaken by the prosecutor.[1]

---

1 HL 3R, 19 February 1996, cols 872–876. See also the earlier amendment, also withdrawn, which differed only in that it did not have an exemption in relation to national security issues; HL Report, 1 February 1996, cols 1581–1583.

3.17 Notwithstanding the streamlined procedure which places a sensitive schedule before the prosecutor together with the reasons for non-disclosure, it must be stressed that the prosecutor's inspection of the material under Pt I of the Act is independent of the earlier assessment by the disclosure officer. The prosecutor will continue to make the assessment as to what prima facie may be considered to be covered by public interest immunity and whether a claim should be made in respect of it. The code does not make a substantive change in this respect; rather, the disclosure officer is given greater guidance by para 6.8 of the code as to what may constitute sensitive material so that the prosecutor would be specifically alerted by the sensitive schedule to the sensitive material and the reason as to why it may not be in the public interest to disclose the material. He may then apply to the court in respect of material which it is not in the public interest to disclose (see para 3.13).[1]

---

1 Although the application will be made to the court in respect of whether material is covered by public interest immunity, it would seem that the judge has the discretion to regard an assurance from an independent competent member of the Bar as sufficient reason for drawing the conclusion that the documents were irrelevant or to look at the documents and decide for himself: *R v W(G); R v W(E)* [1996] 28 LS Gaz R 29, CA.

3.18 The prosecutor may disagree with reasons given for non-disclosure or may consider that the balance of the public interest in non-disclosure is outweighed by the public interest that the accused have disclosure of the material. The prosecutor will also have to be alert to the possibility of content-based public interest immunity claims not raised in the sensitive schedule. Alternatively, the prosecutor may wish to assert public interest immunity in respect of a new class not mentioned in para 6.8, although the recognition of a new class-based public interest immunity requires clear and compelling evidence that it is necessary.[1]

---

1 *R v Chief Constable of the West Midland Police, ex p Wiley* [1995] 1 AC 274, HL.

3.19 Although the prosecutor makes an independent determination as to disclosure, the Act does not give the prosecutor the power to amend the sensitive schedule which the disclosure officer has given. As Baroness Blatch pointed out, the only reason that the prosecutor would want to amend the schedule would be to provide the accused with the amended version. One of two consequences follows from this. The prosecutor could remove from the sensitive schedule everything except sensitive material which falls within the test for disclosure and which is not protected by the public interest test, in which case the accused would receive all the material listed on the schedule and there would be no point in giving the amended schedule to him. Alternatively, the prosecutor could include on the sensitive schedule not only sensitive material which meets the test for disclosure and is not protected by the public interest test but also other sensitive material which is not being disclosed, because it does not meet the test for disclosure or because it is not in the public interest to disclose it. Disclosure of the sensitive schedule in such circumstances would defeat the purpose of listing sensitive material on a separate schedule in the first place.[1]

---

1 HL Report, 5 February 1996, col 40.

3.20 It is worth examining the extent to which para 6.8 follows the case law as to what may constitute class-based public interest immunity.[1] It is important that the examples of sensitive material contained in para 6.8 comprise material which has

3.20 *Criminal investigations*

been held by case law to be protected by class-based public interest immunity or material that may be held to be so protected on the basis of extrapolation from the case law, so that the prosecutor can make an informed decision as to disclosure on the basis of the reasons given in the sensitive schedule, without being faced with a welter of unnecessary material in the sensitive schedule when considering disclosure under Pt I. The common law rules still have application as to what constitutes public interest immunity (s 21(2)) so that the prosecutor will use the case law to assess the sensitive schedule and the reasons given in that schedule for non-disclosure. Paragraph 6.8 is no more than illustrative of material that may be sensitive and therefore may not be considered to be definitive, as is made clear by its wording which states that—

> 'Depending on the circumstances, examples of such [sensitive] material may include the following among others'.

Nevertheless, it will be seen below that the examples given in para 6.8 correlate to the case law on public interest immunity so that it will be unlikely for the disclosure officer to list in the sensitive schedule material not included in those examples.

1 Class-based public interest immunity attaches to a class of documents and the nature of the information contained in the class is irrelevant. Whole content-based public interest immunity attaches to a particular item of information. Public interest immunity prevents disclosure of information in the public interest.

3.21 The code cannot by its nature provide guidance as to content-based public interest immunity, although the code does not preclude the assertion of such content-based public interest immunity. Since class and contents claims are not mutually exclusive, it may be that both a class and contents claim may be asserted in relation to material within para 6.8. Case law has determined the following material mentioned in para 6.8 of the code to be covered by class-based public interest immunity.

3.22 *Material relating to national security, or relating to, or received by, the intelligence and security agencies* It would seem that the judge in criminal proceedings may inspect such material in criminal proceedings as it would be incompatible with the defendant's absolute right to a fair trial to allow the prosecution to make a judgment on the asserted claim to immunity.[1]

1 *R v Ward* [1993] 1 WLR 619 at 681, CA.

3.23 *Material given in confidence* Documents obtained from a third party in a police investigation may be withheld from disclosure on the ground of public interest immunity: see *Marcel v Metropolitan Police Comr*[1] Although *Marcel* involved civil proceedings, it would seem that the reasoning of the case would apply mutatis mutandis to criminal cases.

1 [1995] Ch 225.

3.24 *Material relating to the identity or activities of informants, undercover police officers, or other persons supplying information to the police who may be in danger if identities revealed* Public interest immunity may be asserted in respect of information given by or to a person, the content of the information and the manner in which it was conveyed and

Draft code of practice 3.27

what was done with the information,[1] although disclosure will be ordered where it is necessary to show the innocence of the accused or to prevent a miscarriage of justice.[2]

1   See *Marks v Beyfus* (1890) 25 QBD 494.
2   See *R v Turner* [1995] 1 WLR 264.

3.25 *Material revealing the location of any premises or the identity of any person allowing usage for police surveillance* The public interest immunity that applies to informers has been extended to the identity of a person who has allowed premises to be used for surveillance, as well as the location of those premises.[1] It should be noted that the location of the premises is subject to public interest immunity only to the extent that the identity of the occupier can be extrapolated from that location.[2] This means the code, as phrased, may be more extensive than the common law. A restricted interpretation by the prosecutor in line with the common law is appropriate as concerns the decision as to disclosure under Pt I. But at this stage para 6.8 performs its function of placing material that has the potential to be subject to public interest immunity in the sensitive schedule so that the prosecutor may make a decision as to disclosure under Pt I of the Act.

1   See *R v Rankine* [1986] QB 861.
2   See *R v Johnson (Kenneth)* [1988] 1 WLR 1377 at 1385–86, 1381–82.

3.26 *Material revealing techniques and methods relied upon by police in course of criminal investigation, for example covert surveillance techniques, or other methods of detecting crime* As stated in para 3.5, there is a duty on investigating authorities to destroy all material which is obtained through the issue of a warrant for interception pursuant to the Interception of Communications Act 1985, s 2. When the retention of such material is no longer necessary for the prevention or detection of crime, it must be destroyed so that the material may not be adduced at trial.

Public interest immunity attaches to the police Public Order Manual, which contains operational details of police methods in relation to disorder, demonstrations and riots.[1] In *R v Brown and Daley*[2] the Court of Appeal stated, obiter, that there may be criminal cases where public interest immunity may be successfully asserted to protect information relating to police techniques and methods. Since this contention has not been directly considered, the code cannot be considered to be a definitive statement of the common law. However, the code has fulfilled its role in flagging such material so that it can be placed in a sensitive schedule by the disclosure officer, and an assessment can be made by the prosecutor under Pt I of the Act.

1   See *Goodwin v Chief Constable of Lancashire* [1992] 44 LS Gaz R 35, CA.
2   (1987) 87 Cr App Rep 52 at 59–60.

3.27 *Communications between the police and the CPS* Immunity may be asserted in respect of reports sent from the police to the Director of Public Prosecutions (or the CPS on his behalf), because it is important for the functioning of criminal prosecutions, and in order that police officers should be able to take legal advice.[1]

1   See *Evans v Chief Constable of Surrey* [1988] QB 588; *O'Sullivan v Metropolitan Police Comr* (1995) 139 Sol Jo LB 164.

3.28 *Criminal investigations*

3.28 *Material upon the strength of which a search warrant is obtained* Class-based public interest immunity may be claimed in respect of material upon the strength of which search warrants were obtained. The power to make such an order was derived from the Court's inherent jurisdiction in *Taylor v Anderton*,[1] and although the case involved civil proceedings, the reasoning of the case may be applied mutatis mutandis to criminal cases.

---

1 (1986) Times, 21 October.

3.29 *Material generated by official of body concerned with regulation or supervision of bodies corporate or of persons engaged in financial activities and supplied to investigator during criminal investigation* In *Hamilton v Naviede*,[1] the House of Lords refused public interest immunity for transcripts of interviews under the Insolvency Act 1986, s 236, supplied by Department of Trade and Industry inspectors to the Serious Fraud Office, but it would appear that the decision is dependent on the actual facts of the case; for instance, the House left open the question whether immunity applied to DTI interviews under s 235 of the Insolvency Act 1986, where arguments based on candour would have more force because such investigations depend on the co-operation of those being questioned. As such, given the proper facts, there could be a successful assertion of immunity.

---

1 [1995] 2 AC 75, HL Ref, on appeal from *In Re Arrows (No 4)* [1993] Ch 452, CA.

3.30 *Material generated by local authority social services department or other party and supplied to investigator during criminal investigation relating to child witness* There are civil decisions as concerns this area, but it would seem that this may be justified on general arguments based on candour.[1]

---

1 See *Re D (Infants)* [1970] 1 WLR 599. In *Re G (A Minor) (Social Worker: Disclosure)* [1996] 2 All ER 65, the Court of Appeal held that leave of the court was not required for a social worker to disclose to the police any potentially incriminating information given by the parents. Although the information was covered by public interest immunity, it may be disclosed to fellow members of the child protection team engaged in the investigation of possible child abuse.

3.31 It will be noted that para 6.8 of the code does not list the potentially non-disclosable matters in para 6 of the *A-G's Guidelines: Disclosure of Information to the defence in cases to be tried on indictment*.[1] In *R v Brown*[2] the Court of Appeal stated that it was axiomatic that the duty to disclose extends to material which might arguably undermine the prosecution case or assist a defendant's case, but that it would impose an unnecessary and excessive burden on the Crown to impose a legal duty to disclose material which is only relevant to the credibility of defence witnesses. The Court seemed to reject the disclosure on the grounds of public interest and fairness. It is submitted therefore that the position under the code would be unchanged, notwithstanding the omission from it of para 6 of the Guidelines.[3]

---

1 (1981) 74 Cr App Rep 302 at 303.
2 [1994] 1 WLR 1599.
3 Ibid at 1608.

Draft code of practice 3.35

3.32 The practice in criminal proceedings as to the assertion of public interest immunity is not altered under the code. Accordingly, if no objection is taken to the introduction of evidence which may be covered by public interest immunity, a flexible stance will be manifested in criminal courts so as to allow disclosure where it is relevant to the proceedings. This is the case even though an assertion of public interest immunity is a duty and not a right and so it cannot strictly be waived.[1]

---
1 See *Makanjuola v Metropolitan Police Comr* [1992] 3 All ER 617 at 623.

3.33 *Makanjuola* seems to suggest that where a document is prima facie immune from disclosure, there is no duty to persist in an assertion of privilege where the public interest is in favour of disclosure. In *R v Horseferry Road Magistrates' Court, ex p Bennett (No 2)*[1] the Divisional Court stated that the public interest in the prosecution's use of class documents cannot outweigh the public interest in the defendant having an opportunity of establishing his innocence or furthering his defence. The Court held that it is not necessary in every criminal case for the CPS to seek the court's ruling where, but for public interest immunity, documents would ordinarily fall to be disclosed as part of the material evidence gathered by the prosecution. Subject to safeguards described in the case, voluntary disclosure of class documents to the defence is permissible.

---
1 [1994] 1 All ER 289.

Sensitive material inappropriate for sensitive schedule

3.34 In exceptional circumstances, where an investigator considers that material is so sensitive that its revelation to the prosecutor by means of an entry on the sensitive schedule is inappropriate, the existence of the material must be revealed to the prosecutor separately (para 6.9). Paragraph 6.9 of the code cites as examples material that would be likely to lead directly to the loss of life, or might directly threaten national security if it were compromised. The code provides that in such circumstances, the responsibility for informing the prosecutor lies with the investigator who knows the detail of the sensitive material. The investigator should act as soon as is reasonably practicable after the file is sent to the prosecutor and the investigator should ensure that the prosecutor is able to inspect the material so that he can assess whether it needs to be brought before a court for a ruling on disclosure (para 6.10).

Procedure as to non-disclosure

3.35 Some thought must be given by the prosecutor to the procedure as to non-disclosure. This is outlined in *R v Davis, Johnson and Rowe*.[1] In general, notice should be given to the defence that the prosecution are to apply to the court. The prosecution should give an indication of the category of the material held by it so that the defence is able to resist before the court, if it so wishes. However, there may be cases, where the disclosure of the category of the material would be contrary to the public interest: in these cases, the prosecution should still notify the defence that an application to the court is to be made, but the application will be made ex parte and the category of the material will not be specified. Finally, in highly exceptional cases even the disclosure of an ex parte application would disclose to the defence the

3.35 *Criminal investigations*

material sought to be protected, so that an ex parte application may be made by the prosecution to the court without notification of the application to the defence. In relation to material that comes within para 6.9 of the code, the final procedure described above would be the most appropriate.

1 [1993] 1 WLR 613. At the time of writing, Davis and Rowe have applied to the European Commission of Human Rights for a declaration that their right to a fair trial under Art 6 of the European Convention has been violated. The Court of Appeal had rejected the contention that there should be an inter partes hearing in all cases with disclosure of at least the category of the sensitive material.

Revelation of material to prosecutor

3.36 The disclosure officer must send the schedules to the prosecutor. Wherever practicable this should be at the same time as he sends the file containing the material for the prosecution case (para 7.1). If any material which may fall within the test for primary disclosure has been retained by the disclosure officer, the attention of the prosecutor should be drawn to that material, and it should be explained why the investigator has come to that view (para 7.2). Paragraph 7.3 details the specified material which the disclosure officer must give to the prosecutor in addition to listing material on the schedule.

Subsequent action by officer in charge and disclosure officer

3.37 Paragraphs 8.1 and 8.2 of the code pertain to the situation after primary disclosure has taken place. At the time a schedule is prepared, the officer in charge of an investigation or a disclosure officer will not know what defence the accused is to set out in a defence statement under Pt I of the Act. After a defence statement has been given, the disclosure officer must look again at the material which has been retained and must draw the attention of the prosecutor to any material which might reasonably be expected to assist the defence disclosed by the accused (para 8.1). As s 9 of the Act imposes a continuing duty on the prosecutor to disclose material which meets the test for disclosure against the accused for the duration of the criminal proceedings (subject to public interest considerations); any new material coming to light should be treated in the same way as the earlier material (para 8.2).

EFFECT OF THE CODE OF PRACTICE

3.38 Under s 26(1) a person, other than a police officer, who is charged with the duty of conducting a criminal investigation shall 'have regard' to any relevant provision of a code which would apply if the investigation were conducted by the police. This follows the precedent of the Police and Criminal Evidence Act 1984, s 67(9), so that it would seem that the code will have wide application. Under s 67(9) of the 1984 Act, persons charged with the duty of investigating offences and charging offenders include Customs and Excise officers,[1] officers of the Serious Fraud Office,[2] store detectives or other similar security officers,[3] and inspectors of the RSPCA.[4]

1 *R v Sanusi* [1992] Crim LR 43.
2 *R v Director of Serious Fraud Office, ex p Saunders* [1988] Crim LR 837.
3 *R v Bayliss* (1993) 98 Cr App Rep 235.
4 *RSPCA v Eager* [1995] Crim LR 59.

3.39 At Committee Stage in the House of Lords, amendments were moved to provide that the code should apply to all investigative authorities, and that the investigative agencies should not only have regard to a code of practice but also comply with a code of practice. This argument was resisted by the Government, which argued that the operational practices of the persons mentioned above are different from those of the police and that flexibility was needed to adapt the provisions of the code to their own particular circumstances. Some agencies undertook both investigation and prosecution, and it would not be sensible for the code to require a person to reveal material to himself, and to certify to himself that this had been done.[1]

1 HL Committee, 19 December 1995, cols 1526–1529; HL Report, 5 February 1996, cols 14–16. See also the discussion at Standing Committee B, 16 May 1996, cols 88–94, and 21 May 1996, cols 95–102.

3.40 Sections 26(2), (3) and (4) substantially follow s 67 of the 1984 Act. The provisions of the code are to be admissible in evidence, although a failure by a police officer to comply with any provision of the code, or by a person charged with a duty to investigate to have regard to a provision in the code, shall not in itself render him liable to any criminal or civil proceedings. Nonetheless, a provision of the code, or a failure to comply with or have regard to a provision, may be taken into account in deciding any relevant question arising in the proceedings.

COMMON LAW RULES

3.41 Section 27 deals with the applicability of the common law rules in relation to the revealing of material—
    (a) by a police officer or other person charged with the duty of conducting an investigation with a view to it being ascertained whether a person should be charged with an offence or whether a person charged with an offence is guilty of it; and
    (b) to a person involved in the prosecution of criminal proceedings.

Where a code prepared under s 23 and brought into operation under s 25 applies in relation to a suspected or alleged offence, such rules of common law are no longer applicable.

4 Preparatory hearings

INTRODUCTION

4.1 Part III of the Act reflects one of the major themes of the Runciman Commission, that is, to improve the efficiency of Crown Court proceedings.[1] In the past, issues frequently arose at the trial which needed to be resolved in the absence of the jury, causing disruption and inconvenience, and adding to the length and cost of proceedings. The Act puts in place a statutory scheme for preparatory hearings and binding rulings before trials in cases that are likely to be long and complex, for example, money laundering or international drug trafficking cases, in addition to giving a new general power under Pt IV for judges to make binding rulings in advance of any Crown Court trial. These provisions are modelled on existing arrangements for serious or complex fraud cases introduced by the Criminal Justice Act 1987 which was enacted after the 1986 Fraud Trials Committee Report (the Roskill Report). The detail of the new preparatory hearing provisions also take account of the proposals embodied in, and the responses received to, the Home Office consultation document 'Improving the Effectiveness of Pre-Trial Hearings in the Crown Court'.[2]

---

1. Royal Commission on Criminal Justice (Cm 2263), Chs 6 and 7. The Report recognised that attempts had been made in the past to extend the scope and effectiveness of pre-trial preparations, but concluded that they were ineffective. Despite that, it went on to recommend preparatory hearings as a means to improve the administration of justice.
2. Improving the Effectiveness of Pre-Trial Hearings in the Crown Court (Cm 2924). This proposal was part of a trilogy issued by the Government which built on recommendations of the Runciman Commission (see para 1.1).

4.2 The aim of the provisions in Pts III and IV is to ensure that potentially difficult cases come to court as thoroughly prepared and as well-presented as possible. Under Pt III the judge, either of his own volition, or on application by either party, is given the discretion to order a preparatory hearing if it would be beneficial for the subsequent trial. It is envisaged, however, that this power will only be used for long and complex cases.

4.3 If a case does not have the potential to be sufficiently lengthy or complex to merit the assignment of a judge to oversee its management, then it will not be a case that will warrant or justify a Pt III preparatory hearing. In such instances, pre-trial issues can be resolved by the usual Plea and Directions Hearings (PDHs)[1] and binding rules made under Pt IV of the Act.[2]

---

1. See paras 4.26, 5.5–5.7. In the rare instance where the new preparatory hearing process is used it will not necessarily disturb the existing arrangements for a PDH. Every case (whether or not it is a case involving serious or complex fraud) will be listed as usual for a PDH within four to six weeks of being sent to the Crown Court. A case being considered for a preparatory hearing might then be removed from the PDH scheme by either the presiding judge or the judge assigned to handle the case.
2. Improving the Effectiveness of Pre-Trial Hearings in the Crown Court (Cm 2924), Ch 5.

4.4 The main features of Pt III are that—
  (a) the same judge will conduct both the preparatory hearing and the trial—this would assist the management of difficult cases;
  (b) rulings can be made on points of law, including the admissibility of evidence before the jury is involved; such rulings may be appealed against;
  (c) the judge is given other powers to narrow the issues in dispute and to help the jury to understand the case;
  (d) sanctions are available if either side departs from its case or fails to comply with a requirement imposed at the hearing; and
  (e) such hearings will be subject to reporting restrictions.

PURPOSE OF PREPARATORY HEARINGS

4.5 Preparatory hearings were previously only held in cases of serious or complex fraud. Now any Crown Court case that offers the prospect of a complex or protracted trial may be subject to this new procedure to ensure the case comes to trial as well-prepared and presented as possible by narrowing the issues in a binding way before empanelling the jury. The same judge will conduct both the preparatory hearing and the trial.

4.6 The purpose of a preparatory hearing is to—
  (a) identify issues which are likely to be material to the verdict of the jury;
  (b) assist their comprehension of those issues;
  (c) expedite the proceedings before the jury; and
  (d) assist the judge's management of the trial (s 29(2)).[1]

Obvious trial management benefits may arise from preparatory hearings, such as—
  (a) improving and encouraging the early preparation of cases by the parties, in part by making decisions made at such hearings binding;
  (b) assisting counsel before the trial to identify what evidence and points of law are at issue thereby narrowing the issues in dispute;
  (c) clarifying, defining and simplifying the issues which are to be put before the jury;
  (d) gaining an early estimate of the probable length of the trial and its likely shape;
  (e) delivering efficiency savings as a result of shorter trials and reductions in jury costs (it would generally not be necessary to send out the jury to resolve legal arguments in their absence); and
  (f) reducing inconvenience to witnesses and jurors.

---

1 These are identical purposes to those set out on the Criminal Justice Act 1987, s 7 (preparatory hearings in serious or complex fraud cases).

POWER TO ORDER PREPARATORY HEARING

4.7 Section 29 enables a Crown Court judge, on application of the prosecutor, the accused, or any one of them if there is more than one, or on his own initiative, to order a preparatory hearing in a potentially long or complex case if it appears to him that substantial benefits are likely to accrue from such a hearing (s 29(1), (4)).

4.8   *Preparatory hearings*

4.8   Matters which could be addressed at a preparatory hearing, and on which binding rulings could be made, include—
- (a) those relating to the indictment of such questions as duplicity, severance, separate trials, the joinder of counts in the indictment, and the jurisdiction;
- (b) disputes about prosecution or defence disclosure;
- (c) admissibility of evidence (confession evidence, hearsay rule, previous convictions, identification evidence);
- (d) anonymity of witnesses and which witnesses are to be called; and
- (e) the time that the trial is expected to take.[1]

---

1   Improving the Effectiveness of Pre-Trial Hearings in the Crown Court (Cm 2924), Ch 5.

4.9   Section 29 makes it clear that if an indictment reveals evidence of serious or complex fraud then an order for a preparatory hearing must not be made under this Act but under the corresponding preparatory hearing provisions of the Criminal Justice Act 1987, ss 7–10 which continue to be applicable in such cases (s 29(3)).

4.10   Section 30 specifies the starting point for the arraignment and the trial when the judge does order a preparatory hearing to take place. Unless arraignment has taken place before, it must take place at the start of the preparatory hearing and the trial is deemed to start with the commencement of the preparatory hearing.

JUDGE'S POWERS

4.11   Section 31 sets out the powers exercisable by the judge at a preparatory hearing. These include power to adjourn the hearing, to make rulings on the admissibility of evidence and any other questions of law relating to the case (s 31(2), (3)). The judge may also require the prosecutor to provide the court and the accused with information about the case. This will be in the form of a written case statement setting out the principal facts, witnesses, exhibits, any proposition of law on which the prosecutor proposes to rely in the trial and the consequences for counts in the indictment flowing from the foregoing matters (s 31(4)(a), (5)).

4.12   The judge may then order the accused to provide a written reply setting out generally the terms of the defence and notice of points which the accused will dispute. The judge may order that written notice be given to both the court and the prosecution of any objection the accused has to the case statement and of any point of law and of admissibility of evidence that he will take, and the authorities he will rely on (s 31(6)). Where the prosecution is ordered to give written notice of a list of documents the truth of which in the prosecution's view ought not be contested the judge may order the accused to state the extent to which he agrees with the prosecutor and any reasons if he is not in agreement in relation to the admissibility of any of those documents (s 31(7)). If the judge considers such reasons are inadequate he may require that further or better reasons be provided (s 31(9)).

4.13   Once he has decided to hold a preparatory hearing, the judge is not bound to wait until that hearing takes place before ordering disclosure of information about their respective cases by the two sides. Such orders may be made before or at the hearing (s 32).

Judge's powers 4.19

4.14 These new powers are necessary if the issues in complex cases are to be refined to any worthwhile extent at a preparatory hearing and they distinguish such a hearing from the proposals in Pt IV[1] which empower judges to make binding rulings at any stage after any case has been sent to the Crown Court.

1   See paras 5.1–5.14.

Procedure

4.15 The Home Office[1] envisages that a case will enter the Pt III preparatory hearing regime as a result of the Presiding Judge designating it as suitable for judicial management and that at the same time he will assign a trial judge to handle it. The prosecuting authority would be expected to give advance warning to allow a suitably experienced judge to be assigned the case. Preparatory hearings rules will be produced specifying that an application must be made not later than 28 days after the day the case was sent to the Crown Court for trial but that time may be extended before or after it has expired.

1   Improving the Effectiveness of Pre-Trial Hearings in the Crown Court (Cm 2924), Ch 5.

4.16 The application for a preparatory hearing should be in writing to the appropriate officer of the Crown Court proposed for the trial, setting out briefly the reasons for the application. Copies should be sent simultaneously to the other party. A timetable should then be agreed between prosecution and defence to be put before the judge, who must ensure that the timetable is adhered to.[1]

1   Improving the Effectiveness of Pre-Trial Hearings in the Crown Court (Cm 2924), Ch 5.

4.17 In the case of preparatory hearings the custody time limits expire at the start of the hearing. The preparatory hearing is deemed to be the start of the trial (s 71; see para 4.10).

Non-compliance

4.18 In any instance where the judge, acting under s 31(6) or (7), orders the accused to provide information about his case, the judge must warn the accused of the possible consequences of failing to comply (s 31(8)).

4.19 The consequence or sanction follows the example set by the Criminal Justice and Public Order Act 1994 in relation to failure to mention facts when questioned, or failure or refusal to account for objects, substances or marks, or presence at the scene of the crime.[1] Section 34 of the 1996 Act similarly provides for the drawing of appropriate (adverse) inferences if either the prosecutor or the accused subsequently departs from the case disclosed at the preparatory hearing or fails to comply with a requirement imposed at the hearing.

1   Sections 34, 36, 37 provide that the jury may draw adverse inferences. See also s 35 of the 1994 Act in relation to the effect of failure to testify in court, and the Lord Chief Justice's *Practice Note* (*Crown Court: Defendant's Evidence*) [1995] 2 All ER 499; see *Butterworths Rules of Court—Criminal Court Practice*.

4.20   *Preparatory hearings*

4.20   This sanction corresponds with that provided for defence non-compliance under the new disclosure scheme in Pt I of this Act, whereby the prosecution may deduce evidence at the trial that the accused did not disclose a defence or has changed his defence and the court may draw whatever inference seems appropriate (see para 2.25).

4.21   Section 31(11) makes it clear that any order or ruling made at, or as part of, a preparatory hearing, continues in effect throughout the trial unless, on application, the judge decides to vary or discharge it in the interests of justice.

APPEALS AGAINST PREPARATORY HEARING RULINGS

4.22   Section 35 provides for an appeal to the Court of Appeal, Criminal Division, against a ruling at a preparatory hearing on the admissibility of evidence or any other question of law but only with the leave of the judge who made the ruling or with the leave of the Court of Appeal (s 35(1)). Despite the fact that leave to appeal has been granted, the judge may continue the preparatory hearing but no jury can be sworn in until the appeal has been determined or abandoned (s 35(2)). The Court of Appeal may confirm, reverse, or vary the ruling appealed against (s 35(3)).

4.23   Section 36 provides for appeals to the House of Lords against the decision of the Court of Appeal on preparatory rulings. Again, despite the fact that such an appeal is pending, the judge may continue the preparatory hearing but may not empanel a jury for the trial until that appeal has been resolved or abandoned.

4.24   These two provisions replicate the appeal provisions of the Criminal Justice Act 1987, s 9(11), (12). They appear simple and straightforward but experience of the workings of the corresponding provisions under the 1987 Act in relation to serious or complex fraud preparatory hearings and rulings would indicate the contrary. It has been argued[1] that the intention of Parliament, in providing that pre-trial legal issues in cases of serious fraud should form part of the trial, and might be the subject of appeal before a jury is empanelled, has been defeated by a succession of inconsistent decisions of the Court of Appeal.[2] These decisions are a contradictory minefield, which in the opinion of Alun Jones QC 'chart the decline of the preparatory hearing', in relation to serious fraud cases at least,[3] and may have implications for their adaptation to and usefulness for the trial of other criminal offences.

---

1   Alun Jones QC, 'The Decline and Fall of the Preparatory Hearing' [1996] Crim LR 460.
2   The cases cited, ibid are— *R v Saunders* (cc No T881630) (5 February 1990, unreported); affd [1990] Crim LR 597, CA; *R v Gunawardena* (1990) 91 Cr App Rep 55, CA; *R v Moore (No 115/51/91)* (5 February 1991, unreported), CA; *R v Smith (Wallace)* (1994) 99 Cr App Rep 233, CA; *R v Smith (Gerald) (No 93/3699/S2)* (18 August 1993, unreported), CA; *R v Virani (No 92/3900/S2)* (22 September 1993, unreported), CA; *R v Lindley (No 93/3668/S2)* (23 September 1992, unreported), CA; *R v Jennings* (1993) 98 Cr App Rep 308, CA; *R v Hunt* [1994] Crim LR 747, CA; *R v Smithson* [1994] Crim LR 913, CA; *R v Maxwell (Kevin)* (21 December 1994, unreported); *R v Maxwell (Kevin) (No 94/7352/S2)* (9 February 1995, unreported).
3   Ibid, at 462.

4.25   Section 29(2) of the 1996 Act is in part identical to the wording of the relevant provision of the Criminal Justice Act 1987 (s 7(1)). Consequently the attitude of the judiciary to the new (but identical) provision is likely to be the same. The analysis of Alun Jones QC in relation to fraud-related cases (see para 4.24), inter alia, shows the uncertainty that has occurred as to when an argument of law falls within the preparatory hearing regime. The Court of Appeal has held that s 9(3) of the 1987 Act (an order or ruling at a preparatory hearing on admissibility of evidence or a point of law) must be read subject to s 7(1) (purposes of the preparatory hearing). For example, in his view, the cases which he cites indicate variously that an argument of law will only fall within the 1987 Act if the application relates objectively to the purposes set out in s 7(1) of that Act,[1] or that the purpose of defence counsel is within those purposes, or that the purpose of the judge is within those purposes. Yet another case indicates that the purposes of counsel and of the hearing judge may be disregarded by the Court of Appeal which may itself substitute a purpose.[2] He found no guidance where defence, prosecution or judge have different or mixed purposes, but one case showed that interlocutory appeals will not be heard where an appeal is sought against a 'case management' decision.[3] His analysis also disclosed that some decisions of the Court of Appeal have treated preparatory issues as very narrow and confined to s 7(1) issues of case management (see s 29(2) of the 1996 Act). The Court of Appeal has ruled in several cases that an appeal will lie only if the ruling was fundamentally flawed and unless a case is within this principle, counsel who seek an interlocutory appeal are at risk of an order of costs against them.

1 *R v Gunawardena* [1990] 1 WLR 703, 91 Cr App Rep 55, CA.
2 *R v Maxwell (Kevin)* unreported 94/7352/S2.
3 *R v Smithson* [1994] Crim LR 913, CA.

4.26 The effect would seem to be that the scope for interlocutory appeals by either the prosecution or defence from preparatory hearing rulings or orders is now available, but is limited and does not extend to all the issues which may be raised in hearings occurring after a preparatory hearing has commenced. In comparison, however, in the majority of cases which will be dealt with outside of the preparatory hearing regime, ie at PDHs or further preliminary hearings, there is no right of interlocutory appeal at all against binding rulings including those on disclosure (see paras 5.12–5.14).

REPORTING RESTRICTIONS

4.27 Neither a preparatory hearing nor an application for leave to appeal in relation to such a hearing, nor any actual appeal that takes place, may be reported by the press or media in Great Britain (s 37(1), (2)), unless it contains nothing more than the basic information prescribed by s 37(9) namely, the address of the court and name of the judge, the names, ages, occupations, and addresses of any accused and any witnesses, the offence with which the accused is charged, the names of counsel and solicitors to the proceedings, details about any adjournment, any arrangement for bail, and whether or not legal aid has been granted.

4.28 Alternatively the judge dealing with the hearing may permit it to be reported (s 37(3)). Similarly the Court of Appeal may permit reporting of any application or appeal to it in relation to a preparatory hearing and the House of Lords can do likewise in relation to such applications or appeals to it (s 37(4)). If, however, the accused objects, then the court shall only make the order permitting reporting if, having heard the accused's representations, it appears to be in the interests of justice to do so (s 37(6)).

4.29   *Preparatory hearings*

REPORTING OFFENCES

4.29 If any reporting restriction is breached an offence is committed which results, on summary conviction, in a fine not exceeding £5,000 (s 38(2)). An offence is committed by the proprietor, editor or publisher of a newspaper or periodical, or the person who published it in any other written form and in the case of a report on radio or television, the company responsible for the broadcasting service is liable as is any person responsible for that programme who is in a corresponding position to an editor of a newspaper (s 38(1)). Criminal proceedings for this offence cannot, however, be instituted in England and Wales without the consent of the Attorney-General (s 38(3)).

Scotland

4.30 The reporting restrictions extend to Scotland (s 79(1)). Extending reporting restrictions in this way provides a safeguard against any reporting in Scotland of preparatory hearing proceedings which may be seen or heard by potential English jurors. This is consistent with reporting restrictions under the Criminal Justice Act 1987, s 11, in respect of preparatory hearings in cases of serious or complex fraud.

5 Rulings

INTRODUCTION

5.1 Part IV of the Act gives judges a new power to rule generally on points of law before the start of a Crown Court trial. It is of a wider application and significance than Pt III (preparatory hearings), which only operates in cases of potential length or complexity. Part IV, on the other hand, caters for the majority of cases which although not requiring the full machinery of a preparatory hearing, will nevertheless benefit from a ruling in advance on one or possibly more issues before the jury is empanelled.

BACKGROUND

5.2 Prior to this new legislation there were no statutory provisions for preliminary hearings, except in relation to cases of serious or complex fraud. Practice rules provided a non-statutory form of pre-trial review (PTR) to identify the issues prior to a trial. However, decisions made at the PTR were not binding and could be re-opened at the trial.

5.3 The history, nature and problems of pre-trial reviews were summed up by Watkins LJ in the Court of Appeal—

> 'The review ... has proved to be, when properly conducted and when the prosecution and defence co-operate to maximum expectation, of great assistance to the court and to the administration. It assists in highlighting the issues involved in a trial and has the effect quite often of shortening the length of it. But it does not have the force of law. It is not recognised by statute or regulation ... Thus nothing decided at a pre-trial review is enforceable in the trial ... [the review] remains more or less a form of useful and, in many cases, essentially voluntary discussion about matters affecting a forthcoming trial. The arrangements come to there are more often than not acted upon, but when they are not no penalty is available to ... punish failure to comply with what has been agreed ... or admitted'.[1]

---
1 See Improving the Effectiveness of Pre-Trial Hearings in the Crown Court (Cm 2924), Ch 1, para 6.

5.4 The Runciman Commission proposed that in less complex cases a pre-trial exchange of papers between the parties would be sufficient to improve the effectiveness of pre-trial preparation for Crown Court trial, and that in more complex cases a preparatory hearing should be held.[1]

---
1 Royal Commission on Criminal Justice (Cm 2263) Chs 6, 7.

5.5   *Rulings*

Plea and directions hearings

5.5   The Government did not follow the first of the Commission's proposals (the second is now embodied in Pt III of this Act). It introduced instead a scheme of Plea and Directions Hearings (PDHs) during 1995, and the Home Office has evidence to suggest that this process has reduced the number of cases listed for trial and ensured that cases likely to be uncontested are disposed of more quickly.[1]

1   Improving the Effectiveness of Pre-Trial Hearings in the Crown Court (Cm 2924).

5.6   Subsequently, the Lord Chief Justice issued a *Practice Direction* Plea and Directions Hearings[1] to encourage proper preparation of cases for Crown Court trial. These PDHs are in the form of brief hearings (about 15 minutes) which occur four to six weeks after a case is sent by the magistrates to the Crown Court.

1   [1995] 4 All ER 379; see *Butterworths Rules of Court—Criminal Court Practice.*

5.7   There was, however, one main weakness in the PDH process. At that hearing, if the accused pleaded guilty it was usual to pass sentence at that time unless reports were required. If the accused pleaded not guilty, the PDH was used to identify the issues likely to come up during the trial. Such brief hearings were not designed to deal with detailed pre-trial issues and the judge conducting the PDH was not empowered to make binding rulings in advance of the trial. Even when the judge of a PDH ordered a further preliminary hearing specifically to consider issues of complexity identified at the PDH, he had no power at that additional hearing to make binding rulings. Any rulings or decisions made at either a PDH or a further preliminary hearing were not enforceable at the subsequent trial.[1]

1   See further Improving the Effectiveness of Pre-Trial Hearings in the Crown Court (Cm 2924), Ch 1.

POWER TO MAKE RULINGS

5.8   Part IV remedies this defect in the pre-trial process.[1] Sections 39 and 40 provide that a judge may make binding rulings on the admissibility of evidence or other points of law in any case at a pre-trial hearing after the case has been sent to the Crown Court. This power is distinct from anything that happens at a preparatory hearing under Pt III. This new power is supplementary to, and does not diminish, the scheme of PDHs established prior to the 1996 legislation.

1   See further Improving the Effectiveness of Pre-Trial Hearings in the Crown Court (Cm 2924), Ch 4, para 31.

5.9   A binding ruling may now be made at such a hearing or, more likely, at a further preliminary hearing after the PDH. This new power makes the existing pre-trial hearing process much more effective and will be of relevance to the majority of cases which will benefit from binding rulings on issues such as disclosure, but which do not need a full-scale preparatory hearing, nor the continuity of judge that is essential to that more elaborate process.

5.10 In relation to the making of binding rulings, a change of judge between the pre-trial stage and the jury trial is permissible and in many instances, likely (s 40(6)).[1]

---
1 See para 5.13.

POWER TO MAKE RULINGS

5.11 Binding rulings can be made at a pre-trial hearing in relation to any question of admissibility of evidence and any other question of law relating to the case (s 40(1)) and either party may request such a ruling or a judge may make one of his own volition (s 40(2)). Rulings will have effect until the conclusion of the case; a case is concluded if the accused is acquitted or convicted, or if the prosecution drop the case (s 40(3)). Section 39(3) provides that binding rulings do not signal the start of the trial.

Examples of other matters on which a binding ruling could be usefully made are—
   (a) the number and nature of the counts on which the prosecution will proceed;
   (b) the identity and number of prosecution or defence witnesses to be called at the trial;
   (c) the pleas to be entered by the defence.

Variation of binding ruling

5.12 The power of a judge to make a binding ruling in advance of the trial, if there was a change of judge before the start of the trial (allowed by s 40(6)), would breach the convention that one judge cannot bind another. Consequently s 40(4) provides that the trial judge has the power to vary or discharge a binding ruling made at the pre-trial stage, either of his own volition or on application from either party, if he thinks the interests of justice require it. It is not permissible for either party to re-open the ruling unless there has been a material change of circumstances since the ruling, but the judge may in such circumstances exercise his own initiative to make a variation if he thinks it would be in the interests of justice.

REPORTING RESTRICTIONS

5.13 No pre-trial ruling, application for a ruling, variation of a ruling, or proceedings at a rulings hearing made under Pt IV may be reported by the press or media in Great Britain. However, a judge dealing with any of those matters has the power to permit publication in full detail or to the extent specified by him (s 41(1)–(3)). If there is any objection from one, or any accused (where there is more than one) then the judge must hear representations against disclosure and must only permit media publication if he considers it to be in the interests of justice (s 41(4), (5)). The prohibition on media coverage of pre-trial rulings and matters relating to them do not extend beyond the conclusion of the trial (s 41(6)). Section 42 creates offences in connection with reporting restrictions with a maximum penalty on summary conviction of a £5,000 fine (level 5). Proceedings however, may only be instigated with the consent of the Attorney General.[1]

---
1 See also corresponding provisions in paras 4.27–4.29.

5.14 *Rulings*

RIGHTS OF APPEAL

5.14 There is no right of interlocutory appeal provided to the Court of Appeal, Criminal Division in respect of binding rulings under Pt IV of the Act. As stated in para 5.12, a trial judge may vary a binding ruling if he considers it necessary in the interests of justice.

5.15 Traditionally, the Court of Appeal has limited jurisdiction over matters arising in the course of a trial on the basis that the trial on indictment should not be delayed by interim appeals or reviews of decisions made prior to conviction. If an accused has a complaint about a trial or indictment, he can appeal if he is convicted. As a matter of principle the prosecution is not generally allowed a right of appeal unless it is granted by statute.[1]

1 Improving the Effectiveness of Pre-Trial Hearings in the Crown Court (Cm 2924), Ch 4.

5.16 The position is different, however, in relation to preparatory hearings under Pt III of the Act. There the appeal provisions of the Criminal Justice Act 1987 are replicated in relation to complex and potentially lengthy criminal trials other than those cases of serious or complex fraud.[1]

1 See paras 4.22–4.26.

EFFECT ON CUSTODY TIME LIMITS

5.17 The Prosecution of Offences Act 1985, s 22 is amended to redefine 'the preliminary stage' in order to allow the custody time limit to run right up to the start of the trial proper and not merely up to arraignment. The start of trial on indictment is now defined as when the jury is sworn or when a guilty plea is accepted or, where held, the start of a preparatory hearing (s 71(1)–(3)).[1]

1 Ie, a hearing under Pt III of the 1996 Act or under the Criminal Justice Act 1987.

5.18 This ensures that the custody limits continue to operate effectively where the accused has been arraigned, as is now usually the case, at a PDH before the start of the trial. It should be noted that the making of a binding ruling does not trigger off the start of the trial and consequently the discipline that custody time limits impose on the management of cases will not be diluted.

DISCLOSURE

5.19 This topic is dealt with in Pt I of the Act (see Ch 2) but an application might usefully be made to a judge for a binding ruling before the start of the trial about the extent of disclosure. The prosecution could also use this new process to apply ex parte to protect sensitive material from disclosure.[1]

1 Improving the Effectiveness of Pre-Trial Hearings in the Crown Court (Cm 2924), Ch 4.

6 Committal and transfer

BACKGROUND

6.1 In the words of Lord McIntosh of Haringey, the issue of transfer for trial from the magistrates' court to the Crown Court—

> 'has a history of aborted reform over a considerable period . . . on no fewer than three occasions the Government have tried to come forward with reform and on each occasion reform has been delayed.
>
> ... the Runciman Commission ... recommended in respect of full committals from the magistrates' court, in their present form, that where the defendant makes a submission of no case it is considered on the basis of the papers rather than in person and that the defence is able to advance oral argument in support of a submission but that witnesses should not be called.'[1]

---

1 HL Report, 5 February 1996, cols 73, 74.

6.2 The Government's proposals, which were introduced in amendments at Committee Stage[1] rather than in the Bill as originally published, replace all committals with a transfer for trial scheme. The object was to spare witnesses having to give evidence twice—once at committal and again at the Crown Court trial—and to improve the efficiency of the courts.

---

1 HL Consideration of Commons Amendments, 26 June 1996, col 945.

6.3 The Criminal Justice and Public Order Act 1994, s 44,[1] abolished committal proceedings. It was intended that they be replaced by a paper transfer for trial procedure modelled on the provisions for serious fraud cases under the Criminal Justice Act 1987, to be brought into effect by mid-1995. However, the provisions were not brought into force. The following reason was given by Baroness Blatch—

> 'The transfer for trial scheme set out in the Criminal Justice and Public Order Act 1994 was intended to improve the efficiency of moving cases into the Crown Court. Importantly, it was also intended to resolve the difficulties identified by the Royal Commission and others of vulnerable witnesses being exposed to the double ordeal of giving oral evidence and being cross-examined at committal proceedings as well as at the trial itself.
>
> These aims and objectives are widely shared by all practitioners. The Government are committed to achieving them in a way that is effective and takes a full account of the day-to-day operation of the criminal justice system and the experience of those working within it.
>
> The work on implementation of the transfer procedures highlights certain difficulties and complexities which suggested that the transfer scheme might not in practice offer the gains in efficiency that were originally envisaged. We have concluded that the two central objectives of improved efficiency and the protection of witnesses can be better achieved by a modified form of committals of the kind proposed by the Law Society.'[2]

6.3 Committal and transfer

Part V of the 1996 Act (ss 44–47) and Sch 1 replace the abortive transfer for trial scheme with a modified form of committal proceedings and thus attempt to make the system for moving cases into the Crown Court more efficient and workable as well as shielding witnesses from the stress and inconvenience of having to give evidence in person at two different hearings. Existing transfer provisions contained in the Criminal Justice Act 1987 (serious or complex fraud) and the Criminal Justice Act 1991 (certain cases involving children) will not be affected. Because of the previous uncertainty and the significance of the new arrangements for committal the Home Office's explanation of the legislation and in particular the amendments to the Magistrates' Courts Act 1980 are reproduced in some detail as below.

1 For a commentary on the 1994 Act, see James Morton 'A Guide to the Criminal Justice and Public Order Act 1994' (1994), para 3.16.
2 HL Consideration of Commons Amendments, 26 June 1996, col 945.

CONTESTED COMMITTALS

6.4 Under the new system, the evidence considered by magistrates at a contested committal will be limited to documentary evidence tendered by the prosecution, together with any exhibits. No witnesses will be called to give oral evidence. Magistrates will continue to be able to consider any representations by the defence or the prosecution, in addition to the prosecution evidence, to help them reach their decision. After considering the evidence and hearing any representations, the court will be able either to commit the defendant for trial at Crown Court or discharge him. Otherwise the existing system will remain largely unchanged.

UNCONTESTED COMMITTALS

6.5 For uncontested committals, the requirement on the defendant and the parties to attend will remain. In such cases, the prosecution will tender its evidence in documentary form, with or without exhibits and, as at present, the court will be able to commit a defendant for trial without consideration of the evidence if satisfied that all such evidence complies with certain requirements, unless the defendant is unrepresented. Because safeguards are necessary to ensure his interests will be properly protected without a full hearing, it was therefore, decided to retain the existing arrangements. The Law Society proposal envisaged allowing cases to proceed to the Crown Court for trial without the attendance of any parties at the magistrates' court, at the discretion of the defence.[1] The implementation of such a measure would have required the introduction of some of the very same complex procedural arrangements which had caused concern in the context of the transfer scheme. It would have been necessary to introduce time limits for service of the prosecution papers, and to provide the court with the power to require the defendant to attend court in the considerable number of cases where the charges needed to be amended. For this reason, the Government decided not to make any changes to uncontested committals, but to focus on the principal objective of excluding oral evidence at contested committals. This will involve minimal changes to existing practice and procedure, which will spare witnesses the possible distress of giving evidence at contested hearings, as well as some savings in time and resources. The disclosure provisions will now operate on the basis of committals.

1 HL Consideration of Commons Amendments, 26 June 1996, col 946.

MAGISTRATES' ROLE AND LIMITATION ON EVIDENCE

6.6 The old style committal hearing with oral evidence and witness cross-examination was unsatisfactory and needed to be replaced. Excluding oral evidence will remove the requirement on witnesses, who may also be victims, to give evidence twice—once at committal and again at Crown Court trial. As to limiting the evidence considered to be prosecution evidence, it is not the function of magistrates acting as examining justices at committals to weigh the merits of competing evidence. That must be a matter for the jury at any subsequent trial. The court's role at committals is to decide whether the prosecution has adduced sufficient evidence to put the case before a jury. The new arrangements will make this clearer, thus limiting the evidence considered to prosecution evidence. Prosecution evidence should cover all documentary evidence (for example, videos, tapes etc) in addition to written evidence.

AMENDMENTS MADE BY THE 1996 ACT

6.7 Section 44(2) repeals the Criminal Justice and Public Order Act 1994, s 44, Sch 4, which would have provided for the new system of transfer, and amends Sch 11 to omit the repeals which would have been attributable to the new system of transfer. It also amends ss 34, 36 and 37 of the 1994 Act, which make provision for inferences to be drawn from an accused's silence, by replacing references to an application for dismissal, under the transfer system originally proposed, with references to a magistrates' court conducting the newly modified committal proceedings.

6.8 Section 45 amends the requirement on the prosecutor, where serious or complex fraud cases and certain cases involving children have been transferred under the Criminal Justice Acts 1987 and 1991, to copy a statement of the evidence to the accused and the court. It provides that the prosecutor should simply give copies of the documents containing the evidence to the accused and the court, and that he need not send copies of any documents which have already been sent.

6.9 Section 46 amends the War Crimes Act 1991 by removing the provisions which introduced a transfer procedure for use instead of committal proceedings for certain war crimes in England and Wales. The amendment replicates provisions of the 1994 Act which were not brought into force.[1]

---

1 See s 44(3) of, Sch 4, Pt II, para 72 to, the 1994 Act.

6.10 Section 47 introduces Sch 1 which amends the existing committal provisions and other related provisions contained in the Magistrates' Courts Act 1980. Part II of Sch 1 (paras 1–13) makes the necessary consequential and other related amendments to provisions in other legislation and Part III concerns the commencement of Sch 1.[1]

---

1 For a detailed discussion of Sch 1, see paras 6.11–6.27 et seq.

6.11 *Committal and transfer*

COMMITTAL PROCEEDINGS—THE NEW PROVISIONS

Evidence which is admissible

6.11 Sch 1, para 3 inserts the Magistrates' Court Act 1980, ss 5A–5F. Section 5A indicates evidence which is to be admissible in committal proceedings, limiting it to documentary evidence tendered by the prosecution. Limiting the admissible evidence to prosecution evidence reflects the fact that the function of magistrates acting as examining justices in committal proceedings is to decide whether the prosecution has adduced sufficient prima facie evidence to put the case before a jury, and not to weigh the merits of competing evidence. This new section provides that such evidence must be in the form of written statements complying with s 5B of the 1980 Act, of depositions complying with s 5C of the 1980 Act (together with documents or other exhibits referred to in such statements or depositions, as the case may be), of statements whose maker is unavailable or certain statements made in the course of business (s 5D), or of documents which are 'self-admissible' by virtue of other legislation (s 5E).

Written statements

6.12 Section 5B of the 1980 Act, as so inserted, sets out the formal conditions with which written statements must comply in order to be admissible as evidence in committal proceedings, including a condition that, together with any exhibits, they must be copied to each of the other parties before being tendered in evidence. The effect of s 5B(2), (3) is to preserve the formality and soundness of written statements, at present ensured by the provisions in s 102 of the 1980 Act, which is replaced by s 5B. Subsection (4) provides that, where a court considers the evidence under s 6(1) of the 1980 Act (as inserted by para 4), written statements are to be read out or summarised by leave of the court. Subsection (5) provides that any documents or other exhibit referred to in a statement is to be treated as if it had been produced and identified in court by the maker of the statement. Subsection (6) defines the term 'document' for the purpose of s 5B to provide for the admissibility of written statements and documents attached to them as exhibits at committal proceedings.

Depositions

6.13 Section 5C of the 1980 Act sets out the conditions with which a deposition must comply in order for it to be admissible as evidence in committal proceedings, namely that a copy of the deposition be sent to the prosecutor and that the prosecutor copy it to the other parties before tendering it in evidence. In addition, by virtue of s 5C(3), any document referred to in a deposition as an exhibit should either be copied to the other parties, or the document itself, or a copy of it should be made available for inspection by the other parties. Subsection (4) provides for the reading aloud of depositions which are admitted in evidence. Subsection (5) provides that depositions admitted in evidence by virtue of s 5C are to be treated as if they had been produced as an exhibit and identified in court by the person whose evidence is taken as the deposition. Subsection (6) defines the term 'document' for the purposes s 5C (cf s 5B(6) and para 6.12).

Statements

6.14 The new s 5D provides that for those cases where, for reasons of the death, insanity, illness, absence from the country, or intimidation of a witness, it is not possible to comply with the evidential requirements indicated in ss 5B and 5C of the 1980 Act (as inserted), or in cases involving certain statements made in the course of business, a statement in a document shall nonetheless be admissible as evidence in the newly modified committal proceedings, provided that the prosecutor notifies the court and the other parties that the maker of this statement is unavailable (for the reasons given above) or that this statement is a particular kind of business statement. As in the case of other written evidence, the amendments also provide that such of the statements as are in writing should be read out or summarised at committal proceedings where the court considers the evidence.

Other documents

6.15 Section 5E provides that documentary evidence which is admissible in criminal proceedings by virtue of any other enactment is to be admissible in the newly modified committal proceedings, and makes provision (similar to that for statements and depositions) for the reading out of such evidence in such proceedings.

Proof by production of copy

6.16 Section 5F provides that the prosecutor is to be able to tender copies of any of the statements, depositions, or documents which are admissible in evidence in newly modified committal proceedings, whether or not the originals are still in existence.

Modified system of committal proceedings

6.17 Paragraph 4 substitutes s 6(1), (2) of the 1980 Act to make provision for the newly modified system of committal proceedings. Subsection (1) requires a court to commit the accused for trial in the Crown Court if, after consideration of the evidence, it is of the view that there is sufficient evidence to do so, or otherwise to order that the accused be discharged. The new provision omits the reference in the existing sub-s (1) to any statement of the accused (as it is generally accepted that the right to make an unsworn statement was removed by the Criminal Justice Act 1982, s 71(1)). The requirement of a court to commit or discharge the accused under this subsection continues to be subject to any relevant provisions in the 1980 Act and any other Act relating to the summary trial of indictable offences.

6.18 Section 6(2) provides that if a court is satisfied that all the evidence tendered by the prosecution fulfils the statutory requirements set out in s 5A,[1] it may commit the accused for trial in the Crown Court without consideration of any of the evidence or exhibits, unless the accused or one of the accused is unrepresented, or contests the committal. The new subsection omits any reference to defence evidence, since this will not be admissible in committal proceedings under the newly modified system.

---

1 This was previously required by s 102 of the 1980 Act which is repealed by Sch 1, para 9, and Sch 5 to, the 1996 Act (see para 6.23).

6.19   *Committal and transfer*

New switching of mode of hearing procedure

6.19   Paragraph 5 amends s 25 of the 1980 Act to require (rather than allow, as under the old wording) a court to adjourn the hearing when switching from summary trial to committal proceedings. Such a requirement is needed to enable the prosecution to make the necessary arrangements for such proceedings, for example to ensure that the evidence is in the correct form and to put the charge in indictment form.

6.20   Paragraph 6 repeals s 28 of the 1980 Act, which provided that, where the court changed from committal proceedings to summary trial, evidence given in the committal proceedings did not have to be given again in the summary trial. This provision will no longer apply since there will be no oral evidence given in committal proceedings under the newly modified system.

Summons for committal proceedings

6.21   Paragraph 7 amends s 97 of the 1980 Act, which deals with the issue of a summons to a reluctant witness or a warrant for his arrest with a view to compelling his attendance at court for the purpose of giving evidence, so as to disapply it in respect of committal proceedings. This reflects the fact that witnesses will no longer appear in committal proceedings under the newly modified system.

6.22   Paragraph 8 inserts s 97A of the 1980 Act to make specific provision for the issue of a summons to a reluctant witness or a warrant for his arrest for the purpose of committal proceedings. This section provides that a court may issue a summons or a warrant requiring him to attend in order to have his evidence taken as a deposition, or to produce a document or other exhibit, at an appointed time and place. The appointed time for the taking of the deposition is to be such as will enable the evidence to be taken as a deposition before committal proceedings commence. Section 97A(7) indicates the penalty incurred if the witness refuses to comply with the requirement. It also imposes a requirement on the court to send to the prosecutor a copy of any deposition taken, a copy of any document produced, and an indication of any other non-documentary exhibit produced.

Oral evidence removed from committals

6.23   Paragraph 9 repeals s 102 of the 1980 Act which specified the conditions that must be satisfied before a written statement could be tendered in lieu of oral evidence in existing committal proceedings. Under the newly modified system, oral evidence will be excluded from committal proceedings, and this section therefore no longer performs its primary role.

6.24   Paragraph 10 amends s 103 of the 1980 Act to remove the reference to a child being called as a witness at committal proceedings in certain cases (because witnesses will no longer appear at such proceedings). A child's written statement will still be admissible as evidence under the newly modified committal system.

6.25   Paragraph 11 repeals s 105 of the 1980 Act, which provided that a justice could take the deposition of a person too ill to give oral evidence before examining justices. This provision is no longer appropriate to the newly modified committal system (where no oral evidence will be given before the court), not least because the provision required compliance with a requirement for the accused to have had an opportunity to cross-examine the person making the deposition.

Committal offence amendments

6.26 Paragraph 12 makes two technical amendments to s 106 of the 1980 Act, which provides that it is an offence to tender false written statements in evidence. The first amendment makes it clear that only evidence falling within s 5A(3) (which deals with the types of evidence which are to be admissible in committal proceedings) is admissible in committal proceedings. The second amendment reflects the fact that the conditions with which a written statement must comply in order for it to be admissible as evidence in committal proceedings are now contained in s 5B of the 1980 Act (and no longer in s 102 which is repealed by para 9).

Corporate representation at committals

6.27 Paragraph 13 amends Sch 3 to the 1980 Act, which allows a representative of a corporation to make a statement before examining justices in answer to the charge on behalf of a corporation. This amendment reflects the fact that oral evidence will not be considered in committal proceedings, but that it will still be possible for the parties (and representatives of corporations) to make representations at a committal hearing, as already occurs under the existing provisions.

Miscellaneous amendments

6.28 Paragraph 14 repeals the Criminal Law Amendment Act 1867, ss 6, 7, which deal with statements taken under s 105 of the 1980 Act, which is repealed by para 11 (see para 6.25).

6.29 Paragraphs 15 and 16 amend the Bankers' Books Evidence Act 1879, ss 4, 5, to make it clear that where a copy of an entry in a banker's book is used in evidence at committal proceedings, proof that it was made in the course of the bank's business and that it is a true copy may not be given orally but can only be given by an affidavit.

6.30 Paragraph 17 amends the Administration of Justice (Miscellaneous Provisions) Act 1933, s 2(2), which makes it possible for new or additional counts to be added to, or substituted for, the charge if based on the evidence put before the court. This amendment reflects the fact that, under the newly modified system, no examination or deposition can be taken before a justice in the presence of the accused.

6.31 Paragraph 18 amends the Criminal Justice Act 1948, s 41, which deals with giving evidence by certificate, to remove the reference to such evidence being admissible to the same extent as oral evidence, and the accused's being able to require the attendance of the person who signed the certificate. These amendments are a consequence of the fact that oral evidence and the attendance of witnesses are no longer to be allowed in committal proceedings. Paragraph 19 makes a similar amendment to the Theft Act 1968, s 27, which deals with giving evidence by statutory declaration, to remove the references to such declarations being admissible in committal proceedings to the same extent as oral evidence, and to the accused's being able to require the attendance at such proceedings of the person who made the declaration.

6.32 Committal and transfer

6.32 Paragraph 20 amends s 28 of the 1968 Act (orders for restitution) to reflect the fact that, under the newly modified system, no depositions will be taken before the court in committal proceedings. The effect of the amendment is to replace the reference to depositions *taken* at any committal proceedings with a reference to depositions *tendered* in evidence by the prosecutor at any committal proceedings.

6.33 Paragraph 21 makes a minor technical amendment to the Children and Young Persons Act 1969, Sch 5, which inserted a provision indicating an alternative condition which must be complied with in respect of statements made by children under the age of 14 into the Magistrates' Courts Act 1980, s 102. The amendment reflects the fact that the conditions with which a written statement must comply in order for it to be admissible as evidence in committal proceedings are now contained in new s 5B of the 1980 Act and no longer in s 102.

6.34 Paragraph 22 makes a number of consequential amendments to the Criminal Justice Act 1972, s 46, which makes provision for the admissibility of written statements made outside England and Wales. These changes reflect the new provisions in ss 5A and 5B of the 1980 Act, which replace s 102 of that Act.

6.35 Paragraph 23 amends the Sexual Offences (Amendment) Act 1976, s 3. That section restricts the evidence which is allowed, without the consent of the court, at committal proceedings involving alleged rape offences. This amendment omits references to the adducing of evidence and the asking of questions to avoid any possible ambiguity over the calling of witnesses, which is no longer permissible under the newly modified system.

6.36 Paragraph 24 amends the Police and Criminal Evidence Act 1984, s 71, which provides for the proof of a document by production of a microfilm, and provides that, in committal proceedings, that section is to have effect with the omission of the requirement that the microfilm be 'authenticated in such a manner as the court may approve'. It reflects the fact that, under the newly modified committal procedures, the prosecution cannot be put to prove its evidence.

6.37 Paragraph 25 inserts s 76(9) into the 1984 Act. The effect of the new sub-s (9) is to disapply, in relation to committal proceedings (but not any other proceedings) the provisions of s 76 (which relate to the admissibility of confessions) relating to proof by the prosecution that a confession was not obtained under duress. The effect of the exclusion of oral evidence will be that the prosecution will be unable to prove this at this stage.

6.38 Paragraph 26 inserts s 78(3) of the 1984 Act. Section 78 makes provision for a court to exclude unfair evidence in any proceedings. The effect of the amendment is to disapply the provision to committal proceedings, to reflect the fact that it is not the function of examining justices to determine matters which lie beyond what appears on the face of the evidence.

6.39 Paragraph 27 amends Sch 3 to the 1984 Act, which deals with evidence from computer records. The effect of the amendment is to disapply, in relation to committal proceedings, para 9 which gives the court the discretion to require oral evidence in lieu of a certificate as to the soundness of computer evidence.

6.40 Paragraphs 28 and 29 insert the Criminal Justice Act 1988, ss 23(5), 24(5), to disapply, in the case of newly modified committal proceedings, those sections of the 1988 Act which provide the first-hand hearsay statements contained in documents admissible in criminal proceedings. Certain requirements must be satisfied—for example, if it can be shown that the maker of the statement is dead, ill, or unavailable. As oral evidence is to be excluded from committal proceedings, it will be difficult for the prosecution to satisfy these requirements at that stage. Alternative provision for these matters is made in the new s 5D of the 1980 Act (see para 6.14).

6.41 Paragraphs 30 and 31 amend the Criminal Justice Act 1988, 26, 27, to disapply those sections in the case of committal proceedings. Section 26 enables the court to determine questions of admissibility and is inappropriate in relation to the newly modified committal procedures; and s 27, which deals with the admissibility of copy documents (and is also inappropriate), has been replaced in the case of committal proceedings with provisions specifically tailored to such proceedings (see s 5F of the 1980 Act and para 6.16).

6.42 Paragraph 32 inserts s 30(4A) into the 1988 Act, to ensure that the requirements of s 30 (which provides for the admissibility of expert reports) by reference to the giving or oral evidence, do not apply in relation to committal proceedings.

6.43 Paragraph 33 amends s 32A of the 1988 Act, which provides for the admissibility of video recordings of testimony by child witnesses, to remove what will now be inappropriate references to the possibility of a child being called as a witness in committal proceedings.

6.44 Paragraph 34 amends s 40 of the 1988 Act to enable the Crown Court to include in the indictment a count charging a person with a summary offence if the evidence relating to the offence was disclosed in the newly modified committal proceedings.

6.45 Paragraph 35 inserts s 11(3A) into the 1988 Act. Section 11 provides for the admissibility of a certificate by a constable as to the driver, owner, or user of a vehicle. The amendment ensures that the requirement that the evidence in such a certificate be such as would be admissible in oral evidence, and the opportunity for the accused to require the attendance of the person who signed the certificate is not to apply to committal proceedings.

6.46 Paragraph 36 inserts s 13(7) into the 1988 Act, to provide that the requirement, in relation to committal proceedings, that the evidence in records admissible as evidence be such as would be admissible in oral evidence, and provisions referring to the accused having appeared before the court and admitting a previous conviction or order are not to apply to such proceedings.

6.47 Paragraph 37 inserts sub-s (6A) into s 16 of the 1988 Act, which provides that documentary evidence as to breath, blood, or urine specimens may be given in road traffic offence proceedings. Paragraph 38 inserts sub-s (8A) into s 20 of the 1988 Act, which provides for the admissibility of certain documentary evidence in proceedings relating to speeding offences. These amendments ensure that the reference to the accused being able to require the attendance in court of the person who signed any such document is not to apply to committal proceedings.

6.48 Committal and transfer

COMMENCEMENT

6.48 Part III (para 39) makes provision for the Secretary of State to bring into force Pts I and II of this Schedule by order.

STATEMENTS AND DEPOSITIONS

6.49 Section 68 and Sch 2 relate to the use at the trial of written statements and depositions admitted in evidence in committal proceedings. The effect of these provisions is to ensure, subject to suitable safeguards, that written statements and depositions which have been admitted in evidence in committal proceedings may be admitted at any subsequent trial without the need for those who made the statements or depositions to give evidence orally at the trial, where the other parties do not object. Revised associated Rules of Court necessary to implement the modified procedure will be submitted to the Rule Committee and laid before Parliament, with a view to implementation in the spring of 1997.

7 Magistrates' courts

INTRODUCTION

7.1 Part VI of the Act contains miscellaneous provisions relating to procedure in magistrates' courts. The two main changes to magistrates' court procedure instituted by Pt VI are as follows. First, s 49 provides for the accused to give a plea when brought before a magistrates' court on an information charging him with an offence triable either way. The magistrates' court is not to proceed to consider which mode of trial is more suitable, unless there is an indication of a plea of not guilty. Secondly, s 52 amends the previous law relating to juveniles on remand. The magistrates' court may further remand a juvenile on an adjournment under s 5, 10(1), 17C or 18(4) of the 1980 Act without him being brought before it, and the magistrates' court is given the power to remand a juvenile for up to 28 days, although on the first appearance of a juvenile in court the maximum remand period remains eight days.

7.2 The remainder of Pt VI consists of amending provisions in respect of the circumstances in which a magistrates' court may issue a warrant in the absence of the accused (s 48), the enforcement of the payment of fines (s 50), the summons to a witness and the warrant for his arrest (s 51), and provisions in relation to the attachment of earnings (s 53). The provisions in Pt VI will come into force on a day to be appointed by the Secretary of State.

NON-APPEARANCE OF ACCUSED—ISSUE OF WARRANT

7.3 Section 48 amends the Magistrates' Court Act 1980, s 13(2), so that where a summons has been issued, the court shall not issue a warrant for arrest under s 13 unless the conditions in the new sub-ss (2A) or (2B) are fulfilled. The condition in sub-s (2A) is that it is proved to the satisfaction of the court, on oath or in such manner as may be prescribed, that the summons was served on the accused within what appears to the court to be a reasonable time before the trial or adjourned trial. The conditions in sub-s (2B) are that—
- (a) the adjournment is a second or subsequent adjournment of the trial,
- (b) the accused was present on the last (or only) occasion when the trial was adjourned, and
- (c) on that occasion the court determined the time for the hearing at which the adjournment is now being made.

EITHER WAY OFFENCES—ACCUSED'S INTENTION AS TO PLEA

7.4 Section 49(2) inserts the Magistrates' Court Act 1980, ss 17A and 17B,[1] to provide for the magistrates' court to invite the accused, or his representative in certain circumstances, to give an indication as to plea where the accused appears or is brought before the court on an information charging him with an offence triable

7.4 Magistrates' courts

either way. If there is an indication of a plea of not guilty, the court is to proceed to decide whether the case is more suitable for summary trial or for trial on indictment. The position before the amendments introduced by the Act was that pleas could not be entered when the magistrates' court was considering which mode of trial appeared more suitable. Where trial on indictment appeared more suitable to the magistrates' court, or the accused did not consent to a summary trial, the court proceeded to inquire into the information as examining magistrates (ss 20(3)(b), 21 of the 1980 Act).[2]

---

[1] Section 49(2) also inserts a new s 17C into the 1980 Act, which provides for adjournments and consequential amendments; see para 7.14.
[2] The transfer for trial provisions in the Criminal Justice and Public Order Act 1994, s 44, Sch 4, are repealed; see ss 44, 80, Sch 5, Pt I. See Ch 6.

7.5 The new sections follow from one of the proposals contained in a Home Office Consultation Document.[1] It is hoped that these provisions will result in the retention of significantly more work at magistrates' courts, as two-thirds of committals to the Crown Court are the result of magistrates' refusing jurisdiction. Therefore, there is potential to retain a larger amount of business in the magistrates' court than may be achieved by limiting the defendant's right to elect for Crown Court trial. In this respect, the figure in the Consultation Document was confirmed by the Runciman Commission, which cites evidence that 64% of either way offences were sent to the Crown Court by magistrates in 1990, presumably because they thought their sentencing powers were insufficient or that the case was otherwise too serious for them. However, in 62% of the cases in which the magistrates declined jurisdiction, the Crown Court imposed a sentence that would have been within the power of the magistrates' court to impose.[2] A second rationale for these provisions given in the consultation document is that the defendant should be prevented from exercising the right of election in order to select the sentencing forum.

---

[1] Mode of Trial: A Consultation Document (Cm 2908), paras 19–25.
[2] The Royal Commission on Criminal Justice (Cm 2263), Ch 6, para 4.

7.6 Section 17A deals with the procedure where the accused is present in court (s 17A(2)), while s 17B deals with the situation where the accused person is represented by a legal representative, since the court considers that by reason of the accused's disorderly conduct before the court it is not practicable for proceedings under s 17A to be conducted in his presence, and that it should proceed in his absence (s 17B(1)(b)–(d)). The discussion that follows below should be seen against this distinction between the two sections.

7.7 Both ss 17A and 17B have effect where the person who appears or is brought before a magistrates' court on an information charging him with an either way offence has attained the age of 18 years. Apart from the distinction mentioned in para 7.6, the procedure under ss 17A and 17B is similar—

(a) the court shall cause the charge to be written down, if this has not already been done, and to be read to the accused or to the legal representative, as appropriate (s 17A(3); s 17B(2)(a)). Section 49(4) amends s 19(2)(a) so that this does not have to be repeated if the court goes on to consider which mode of trial is more suitable under s 19.

(b) the court shall then explain to the accused that he may indicate whether (if the offence were to proceed to trial) he would plead guilty or not

Either way offences 7.10

guilty (s 17A(4)). The court shall also explain the procedure in the event of a guilty plea, and that there is a power of committal for sentence. There is no need for such a provision in s 17B, given that the accused is being represented by a legal representative.

(c) the court shall then ask the accused, or the legal representative, whether (if the offence were to proceed to trial) the accused would plead guilty or not guilty (s 17A(5); s 17B(2)(b)).

(d) if the accused, or the legal representative on behalf of the accused, indicates a plea of guilty, the court shall proceed as if the proceedings constituted from the beginning the summary trial of the information, and as if s 9(1) of the 1980 Act was complied with and the accused pleaded guilty under it (s 17A(6); s 17B(2)(c)). Section 9(1) provides that on the summary trial of an information, the court shall, if the accused appears, state to him the substance of the information, and ask whether he pleads guilty or not guilty.

(e) if the accused, or the legal representative on behalf of the accused, indicates a plea of not guilty, s 18(1) of the 1980 Act applies (s 17A(7); s 17B(2)(d)). In other words, in the case of an indication of a plea of not guilty, the normal procedure as to mode of trial will apply, as set out in s 18(1) and ss 19–23 of the 1980 Act to which s 18(1) refers. Section 18(1) is amended by s 17C(3) to incorporate the procedure under ss 17A and 17B.

(f) if the accused, or the legal representative on behalf of the accused, fails to indicate a plea he shall be taken for the purposes of ss 17A and 17B, as appropriate, and of s 18(1), of the 1980 Act, to indicate that he would plead not guilty (s 17A(8); s 17B(3)).

7.8 Section 17A(4)(b) provides that when the court explains to the accused, in ordinary language, that he may plead guilty, it shall explain that he may be committed for sentence to the Crown Court under s 38(2) of the 1980 Act. The effect of s 38(2) is that where a person is convicted on the summary trial of an offence triable either way, the court may commit that person to the Crown Court for sentencing. The committing magistrates' court must be of the opinion—

(a) that the offence or the combination of the offence and one or more offences associated with it was so serious that greater punishment should be inflicted for the offence than the court has power to impose; or

(b) in the case of a violent or sexual offence committed by a person who is not less than 21 years old, that a sentence of imprisonment for a term longer than the court has power to impose is necessary to protect the public from serious harm from him.

7.9 It must be noted that an explanation of the effect of s 38 is not necessary when the court proceeds under s 17B because there will be a legal representative acting on behalf of the accused. Section 38 of the 1980 Act applies to both ss 17A and 17B; both sections provide that in the case of a guilty plea the court shall proceed as if the proceedings constituted from the beginning the summary trial of the information and that the accused pleaded guilty under s 9 of the 1980 Act, so that s 38 becomes applicable as it does to a guilty plea in summary proceedings.

7.10 It is important to examine the extent to which ss 17A and 17B will achieve the Government's objective, as set out in the consultation document,[1] of reducing unnecessary committals to the Crown Court. The first objective of these provisions is to reduce committals by the magistrates' court. The court's discretion as to mode of trial was previously structured under s 19(3) of the 1980 Act by a number of factors. The court had to have regard to the nature of the case, whether the circumstances made the offence one of serious character, whether the punishment which a magistrates' court had the power to inflict for it would be adequate, and any other circumstances which appeared to the court to make it more suitable for the offence to be tried in one way rather than the other.[2]

1   Mode of Trial: A Consultation Document (Cm 2908). See para 7.5.
2   See also National Mode of Trial Guidelines 1995; see *Stone's Justices' Manual 1996*.

7.11 The position remains the same where a not guilty plea is indicated, but where a guilty plea is considered the court must consider sentencing as if there had been a summary trial, and then commit to the Crown Court under s 38 if its sentencing powers are not sufficient. This may serve to reduce the number of committals to the Crown Court in that the magistrates' court will consider the exercise of its sentencing powers in the event of an indication of a plea of guilty. The magistrates' court will take into account that there will not be a contested trial, and that the appropriate discount may be given for a guilty plea.

7.12 At the same time, it must be remembered that the same criteria used to determine whether there should be a committal to the Crown Court under s 19 are to be found in s 38(2) as concerns committal for sentence. It seems likely, then, that in many cases there will be a committal to the Crown Court under s 38(2) after a guilty plea has been made in the magistrates' court, where previously there would have been a committal after the magistrates' court had considered mode of trial under s 19.

7.13 The second objective of ss 17A and 17B of the 1980 Act is to prevent the accused electing for the Crown Court because he wishes to choose the sentencing forum. Sections 17A and 17B state that where the accused indicates that he would plead not guilty, s 18 of the 1980 Act applies. This means that it is still possible for the accused to indicate that he would plead not guilty and elect for the Crown Court on sentencing grounds, even though the accused intends to plead guilty at the Crown Court. This is not to suggest that the accused's perception as to the advantage of being sentenced by the Crown Court is justified.[1]

1   Royal Commission on Criminal Justice (Cm 2263), Ch 6, para 8.

INTENTION AS TO PLEA—ADJOURNMENT

7.14 Section 49(2) inserts the Magistrates' Courts Act 1980, s 17C, which provides that a magistrates' court proceeding under s 17A or 17B of the 1980 Act may adjourn the proceedings at any time, and on doing so on any occasion when the accused is present, may remand him. The court shall remand the accused if—
  (a) on the occasion on which he first appeared, or was brought before the court to answer to the information, he was in custody or, having been released on bail, surrendered to the custody of the court; or
  (b) he has been remanded at any time in the course of proceedings on the information.

Where the court remands the accused, the time fixed for the resumption of proceedings shall be that at which he is required to appear or be brought before the court in pursuance of the remand, or would be required to be brought before the court but for s 128(3A) of the 1980 Act. Section 128(3A), together with its other subsections, confines and structures the discretion of the court to further remand a person who has been remanded in custody under s 17C, so that the court may further remand a person under s 17C without bringing him before the court. Consequential amendments are made to s 128(1A), (3A), (3C) and (3E) of the 1980 Act, and to s 130(1) which deals with the transfer of remand hearings, so as to bring s 17C within their ambit.[1]

---

1 See paras 7.20 and 7.21 for a discussion of amendments relating to remand hearings in respect of persons who have not attained the age of 17 years.

ENFORCEMENT OF PAYMENT OF FINES

7.15 Section 50 amends the Magistrates' Court Act 1980, s 87. Section 87(1) of the 1980 Act provides that payment of a sum adjudged to be paid by a conviction of the magistrates' court may be enforced by the High Court or a county court (otherwise than by a writ of fieri facias or other process against goods or by imprisonment, or attachment of earnings) as if the sum were due to a clerk of the magistrates' court in pursuance of a judgment or order of the High Court or county court, as the case may be. Section 87(3) had required that the clerk of the magistrates' court should not take proceedings under s 87(1) to recover any sums adjudged to be paid by a conviction of the court from any person unless authorised to do so by the court after an inquiry into that person's means under s 82 of the 1980 Act.

7.16 As amended, the effect of s 87(3) is that the clerk of the magistrates' court should not take proceedings under s 87(1) unless there has been an inquiry under s 82 into that person's means, and he appeared to the court to have sufficient means to pay the sum forthwith. It should be noticed that there is no longer any need for authorisation by the court, so that the magistrates' clerk may take proceedings in the High Court or county court to enforce the payment of the sum, provided that an inquiry as to means has indicated that the person against whom the sum was levied has sufficient means to pay it.

SUMMONS TO WITNESS AND WARRANT FOR ARREST OF WITNESS

7.17 Section 51 inserts a new s 97(2B) and (2C) into the 1980 Act. Section 97(1) of the 1980 Act provides that where a justice of the peace is satisfied that any person in England and Wales is likely to be able to give material evidence, or produce any document or thing likely to be material evidence at the summary trial of an information or hearing of a complaint, and that that person will not voluntarily attend as a witness or produce the document or thing, the justice shall issue a summons directed to that person requiring him to attend before the magistrates' court at the time and place appointed in the summons to give evidence or to produce the document or thing.-

7.18 Section 97(2) provides that if a justice of the peace is satisfied by evidence on oath of the matters mentioned in s 97(1), and that it is probable that such a summons would not procure the attendance of the person in question, the justice may issue a warrant to arrest that person and bring him before such a court or justice, as the case may be, as aforesaid at a time and place specified in the warrant. A warrant shall not be issued where the attendance is required for the hearing of a complaint.

7.19 The effect of s 97(2B) is that a justice may refuse to issue a summons under s 97(1) in relation to a summary trial of an information if he is not satisfied that an application for the summons was made by a party to a case as soon as reasonably practicable after the accused pleaded not guilty. In relation to a summary trial of an information, s 97(2) is to be read as if the reference to the matters mentioned in s 97(1) included a reference to the matter mentioned in s 97(2B) (s 97(2C)).

REMAND

7.20 Section 52(1) removes the age restrictions to be found in ss 128(1A)(c) and (3A)(c) of the 1980 Act, and s 52(2) removes the age restriction in s 128A(1). Section 128(3A) had required that where a person was remanded in custody, and the remand was not a remand under s 128A for a period exceeding eight clear days, the court may further remand him (otherwise than under that section) on an adjournment under ss 5, 10(1), 17C or 18(4) of the 1980 Act without him being brought before it. Under s 128(3A)(c) the court had to be satisfied that he had attained the age of 17 years when he consented to the hearing or determination of such applications in his absence. A consequential amendment is made to s 128(1A)(c) so that the explanation and information given to the person as to the procedure of further remands applies to a person who has not attained the age of 17 years. Section 128A permits the magistrates' court, pursuant to an order made by statutory instrument by the Secretary of State bringing the section into effect[1] to remand the accused in custody for a period exceeding eight clear days. By s 128A(1) the section had effect only in relation to any accused person who had attained the age of 17 years.

1 See the Magistrates' Courts (Remands in Custody) Order 1989, SI 1989/970 and the Magistrates' Courts (Remands in Custody Order 1991, SI 1991/2667, which have given effect to s 128A as from 2 December 1991.

7.21 The Act now assimilates the position of those who have not yet attained the age of 17 years and adults in respect of remand. This means that after the first appearance the juvenile may be remanded for up to 28 days under s 128A. The rationale behind this amendment was stated by Baroness Blatch in the House of Lords to be that 'frequent court appearances can be disruptive for young people and not in their best interests'.[1] Further, under s 128(3A) a magistrates' court may remand the juvenile in custody on an adjournment under s 5, 10(1), 17C or 18(4), subject to the conditions set out, without his being brought before it.

1 HL 2R, 27 November 1995, col 466.

ATTACHMENT OF EARNINGS

7.22 Section 53 inserts the Attachment of Earnings Act 1971, ss 3(3B) and (3C). Sections 3(3B) and (3C) apply where a magistrates' court imposes a fine on a person in respect of an offence or, in the case of a person convicted of an offence, the magistrates' court makes a compensation order under the Powers of Criminal Courts Act 1973, s 35, requiring him to pay compensation or to make other payment, and that person consents to such an order. In such circumstances, an application does not have to be made for an attachment of earnings order: the court may at the time it imposes the fine or compensation order make an attachment of earnings order, with the consent of the person to whom such an order relates, to secure the payment of the fine or of the compensation, or other payments, rather than only on default.

8 Miscellaneous and general provisions

INTRODUCTION

8.1 Part VII contains a number of miscellaneous provisions, their only connection being that they effect changes in the criminal law and the law of criminal procedure and evidence. Sections 54–57 do however, effect a significant change in the criminal law relating to acquittals tainted by intimidation.

ACQUITTALS TAINTED BY INTIMIDATION

8.2 Sections 54–57 of the Act give effect to the recommendation of the Runciman Commission's recommendations[1] with regard to the mischief of acquittals achieved as a result of interference with, or intimidation of, jurors or witnesses. The Government recognised that the above provisions were novel, but like the Royal Commission, believed that the threats posed by interference and intimidation justify re-trials in such circumstances.[2]

---

1 Royal Commission on Criminal Justice (Cm 2263), Ch 10, para 72.
2 HL Report, 19 December 1995, cols 1581–1583, HL Report, 5 February 1996, cols 78–83.

8.3 Section 54 provides for acquittals to be quashed where there has been a conviction for an administration of justice offence in the proceedings which led to the acquittal (s 54(1)).[1] The relevant administration of justice offences are—

(a) perverting the course of justice;
(b) the intimidation of witnesses, jurors, and others contrary to the Criminal Justice and Public Order Act 1994, s 51(1);
(c) aiding, abetting, counselling, procuring, suborning, or inciting another person to commit perjury under the Perjury Act 1911, s 1 (s 54(6)).

It should be noted that the offences under the Perjury Act 1911 do not of necessity require intimidation of or interference with witnesses or jurors, although it is suggested that this is a requirement of these offences for the purposes of s 54.

---

1 The accused can of course be convicted of such offences.

8.4 A re-trial can only follow a person's acquittal where there are firm grounds for believing that the course of justice has been perverted, and where it is held to be in the interests of justice to pursue this course of action.

Procedure

8.5 The procedure to be observed for the quashing of an acquittal under ss 54–57 of the Act is as follows. The court before which the person was acquitted must certify that there is a real possibility that, but for the interference or intimidation, the acquitted person would not have been acquitted (s 54(2)).[1] Following certification, the High Court, on application to that court, if the conditions in s 55(1)–(4) are satisfied, may order that proceedings may be taken against the acquitted person for the offence for which he was acquitted (s 54(4)).

---
1 See also s 54(5) which prevents certification if it would be contrary to the interests of justice to take proceedings against the acquitted person.

8.6 The four conditions in s 55(1)–(4) are as follows. First, that it appears likely to the Court that, but for the interference or intimidation, the acquitted person would have been convicted (s 55(1)). Secondly, that it does not appear to the Court to be contrary to the interests of justice, because of time lapsed or any other reason, to renew proceedings against the acquitted person (s 55(2)). Thirdly, that it appears that the acquitted person has had a reasonable opportunity to make written representations to the Court (s 55(3)). Fourthly, it must appear to the High Court that the conviction for the administration of justice offence will stand (s 55(4)). In making this determination the court must take into account all the information before it but shall ignore the possibility of new factors coming to light (s 55(5)). Furthermore the court shall not make an order quashing an acquittal, for example, if it appears to the court that any time allowed for the giving of notice of appeal has not expired, or that an appeal is pending (s 55(6)). An order may be made by the High Court quashing an acquittal under s 54(3) in respect of an offence in which proceedings must be instituted within a prescribed time limit. In such cases the time limit is to be regarded as commencing not when the offence was committed, but from the time the order under s 54(3) was made (s 56(1)). The principal offences which will be subject to this provision are those which are also subject to the Magistrates' Courts Act 1980, s 127(1), but this provision applies to other offences specified in s 56(2) of the Act.

8.7 Section 57(1) amends s 45 of the Offences Against the Person Act 1861, by determining that a certificate issued under s 44 of the 1861 Act, or a conviction for an assault, although a bar to other proceedings, is nevertheless subject to s 54(4) of the 1996 Act. Section 57 also amends the Contempt of Court Act 1981. Section 57(2) provides that s 4(2) of the 1981 Act (contemporary reports of proceedings) shall apply to proceedings which are subject to s 54 of the Act.[1]

---
1 Section 54(4) also provides that where s 54 applies to proceedings taken under the 1981 Act, the initial step of the proceedings is a certification under s 54(2), and that the procedural steps for undertaking a prosecution under the provisions of the 1981 Act are thereby subject to this. See Sch 1, paras 4, 4A to the 1981 Act, as amended by s 57(4).

DEROGATORY ASSERTIONS

8.8 Section 58 of the Act provides that when a court of trial or an appeal court is either—

      (a) determining a sentence,[1]
      (b) determining whether a party should be committed to the Crown Court for sentence,
      (c) hearing an appeal against or reviewing a sentence, or
      (d) determining whether to grant leave to appeal against sentence,

and a speech in mitigation, or a submission relating to the sentence is made which contains, or which the court has substantial grounds for believing contains, derogatory assertions of a person's character, and which is either false or irrelevant to the issue of

8.8 Miscellaneous and general provisions

sentence, then the court may under prescribed circumstances make a full or interim restriction order in respect of such assertions (see s 58(7), (8) and para 8.9 et seq).

---

1   See s 58(9) for a definition of what constitutes a determination for the purposes of s 58.

8.9   The power of the court to make interim restriction orders recognises the fact that the court will not be in a position when an assertion is first made to judge whether a full restriction order is justified. An interim order will therefore be more appropriate, as it may be discharged at any time by the court, and in any event will be discharged when the court makes a determination with regard to sentencing (s 58(7)). An interim order can be made if there is a 'real possibility' that the assertion is derogatory and false or irrelevant (s 58(3)). The court, having heard the rest of the mitigation, and having made enquiries, can then determine whether a full restriction order is justified. The Runciman Commission recommended that the power to make a full restriction order should only be exercised as a matter of last resort. The test for the making of a full restriction order is therefore higher than the test for the making of an interim restriction order, requiring that there are substantial grounds for believing that the assertion is derogatory and false or irrelevant (s 58(4), (8)). A full order is subject to revocation by the court, but in any event ceases to have effect 12 months from the date it was made (s 58(8)).

8.10   The court cannot make an interim or a full restriction order in relation to any assertion if it appears to the court that the assertion was previously made—
   (a)   at the trial at which the person was convicted of the offence, or
   (b)   during any other proceedings relating to the offence (s 58(5)).

8.11   The effect of a restriction order is that the assertion to which the restriction order relates may not be published in a written publication or included in a relevant programme for reception in Great Britain (s 59(1)). These terms are defined by s 59(2) of the Act. An assertion is published in contravention of a restriction order if the wording or substance of the assertion is reproduced, and the person about whom the assertion is made is named, or their identity is effectively revealed (s 59(3)).

8.12   Any person, including a body corporate, who is a party to the publication of an assertion contrary to a restriction order is guilty of an offence, and subject to a fine on summary conviction not exceeding level 5 on the standard scale (s 60(1), (2)). It is however, a defence for a party charged with an offence under s 60 to establish that they or the Corporation were not aware, and neither suspected nor had reason to suspect that the assertion which was published or included in a relevant programme was subject to a restriction order (s 60(3)). Where an offence committed under this section is attributed to a body corporate, any individual directing the corporation and who may be regarded as an officer of that body may be held jointly liable with the corporation for the offence (s 60(4), (5)).

8.13   Section 61 provides that an offence in respect of a restriction order can only take place on or after the day appointed by the Secretary of State for the coming into force of s 58. Section 61(3) also provides that the operation of ss 58 and 59 are without prejudice to the prohibition or restriction on the publication or broadcasting of material under any other statutory provision. The Law of Libel Amendment Act 1888, ss 3, 8 are neither subject to, nor affected by, ss 58–60 of the Act (s 61(4), (5)). However, the making of a restriction order by the Crown Court is subject to appeal to the Court of Appeal under the Criminal Justice Act 1988, s 159 (as amended by s 61(6) of the 1996 Act).

EVIDENCE—SPECIAL PROVISIONS

Television and video

8.14 Section 62 amends the Criminal Justice Act 1988, s 32. Where a witness under the age of 14 has been given leave to give evidence through a live television link under s 32, he may not give evidence otherwise than through that link, unless the court permits otherwise. The court will grant such permission if it appears to the court to be in the interests of justice to do so (s 32(3C) (3D) of the 1988 Act as inserted by s 62(1)). Permission may be granted either by the court on its own motion, or on the application of a party to the case. The court will not entertain an application unless there has been a material change of circumstances since the court granted leave for the witness to give evidence through the live television link (s 32(3E) of the 1988 Act, as so inserted). Similar provision is made with respect to the giving of evidence by a child witness by video recording (s 32(6A)–(6D) of the 1988 Act inserted by s 62(2)). These amendments enable the court to make rulings at pre-trial hearings as to how children may give evidence at a trial. Children may therefore prepare themselves for the giving of evidence on that basis, rendering their evidence the more valuable. It is unlikely that a child witness will be faced at short notice with the trauma of having to give evidence in court. These provisions should ensure that once a decision has been made that a child should give evidence by live television link or by video recording, it cannot lightly be reversed. They do however retain some flexibility empowering a court to permit the child to give evidence in person, notwithstanding an earlier ruling that the child witness should give evidence by television link or by video recording—the discretion of the court in this regard is open-ended.

ROAD TRAFFIC—PROVISION OF SPECIMENS

8.15 The Road Traffic Act 1988, s 7(3), requires a party to provide a specimen of blood or urine for analysis in the course of a police investigation of the commission of certain road traffic offences. This can be made at a police station if certain circumstances are satisfied. One such circumstance is that a device for taking a breath sample is not available at the police station. Section 63(1) of the 1996 Act amends s 7(3) to permit the taking of blood or urine samples at a police station where the station does have a device for taking breath samples, but the constable requiring the specimen of breath has reasonable cause to believe the device is unreliable (s 7(3)(bb) of the 1988 Act). Similar provision is made by of the Transport and Works Act 1992, s 31(4) (as amended by s 63(2) of the 1996 Act).[1]

---

[1] The rationale behind this provision is that the police will be able to make full use of new evidential breath-testing equipment, which will shortly be available to police forces, by continuing to be able to exercise their existing discretion to require blood or urine samples from suspected drink-drivers. A similar provision is inserted into the 1992 Act, which provides a scheme for dealing with railway employees suspected of exceeding the alcohol limit. Previously s 7(3) of the 1988 Act did not allow specimens of blood or urine to be required in situations where a working breath-testing machine was available. The new provisions extend the police discretion to allow specimens to be taken in such situations, if the reliability of the breath-testing machine is in question.

8.16 *Miscellaneous and general provisions*

CHECKS AGAINST FINGERPRINTS AND DNA

8.16 Section 64 of the Act substitutes the Police and Criminal Evidence Act 1984, s 63A (1), (1A), (2).[1] The new provisions enable the police in England and Wales to make speculative searches of DNA and fingerprint information that has been taken under powers conferred by Pt V of the 1984 Act from any person who has been charged with or informed that he will be reported for a recordable offence. The new provision will also enable the police to cross-search that information against any other such information which has been taken and retained lawfully as part of the investigation of an offence anywhere in the United Kingdom.

---

1 Section 63A was inserted by the Criminal Justice and Public Order Act 1994, s 56.

8.17 Previously s 63A of the 1984 Act (which governed the power of search), did not cover fingerprints or samples taken from a person who had not been arrested, convicted, or cautioned. Neither did these provisions as drafted contain any specific authority to cross-search information collected in different jurisdictions within the United Kingdom.

8.18 The new powers which have been conferred on the police by s 64 already apply to Scotland under Scottish common law.

WITNESS ORDERS AND SUMMONSES

8.19 Section 65 abolishes the power of examining justices to order witnesses to attend and give evidence before the Crown Court, and references to witness orders in both the Criminal Procedure (Attendance of Witnesses) Act 1965, and the Magistrates' Courts Act 1980 are accordingly omitted.

8.20 Section 66 of the Act substitutes the Criminal Procedure (Attendance of Witnesses) Act 1965, s 2 and inserts new ss 2A–2E, relating to the issue of a summons to a witness to attend the Crown Court. Section 2 of the 1965 Act as substituted provides that the Crown Court may issue a witness summons if it is satisfied—
 (a) that the person in respect of whom the summons is issued is likely—
  (i) to be able to give material evidence, or
  (ii) to be able to produce any document or thing which is itself likely to constitute material evidence;
 (b) that the giving of evidence or the production of any document or thing is for the purpose of any criminal proceedings before the Crown Court, and
 (c) the person concerned will not voluntarily attend as a witness, or produce the document or thing.

In these circumstances, subject to the provisions of s 2, the Crown Court will issue a witness summons requiring the party to attend the Crown Court at a stated time and place, and to give the evidence or produce the document or thing (s 2(1), (2)). A witness summons will only be issued following an application (s 2(3)). The Crown Court may refuse to issue any summons if any requirement relating to the application is not fulfilled (s 2C(4)).

8.21 An application for a witness summons should be made as soon as is practicable after committal for trial, or after transfer of the case to the Crown Court (s 2(4), (5)).[1] Section 2(7) of the 1965 Act authorises the making of new Crown Court rules to give effect to the new provisions.

---

1 See also s 2(6) of the 1965 Act which concerns proceedings relating to a bill of indictment preferred under the Administration of Justice (Miscellaneous Provisions) Act 1933, s 2(2)(b).

8.22 Where a court issues a witness summons in respect of a document or thing, the court may require advance production of that document or item, in order that the applicant who sought the witness summons may inspect the evidence prior to the Crown Court hearing (s 2A). The applicant for a witness summons may, if he has inspected a document or thing under this advanced production procedure conclude that there is no further need for the continuation of the summons. In such a case he may apply to the court for a direction that the summons shall be of no further effect (s 2B(1)).

8.23 A person to whom a witness summons is directed may apply to the Crown Court to have the summons made ineffective. The applicant must satisfy the court that he was not served with notice of the application to issue the summons, that he was unrepresented and not present at the hearing which considered whether the summons should be issued, and that he cannot give evidence, or produce any document or thing likely to be of material value at the substantive hearing (s 2C(1)). For these purposes, it is irrelevant whether or not Crown Court rules may require service with notice of any application to issue a witness summons, or whether such rules permit the person the subject of the summons to be present and to be heard at the hearing (s 2C(2)). The Crown Court may refuse to direct that a witness summons be rendered ineffective if any requirement relating to the application to make the summons ineffective is not fulfilled (s 2C(4)). Any application must be made in accordance with Crown Court rules (s 2C(6), (7)).

8.24 Provision is made for the party who sought the issue of a witness summons to pay the costs of the party who is successful in obtaining from the court a direction to have a witness summons rendered ineffective. Any such costs are to be taxed and payment enforced as if they were costs incurred in a civil case in the High Court, or as a sum adjudged summarily to be paid as a civil debt (s 2C(9)).

8.25 The Crown Court may issue a witness summons of its own motion. Any party who is the subject of such a summons may apply to the court to have the summons made ineffective on the ground that he cannot provide evidence or any document or thing which is likely to constitute material evidence (ss 2D, 2E). Any person who without just excuse disobeys the requirements of a witness summons under s 2A of the 1965 Act is guilty of a contempt of court and may be punished summarily by the court as if the contempt had been committed in the face of the court (s 3(1A) of the 1965 Act as amended by s 66(3)). Section 67 amends s 4(1) of the 1965 Act to provide that a Crown Court judge may issue a warrant to arrest a person the subject of a witness summons so as to secure the attendance of that person before the court.

MISCELLANEOUS PROVISIONS

Written statements and depositions

8.26 Section 68 and Sch 2 define the admissibility of statements and depositions in evidence at the trial of an accused where such statements and depositions have been admitted in evidence in proceedings before a magistrates' court inquiring into an offence as examining justices (see also para 6.49).

8.27 The Criminal Justice Act 1967, s 9, provides that a written statement by any person shall, if the conditions prescribed in that section are satisfied, be admissible in criminal proceedings (other than committal proceedings) as evidence to the same extent as the oral evidence of that person. One of those conditions was that if the person making the statement was under the age of 21, the age of the person had to be set out in the statement. Section 69 substitutes the age of 18 for the age of 21.

Indemnification of justices and justices' clerks

8.28 The Justices of the Peace Act 1979, s 53, which provides that justices and justices' clerks may be indemnified out of local funds in respect of costs ordered to be paid by either of those parties in respect of proceedings, ie the costs of a successful appeal, is amended by s 70 of the 1996 Act. Previously indemnification would be available if, in respect of the matters giving rise to the proceedings or claim, the justice or justices' clerk had acted reasonably and in good faith. Section 70 inserts sub-s (1A) in s 53 of the 1979 Act to provide that justices and their clerks shall, in the exercise of their criminal jurisdiction, be entitled to be indemnified in respect of proceedings, *unless* it is proved in respect of the matters giving rise to the proceedings or claims that they acted in bad faith. Accordingly s 53 as amended does not remove the total risk of the liability for costs, but the liability arises only if the justice or justices' clerk acted in bad faith, or if it is so proved.

Custody time limits

8.29 Section 71 amends the Prosecution of Offences Act 1985, s 22 and the Prosecution of Offences (Custody Time Limits) Regulations 1987, SI 1987/299. Section 22 of the 1985 Act determines maximum custody time limits. Under this section, the Secretary of State may by regulations make provision, with respect to any specified preliminary stage of proceedings for an offence, as to the maximum period—
    (a) to be allowed to the prosecution to complete that stage;
    (b) during which the accused may, while awaiting completion of that stage, be—
        (i) in the custody of a magistrates' court; or
        (ii) in the custody of the Crown Court;
in relation to that offence.

8.30 Section 71 amends s 22(11) of the 1985 Act which defines 'preliminary stage', ie the factor which governs maximum custody time limits, as the start of a trial. The 'preliminary stage' does not by virtue of s 71 include any stage after the start of the trial. The start of a trial on indictment shall be regarded as having occurred in the following circumstances—

(a) when a jury is sworn to consider the issue of guilt or fitness to plead;
(b) if the court accepts a plea of guilty before a jury is sworn, and the plea is accepted.

This is subject to a judge ordering a preparatory hearing, when the trial shall start with that hearing.

Fraud

8.31 Section 72 and Sch 3 amend provisions in the Criminal Justice Act 1987 relating to preparatory hearings conducted in cases of serious or complex fraud. The principal effect of Sch 3 is to incorporate into the provisions of the 1987 Act (which govern preparatory hearings in the case of serious or complex fraud) provisions equivalent to ss 34, 37 and 38 of the 1996 Act, which apply to preparatory hearings conducted under the authority of Pt III. The nature and effect of these provisions have been considered in Ch 4.

Scotland

8.32 Section 73 amends the Criminal Procedure (Scotland) Act 1995. It does so in three ways. First, s 27(4A) is inserted to apply existing evidential presumptions to the new arrangements for tackling the problem of offending by persons whilst they are on bail, which was introduced in the Criminal Justice (Scotland) Act 1995. Secondly, it amends s 65(1) of the 1995 Act to provide for the time limits in s 65 for the commencement of trials to apply to proceedings on indictment only. The third amendment (to Sch 9) corrects a textual error made in the recent consolidation of Scottish criminal procedure legislation.

Alibi

8.33 Section 74 amends the Criminal Justice Act 1967, s 11, providing that notice of alibi shall cease to have effect except in certain cases tried before a court martial. By s 74(4), reference to alibi notice in the Criminal Justice Act 1987, s 9(6), which relates to disclosure in cases involving fraud is replaced by reference to the disclosure of an alibi defence under s 5(7) of the 1996 Act, (see para 2.17).

GENERAL PROVISIONS

8.34 Section 75 determines the time when alleged offences are to be regarded as having been committed for the purposes of ss 52(3), 55(7) of the Act.

8.35 Section 76 ensures that anything which a magistrates' court may do under the Act may be done by any other magistrates' court acting for the same petty sessional area. This principle already operates for magistrates' courts proceedings under the Magistrates' Courts Act 1980.

8.36 Section 77 sets out the powers of the Secretary of State to make orders and regulations under the Act, and prescribes what matters may be set out in any regulations or orders. In particular s 77(5) provides that a code of practice prepared by the Secretary of State under s 25 shall have no effect unless approved by a resolution of each House of Parliament.

8.37 Miscellaneous and general provisions

8.37 It is a long-established principle of criminal justice that courts dealing with the armed forces should follow the same procedures as those observed in civilian criminal courts. Section 78 reflects this principle by giving the Secretary of State power to make an order for the purpose of proceedings before a court martial and Standing Civilian Court, and for supporting investigations. Any such order may contain provisions equivalent to those in Pts I and II relating to disclosure and to a code of practice governing the investigation of an offence (s 78(2)). Section 78 makes it clear that subject to an order being made, nothing in the Act applies to such proceedings or to supporting investigations (s 78(1)).

8.38 Section 79 concerns the extent of the Act. It should be noted that Sch 4 modifies the Act in relation to Northern Ireland, to ensure that the sections of the Act which are in force in Northern Ireland are assimilated to the rules of criminal procedure applicable to Northern Ireland. Otherwise the operation of those provisions of the Act are broadly similar to their operation in England and Wales.

Appendix

Criminal Procedure and Investigations Act 1996

Criminal Procedure and Investigations Act 1996

(1996 c 25)

ARRANGEMENT OF SECTIONS

PART I
DISCLOSURE

Introduction

Section
1 Application of this Part
2 General interpretation

The main provisions

3 Primary disclosure by prosecutor
4 Primary disclosure: further provisions
5 Compulsory disclosure by accused
6 Voluntary disclosure by accused
7 Secondary disclosure by prosecutor
8 Application by accused for disclosure
9 Continuing duty of prosecutor to disclose
10 Prosecutor's failure to observe time limits
11 Faults in disclosure by accused

Time limits

12 Time limits
13 Time limits: transitional

Public interest

14 Public interest: review for summary trials
15 Public interest: review in other cases
16 Applications: opportunity to be heard

Confidentiality

17 Confidentiality of disclosed information
18 Confidentiality: contravention

Other provisions

19 Rules of court
20 Other statutory rules as to disclosure
21 Common law rules as to disclosure

PART II
CRIMINAL INVESTIGATIONS

22 Introduction
23 Code of practice
24 Examples of disclosure provisions
25 Operation and revision of code
26 Effect of code
27 Common law rules as to criminal investigations

PART III
PREPARATORY HEARINGS

Introduction
28　Introduction

Preparatory hearings
29　Power to order preparatory hearing
30　Start of trial and arraignment
31　The preparatory hearing
32　Orders before preparatory hearing
33　Crown Court Rules
34　Later stages of trial

Appeals
35　Appeals to Court of Appeal
36　Appeals to House of Lords

Reporting restrictions
37　Restrictions on reporting
38　Offences in connection with reporting

PART IV
RULINGS

39　Meaning of pre-trial hearing
40　Power to make rulings
41　Restrictions on reporting
42　Offences in connection with reporting
43　Application of this Part

PART V
COMMITTAL, TRANSFER, ETC

44　Reinstatement of certain provisions
45　Notices of transfer
46　War crimes: abolition of transfer procedure
47　Committal proceedings

PART VI
MAGISTRATES' COURTS

48　Non-appearance of accused: issue of warrant
49　Either way offences: accused's intention as to plea
50　Enforcement of payment of fines
51　Summons to witness and warrant for his arrest
52　Remand
53　Attachment of earnings

PART VII
MISCELLANEOUS AND GENERAL

Tainted acquittals
54　Acquittals tainted by intimidation etc
55　Conditions for making order
56　Time limits for proceedings
57　Tainted acquittals: supplementary

Criminal Procedure and Investigations Act 1996

Derogatory assertions
58 Orders in respect of certain assertions
59 Restriction on reporting of assertions
60 Reporting of assertions: offences
61 Reporting of assertions: commencement and supplementary

Evidence: special provisions
62 Television links and video recordings
63 Road traffic and transport: provision of specimens
64 Checks against fingerprints etc

Witness orders and summonses
65 Abolition of witness orders
66 Summons to witness to attend Crown Court
67 Witness summons: securing attendance of witness

Other miscellaneous provisions
68 Use of written statements and depositions at trial
69 Proof by written statement
70 Indemnification of justices and justices' clerks
71 Meaning of preliminary stage of criminal proceedings
72 Fraud
73 Amendments to the Criminal Procedure (Scotland) Act 1995
74 Alibi

General
75 Time when alleged offence committed
76 Power of magistrates' courts
77 Orders and regulations
78 Application to armed forces
79 Extent
80 Repeals
81 Citation

SCHEDULES
    Schedule 1—Committal Proceedings
      Part I—Magistrates' Courts Act 1980
      Part II—Other Provisions
      Part III—Commencement
    Schedule 2—Statements and depositions
    Schedule 3—Fraud
    Schedule 4—Modifications for Northern Ireland
    Schedule 5—Repeals

An Act to make provision about criminal procedure and criminal investigations.

[4 July 1996]

Parliamentary debates
House of Lords.
2nd Reading 27 November 1995: 567 HL Official Report (5th series) col 462.
Committee Stage 18 December 1995: 567 HL Official Report (5th series) col 1407; 19 December 1995: 567 HL Official Report (5th series) col 1518.
Report 1 February 1996: 568 HL Official Report (5th series) col 1558; 5 February 1996: 569 HL Official Report (5th series) col 10.
3rd Reading 19 February 1996: 569 HL Official Report (5th series) col 865.
Consideration of Commons Amendments 26 June 1996: 573 HL Official Report (5th series) col 945.
House of Commons.
2nd Reading 27 February 1996: 272 HC Official Report (6th series) col 738.
Committee Stage 30 April–21 May 1996: HC Official Report, SC B (Criminal Procedure and Investigations Bill).
3rd Reading 12 June 1996: 279 HC Official Report (6th series) col 329.

PART I
DISCLOSURE

Introduction

1 Application of this Part

(1) This Part applies where—
    (a) a person is charged with a summary offence in respect of which a court proceeds to summary trial and in respect of which he pleads not guilty,
    (b) a person who has attained the age of 18 is charged with an offence which is triable either way, in respect of which a court proceeds to summary trial and in respect of which he pleads not guilty, or
    (c) a person under the age of 18 is charged with an indictable offence in respect of which a court proceeds to summary trial and in respect of which he pleads not guilty.

(2) This Part also applies where—
    (a) a person is charged with an indictable offence and he is committed for trial for the offence concerned,
    (b) a person is charged with an indictable offence and proceedings for the trial of the person on the charge concerned are transferred to the Crown Court by virtue of a notice of transfer given under section 4 of the Criminal Justice Act 1987 (serious or complex fraud),
    (c) a person is charged with an indictable offence and proceedings for the trial of the person on the charge concerned are transferred to the Crown Court by virtue of a notice of transfer served on a magistrates' court under section 53 of the Criminal Justice Act 1991 (certain cases involving children),
    (d) a count charging a person with a summary offence is included in an indictment under the authority of section 40 of the Criminal Justice Act 1988 (common assault etc), or
    (e) a bill of indictment charging a person with an indictable offence is preferred under the authority of section 2(2)(b) of the Administration of Justice (Miscellaneous Provisions) Act 1933 (bill preferred by direction of Court of Appeal, or by direction or with consent of a judge).

(3) This Part applies in relation to alleged offences into which no criminal investigation has begun before the appointed day.

(4) For the purposes of this section a criminal investigation is an investigation which police officers or other persons have a duty to conduct with a view to it being ascertained—
    (a) whether a person should be charged with an offence, or
    (b) whether a person charged with an offence is guilty of it.

(5) The reference in subsection (3) to the appointed day is to such day as is appointed for the purposes of this Part by the Secretary of State by order.

References   See paras 2.2–2.6.

2 General interpretation

(1) References to the accused are to the person mentioned in section 1(1) or (2).

(2) Where there is more than one accused in any proceedings this Part applies separately in relation to each of the accused.

(3) References to the prosecutor are to any person acting as prosecutor, whether an individual or a body.

(4) References to material are to material of all kinds, and in particular include references to—
    (a) information, and
    (b) objects of all descriptions.

(5) References to recording information are to putting it in a durable or retrievable form (such as writing or tape).

(6) This section applies for the purposes of this Part.

References   See para 2.7.

The main provisions

3 Primary disclosure by prosecutor

(1) The prosecutor must—
    (a) disclose to the accused any prosecution material which has not previously been disclosed to the accused and which in the prosecutor's opinion might undermine the case for the prosecution against the accused, or
    (b) give to the accused a written statement that there is no material of a description mentioned in paragraph (a).

(2) For the purposes of this section prosecution material is material—
    (a) which is in the prosecutor's possession, and came into his possession in connection with the case for the prosecution against the accused, or
    (b) which, in pursuance of a code operative under Part II, he has inspected in connection with the case for the prosecution against the accused.

(3) Where material consists of information which has been recorded in any form the prosecutor discloses it for the purposes of this section—
    (a) by securing that a copy is made of it and that the copy is given to the accused, or
    (b) if in the prosecutor's opinion that is not practicable or not desirable, by allowing the accused to inspect it at a reasonable time and a reasonable place or by taking steps to secure that he is allowed to do so;

and a copy may be in such a form as the prosecutor thinks fit and need not be in the same form as that in which the information has already been recorded.

(4) Where material consists of information which has not been recorded the prosecutor discloses it for the purposes of this section by securing that it is recorded in such form as he thinks fit and—
    (a) by securing that a copy is made of it and that the copy is given to the accused, or
    (b) if in the prosecutor's opinion that is not practicable or not desirable, by allowing the accused to inspect it at a reasonable time and a reasonable place or by taking steps to secure that he is allowed to do so.

(5) Where material does not consist of information the prosecutor discloses it for the purposes of this section by allowing the accused to inspect it at a reasonable time and a reasonable place or by taking steps to secure that he is allowed to do so.

(6) Material must not be disclosed under this section to the extent that the court, on an application by the prosecutor, concludes it is not in the public interest to disclose it and orders accordingly.

Criminal Procedure and Investigations Act 1996, s 3

(7) Material must not be disclosed under this section to the extent that—
    (a) it has been intercepted in obedience to a warrant issued under section 2 of the Interception of Communications Act 1985, or
    (b) it indicates that such a warrant has been issued or that material has been intercepted in obedience to such a warrant.

(8) The prosecutor must act under this section during the period which, by virtue of section 12, is the relevant period for this section.

Definitions   For "the accused", see, by virtue of s 2(1), (6), s 1(1), (2), and note also s 2(2); for "the prosecutor", see s 2(3), (6); for "material", see s 2(4), (6); as to the recording of information, see s 2(5), (6). Note as to "prosecution material", sub-s (2) above.
References   See paras 1.2, 2.8, 2.9–2.12, 2.15, 2.18, 2.19.

4 Primary disclosure: further provisions

(1) This section applies where—
    (a) the prosecutor acts under section 3, and
    (b) before so doing he was given a document in pursuance of provision included, by virtue of section 24(3), in a code operative under Part II.

(2) In such a case the prosecutor must give the document to the accused at the same time as the prosecutor acts under section 3.

Definitions   For "the accused", see, by virtue of s 2(1), (6), s 1(1), (2), and note also s 2(2); for "the prosecutor", see s 2(3), (6).
References   See para 2.13.

5 Compulsory disclosure by accused

(1) Subject to subsections (2) to (4), this section applies where—
    (a) this Part applies by virtue of section 1(2), and
    (b) the prosecutor complies with section 3 or purports to comply with it.

(2) Where this Part applies by virtue of section 1(2)(b), this section does not apply unless—
    (a) a copy of the notice of transfer, and
    (b) copies of the documents containing the evidence,
have been given to the accused under regulations made under section 5(9) of the Criminal Justice Act 1987.

(3) Where this Part applies by virtue of section 1(2)(c), this section does not apply unless—
    (a) a copy of the notice of transfer, and
    (b) copies of the documents containing the evidence,
have been given to the accused under regulations made under paragraph 4 of Schedule 6 to the Criminal Justice Act 1991.

(4) Where this Part applies by virtue of section 1(2)(e), this section does not apply unless the prosecutor has served on the accused a copy of the indictment and a copy of the set of documents containing the evidence which is the basis of the charge.

(5) Where this section applies, the accused must give a defence statement to the court and the prosecutor.

(6) For the purposes of this section a defence statement is a written statement—
    (a) setting out in general terms the nature of the accused's defence,
    (b) indicating the matters on which he takes issue with the prosecution, and
    (c) setting out, in the case of each such matter, the reason why he takes issue with the prosecution.

(7) If the defence statement discloses an alibi the accused must give particulars of the alibi in the statement, including—
- (a) the name and address of any witness the accused believes is able to give evidence in support of the alibi, if the name and address are known to the accused when the statement is given;
- (b) any information in the accused's possession which might be of material assistance in finding any such witness, if his name or address is not known to the accused when the statement is given.

(8) For the purposes of this section evidence in support of an alibi is evidence tending to show that by reason of the presence of the accused at a particular place or in a particular area at a particular time he was not, or was unlikely to have been, at the place where the offence is alleged to have been committed at the time of its alleged commission.

(9) The accused must give a defence statement under this section during the period which, by virtue of section 12, is the relevant period for this section.

Definitions For "the accused", see, by virtue of s 2(1), (6), s 1(1), (2), and note also s 2(2); for "the prosecutor", see s 2(3), (6). Note as to "defence statement", sub-s (6) above, and as to "evidence in support of an alibi", sub-s (8) above.
References See paras 2.14–2.17, 2.19.

6 Voluntary disclosure by accused

(1) This section applies where—
- (a) this Part applies by virtue of section 1(1), and
- (b) the prosecutor complies with section 3 or purports to comply with it.

(2) The accused—
- (a) may give a defence statement to the prosecutor, and
- (b) if he does so, must also give such a statement to the court.

(3) Subsections (6) to (8) of section 5 apply for the purposes of this section as they apply for the purposes of that.

(4) If the accused gives a defence statement under this section he must give it during the period which, by virtue of section 12, is the relevant period for this section.

Definitions For "the accused", see, by virtue of s 2(1), (6), s 1(1), (2), and note also s 2(2); for "the prosecutor", see s 2(3), (6); for "defence statement" see, by virtue of sub-s (3) above, s 5(6).
References See paras 2.18, 2.19.

7 Secondary disclosure by prosecutor

(1) This section applies where the accused gives a defence statement under section 5 or 6.

(2) The prosecutor must—
- (a) disclose to the accused any prosecution material which has not previously been disclosed to the accused and which might be reasonably expected to assist the accused's defence as disclosed by the defence statement given under section 5 or 6, or
- (b) give to the accused a written statement that there is no material of a description mentioned in paragraph (a).

(3) For the purposes of this section prosecution material is material—
- (a) which is in the prosecutor's possession and came into his possession in connection with the case for the prosecution against the accused, or

(b) which, in pursuance of a code operative under Part II, he has inspected in connection with the case for the prosecution against the accused.

(4) Subsections (3) to (5) of section 3 (method by which prosecutor discloses) apply for the purposes of this section as they apply for the purposes of that.

(5) Material must not be disclosed under this section to the extent that the court, on an application by the prosecutor, concludes it is not in the public interest to disclose it and orders accordingly.

(6) Material must not be disclosed under this section to the extent that—
    (a) it has been intercepted in obedience to a warrant issued under section 2 of the Interception of Communications Act 1985, or
    (b) it indicates that such a warrant has been issued or that material has been intercepted in obedience to such a warrant.

(7) The prosecutor must act under this section during the period which, by virtue of section 12, is the relevant period for this section.

Definitions For "the accused", see, by virtue of s 2(1), (6), s 1(1), (2), and note also s 2(2); for "the prosecutor", see s 2(3), (6); for "material", see s 2(4), (6). Note as to "prosecution material", sub-s (3) above.
References See paras 2.19–2.20.

8 Application by accused for disclosure

(1) This section applies where the accused gives a defence statement under section 5 or 6 and the prosecutor complies with section 7 or purports to comply with it or fails to comply with it.

(2) If the accused has at any time reasonable cause to believe that—
    (a) there is prosecution material which might be reasonably expected to assist the accused's defence as disclosed by the defence statement given under section 5 or 6, and
    (b) the material has not been disclosed to the accused,

the accused may apply to the court for an order requiring the prosecutor to disclose such material to the accused.

(3) For the purposes of this section prosecution material is material—
    (a) which is in the prosecutor's possession and came into his possession in connection with the case for the prosecution against the accused,
    (b) which, in pursuance of a code operative under Part II, he has inspected in connection with the case for the prosecution against the accused, or
    (c) which falls within subsection (4).

(4) Material falls within this subsection if in pursuance of a code operative under Part II the prosecutor must, if he asks for the material, be given a copy of it or be allowed to inspect it in connection with the case for the prosecution against the accused.

(5) Material must not be disclosed under this section to the extent that the court, on an application by the prosecutor, concludes it is not in the public interest to disclose it and orders accordingly.

(6) Material must not be disclosed under this section to the extent that—
    (a) it has been intercepted in obedience to a warrant issued under section 2 of the Interception of Communications Act 1985, or
    (b) it indicates that such a warrant has been issued or that material has been intercepted in obedience to such a warrant.

Definitions For "the accused", see, by virtue of s 2(1), (6), s 1(1), (2), and note also s 2(2); for "the prosecutor", see s 2(3), (6); for "material", see s 2(4), (6). Note as to "prosecution material", sub-s (3) above.
References See paras 2.21, 2.22.

9 Continuing duty of prosecutor to disclose

(1) Subsection (2) applies at all times—
   (a) after the prosecutor complies with section 3 or purports to comply with it, and
   (b) before the accused is acquitted or convicted or the prosecutor decides not to proceed with the case concerned.

(2) The prosecutor must keep under review the question whether at any given time there is prosecution material which—
   (a) in his opinion might undermine the case for the prosecution against the accused, and
   (b) has not been disclosed to the accused;

and if there is such material at any time the prosecutor must disclose it to the accused as soon as is reasonably practicable.

(3) In applying subsection (2) by reference to any given time the state of affairs at that time (including the case for the prosecution as it stands at that time) must be taken into account.

(4) Subsection (5) applies at all times—
   (a) after the prosecutor complies with section 7 or purports to comply with it, and
   (b) before the accused is acquitted or convicted or the prosecutor decides not to proceed with the case concerned.

(5) The prosecutor must keep under review the question whether at any given time there is prosecution material which—
   (a) might be reasonably expected to assist the accused's defence as disclosed by the defence statement given under section 5 or 6, and
   (b) has not been disclosed to the accused;

and if there is such material at any time the prosecutor must disclose it to the accused as soon as is reasonably practicable.

(6) For the purposes of this section prosecution material is material—
   (a) which is in the prosecutor's possession and came into his possession in connection with the case for the prosecution against the accused, or
   (b) which, in pursuance of a code operative under Part II, he has inspected in connection with the case for the prosecution against the accused.

(7) Subsections (3) to (5) of section 3 (method by which prosecutor discloses) apply for the purposes of this section as they apply for the purposes of that.

(8) Material must not be disclosed under this section to the extent that the court, on an application by the prosecutor, concludes it is not in the public interest to disclose it and orders accordingly.

(9) Material must not be disclosed under this section to the extent that—
   (a) it has been intercepted in obedience to a warrant issued under section 2 of the Interception of Communications Act 1985, or
   (b) it indicates that such a warrant has been issued or that material has been intercepted in obedience to such a warrant.

Definitions For "the accused", see, by virtue of s 2(1), (6), s 1(1), (2), and note also s 2(2); for "the prosecutor", see s 2(3), (6); for "material", see s 2(4), (6). Note as to "prosecution material", sub-s (6) above.
References See para 2.23.

10 Prosecutor's failure to observe time limits

(1) This section applies if the prosecutor—
   (a) purports to act under section 3 after the end of the period which, by virtue of section 12, is the relevant period for section 3, or
   (b) purports to act under section 7 after the end of the period which, by virtue of section 12, is the relevant period for section 7.

(2) Subject to subsection (3), the failure to act during the period concerned does not on its own constitute grounds for staying the proceedings for abuse of process.

(3) Subsection (2) does not prevent the failure constituting such grounds if it involves such delay by the prosecutor that the accused is denied a fair trial.

Definitions For "the prosecutor", see s 2(3), (6).
References See para 2.24.

11 Faults in disclosure by accused

(1) This section applies where section 5 applies and the accused—
   (a) fails to give a defence statement under that section,
   (b) gives a defence statement under that section but does so after the end of the period which, by virtue of section 12, is the relevant period for section 5,
   (c) sets out inconsistent defences in a defence statement given under section 5,
   (d) at his trial puts forward a defence which is different from any defence set out in a defence statement given under section 5,
   (e) at his trial adduces evidence in support of an alibi without having given particulars of the alibi in a defence statement given under section 5, or
   (f) at his trial calls a witness to give evidence in support of an alibi without having complied with subsection (7)(a) or (b) of section 5 as regards the witness in giving a defence statement under that section.

(2) This section also applies where section 6 applies, the accused gives a defence statement under that section, and the accused—
   (a) gives the statement after the end of the period which, by virtue of section 12, is the relevant period for section 6,
   (b) sets out inconsistent defences in the statement,
   (c) at his trial puts forward a defence which is different from any defence set out in the statement,
   (d) at his trial adduces evidence in support of an alibi without having given particulars of the alibi in the statement, or
   (e) at his trial calls a witness to give evidence in support of an alibi without having complied with subsection (7)(a) or (b) of section 5 (as applied by section 6) as regards the witness in giving the statement.

(3) Where this section applies—
   (a) the court or, with the leave of the court, any other party may make such comment as appears appropriate;
   (b) the court or jury may draw such inferences as appear proper in deciding whether the accused is guilty of the offence concerned.

(4) Where the accused puts forward a defence which is different from any defence set out in a defence statement given under section 5 or 6, in doing anything under subsection (3) or in deciding whether to do anything under it the court shall have regard—
   (a) to the extent of the difference in the defences, and
   (b) to whether there is any justification for it.

(5) A person shall not be convicted of an offence solely on an inference drawn under subsection (3).

(6) Any reference in this section to evidence in support of an alibi shall be construed in accordance with section 5.

Definitions For "the accused", see, by virtue of s 2(1), (6), s 1(1), (2), and note also s 2(2); for "the prosecutor", see s 2(3), (6).
References See paras 2.25–2.27.

Time limits

12 Time limits

(1) This section has effect for the purpose of determining the relevant period for sections 3, 5, 6 and 7.

(2) Subject to subsection (3), the relevant period is a period beginning and ending with such days as the Secretary of State prescribes by regulations for the purposes of the section concerned.

(3) The regulations may do one or more of the following—
   (a) provide that the relevant period for any section shall if the court so orders be extended (or further extended) by so many days as the court specifies;
   (b) provide that the court may only make such an order if an application is made by a prescribed person and if any other prescribed conditions are fulfilled;
   (c) provide that an application may only be made if prescribed conditions are fulfilled;
   (d) provide that the number of days by which a period may be extended shall be entirely at the court's discretion;
   (e) provide that the number of days by which a period may be extended shall not exceed a prescribed number;
   (f) provide that there shall be no limit on the number of applications that may be made to extend a period;
   (g) provide that no more than a prescribed number of applications may be made to extend a period;

and references to the relevant period for a section shall be construed accordingly.

(4) Conditions mentioned in subsection (3) may be framed by reference to such factors as the Secretary of State thinks fit.

(5) Without prejudice to the generality of subsection (4), so far as the relevant period for section 3 or 7 is concerned—
   (a) conditions may be framed by reference to the nature or volume of the material concerned;
   (b) the nature of material may be defined by reference to the prosecutor's belief that the question of non-disclosure on grounds of public interest may arise.

(6) In subsection (3) "prescribed" means prescribed by regulations under this section.

Definitions For "the prosecutor", see s 2(3), (6); for "material", see s 2(4), (6). Note as to "prescribed", sub-s (6) above.
References See para 2.12.

13 Time limits: transitional

(1) As regards a case in relation to which no regulations under section 12 have come into force for the purposes of section 3, section 3(8) shall have effect as if it read—

> "(8) The prosecutor must act under this section as soon as is reasonably practicable after—
> (a) the accused pleads not guilty (where this Part applies by virtue of section 1(1)),
> (b) the accused is committed for trial (where this Part applies by virtue of section 1(2)(a)),
> (c) the proceedings are transferred (where this Part applies by virtue of section 1(2)(b) or (c)),
> (d) the count is included in the indictment (where this Part applies by virtue of section 1(2)(d)), or
> (e) the bill of indictment is preferred (where this Part applies by virtue of section 1(2)(e))."

(2) As regards a case in relation to which no regulations under section 12 have come into force for the purposes of section 7, section 7(7) shall have effect as if it read—

> "(7) The prosecutor must act under this section as soon as is reasonably practicable after the accused gives a defence statement under section 5 or 6."

Definitions For "the accused", see, by virtue of s 2(1), (6), s 1(1), (2), and note also s 2(2); for "the prosecutor", see s 2(3), (6); for "defence statement", see, partly by virtue of s 6(3), s 5(6).
References See para 2.12.

Public interest

14 Public interest: review for summary trials

(1) This section applies where this Part applies by virtue of section 1(1).

(2) At any time—
  (a) after a court makes an order under section 3(6), 7(5), 8(5) or 9(8), and
  (b) before the accused is acquitted or convicted or the prosecutor decides not to proceed with the case concerned,

the accused may apply to the court for a review of the question whether it is still not in the public interest to disclose material affected by its order.

(3) In such a case the court must review that question, and if it concludes that it is in the public interest to disclose material to any extent—
  (a) it shall so order, and
  (b) it shall take such steps as are reasonable to inform the prosecutor of its order

(4) Where the prosecutor is informed of an order made under subsection (3) he must act accordingly having regard to the provisions of this Part (unless he decides not to proceed with the case concerned).

Definitions For "the accused", see, by virtue of s 2(1), (6), s 1(1), (2), and note also s 2(2); for "the prosecutor", see s 2(3), (6); for "material", see s 2(4), (6).
References See para 2.28.

15 Public interest: review in other cases

(1) This section applies where this Part applies by virtue of section 1(2).

(2) This section applies at all times—
   (a) after a court makes an order under section 3(6), 7(5), 8(5) or 9(8), and
   (b) before the accused is acquitted or convicted or the prosecutor decides not to proceed with the case concerned.

(3) The court must keep under review the question whether at any given time it is still not in the public interest to disclose material affected by its order.

(4) The court must keep the question mentioned in subsection (3) under review without the need for an application; but the accused may apply to the court for a review of that question.

(5) If the court at any time concludes that it is in the public interest to disclose material to any extent—
   (a) it shall so order, and
   (b) it shall take such steps as are reasonable to inform the prosecutor of its order.

(6) Where the prosecutor is informed of an order made under subsection (5) he must act accordingly having regard to the provisions of this Part (unless he decides not to proceed with the case concerned).

Definitions For "the accused", see, by virtue of s 2(1), (6), s 1(1), (2), and note also s 2(2); for "the prosecutor", see s 2(3), (6); for "material", see s 2(4), (6).
References See para 2.29.

16 Applications: opportunity to be heard

Where—
   (a) an application is made under section 3(6), 7(5), 8(5), 9(8), 14(2) or 15(4),
   (b) a person claiming to have an interest in the material applies to be heard by the court, and
   (c) he shows that he was involved (whether alone or with others and whether directly or indirectly) in the prosecutor's attention being brought to the material,

the court must not make an order under section 3(6), 7(5), 8(5), 9(8), 14(3) or 15(5) (as the case may be) unless the person applying under paragraph (b) has been given an opportunity to be heard

Definitions For "the prosecutor", see s 2(3), (6); for "material", see s 2(4), (6).
References See paras 2.29, 2.30.

Confidentiality

17 Confidentiality of disclosed information

(1) If the accused is given or allowed to inspect a document or other object under—
   (a) section 3, 4, 7, 9, 14 or 15, or
   (b) an order under section 8,

then, subject to subsections (2) to (4), he must not use or disclose it or any information recorded in it.

Criminal Procedure and Investigations Act 1996, s 17

(2) The accused may use or disclose the object or information—
    (a) in connection with the proceedings for whose purposes he was given the object or allowed to inspect it,
    (b) with a view to the taking of further criminal proceedings (for instance, by way of appeal) with regard to the matter giving rise to the proceedings mentioned in paragraph (a), or
    (c) in connection with the proceedings first mentioned in paragraph (b).

(3) The accused may use or disclose—
    (a) the object to the extent that it has been displayed to the public in open court, or
    (b) the information to the extent that it has been communicated to the public in open court;

but the preceding provisions of this subsection do not apply if the object is displayed or the information is communicated in proceedings to deal with a contempt of court under section 18.

(4) If—
    (a) the accused applies to the court for an order granting permission to use or disclose the object or information, and
    (b) the court makes such an order,

the accused may use or disclose the object or information for the purpose and to the extent specified by the court.

(5) An application under subsection (4) may be made and dealt with at any time, and in particular after the accused has been acquitted or convicted or the prosecutor has decided not to proceed with the case concerned; but this is subject to rules made by virtue of section 19(2).

(6) Where—
    (a) an application is made under subsection (4), and
    (b) the prosecutor or a person claiming to have an interest in the object or information applies to be heard by the court,

the court must not make an order granting permission unless the person applying under paragraph (b) has been given an opportunity to be heard.

(7) References in this section to the court are to—
    (a) a magistrates' court, where this Part applies by virtue of section 1(1);
    (b) the Crown Court, where this Part applies by virtue of section 1(2).

(8) Nothing in this section affects any other restriction or prohibition on the use or disclosure of an object or information, whether the restriction or prohibition arises under an enactment (whenever passed) or otherwise.

Definitions For "the accused", see, by virtue of s 2(1), (6), s 1(1), (2), and note also s 2(2); for "the prosecutor", see s 2(3), (6); as to the recording of information, see s 2(5), (6). Note as to "the court", sub-s (7) above.
References See paras 2.31, 2.32.

18 Confidentiality: contravention

(1) It is a contempt of court for a person knowingly to use or disclose an object or information recorded in it if the use or disclosure is in contravention of section 17.

(2) The following courts have jurisdiction to deal with a person who is guilty of a contempt under this section—
    (a) a magistrates' court, where this Part applies by virtue of section 1(1);
    (b) the Crown Court, where this Part applies by virtue of section 1(2).

(3) A person who is guilty of a contempt under this section may be dealt with as follows—
  (a) a magistrates' court may commit him to custody for a specified period not exceeding six months or impose on him a fine not exceeding £5,000 or both;
  (b) the Crown Court may commit him to custody for a specified period not exceeding two years or impose a fine on him or both.

(4) If—
  (a) a person is guilty of a contempt under this section, and
  (b) the object concerned is in his possession,

the court finding him guilty may order that the object shall be forfeited and dealt with in such manner as the court may order.

(5) The power of the court under subsection (4) includes power to order the object to be destroyed or to be given to the prosecutor or to be placed in his custody for such period as the court may specify.

(6) If—
  (a) the court proposes to make an order under subsection (4), and
  (b) the person found guilty, or any other person claiming to have an interest in the object, applies to be heard by the court,

the court must not make the order unless the applicant has been given an opportunity to be heard.

(7) If—
  (a) a person is guilty of a contempt under this section, and
  (b) a copy of the object concerned is in his possession,

the court finding him guilty may order that the copy shall be forfeited and dealt with in such manner as the court may order.

(8) Subsections (5) and (6) apply for the purposes of subsection (7) as they apply for the purposes of subsection (4), but as if references to the object were references to the copy.

(9) An object or information shall be inadmissible as evidence in civil proceedings if to adduce it would in the opinion of the court be likely to constitute a contempt under this section; and "the court" here means the court before which the civil proceedings are being taken.

(10) The powers of a magistrates' court under this section may be exercised either of the court's own motion or by order on complaint.

Definitions For "the prosecutor", see s 2(3), (6); as to the recording of information, see s 2(5), (6).
References See paras 2.31, 2.32.

Other provisions

19 Rules of court

(1) Without prejudice to the generality of subsection (1) of—
  (a) section 144 of the Magistrates' Courts Act 1980 (magistrates' court rules), and
  (b) section 84 of the Supreme Court Act 1981 (rules of court),

the power to make rules under each of those sections includes power to make provision mentioned in subsection (2).

(2) The provision is provision as to the practice and procedure to be followed in relation to—
    (a) proceedings to deal with a contempt of court under section 18;
    (b) an application under section 3(6), 7(5), 8(2) or (5), 9(8), 14(2), 15(4), 16(b), 17(4) or (6)(b) or 18(6);
    (c) an application under regulations made under section 12;
    (d) an order under section 3(6), 7(5), 8(2) or (5), 9(8), 14(3), 17(4) or 18(4) or (7);
    (e) an order under section 15(5) (whether or not an application is made under section 15(4));
    (f) an order under regulations made under section 12.

(3) Rules made under section 144 of the Magistrates' Courts Act 1980 by virtue of subsection (2)(a) above may contain or include provision equivalent to Schedule 3 to the Contempt of Court Act 1981 (proceedings for disobeying magistrates' court order) with any modifications which the Lord Chancellor considers appropriate on the advice of or after consultation with the rule committee for magistrates' courts.

(4) Rules made by virtue of subsection (2)(b) in relation to an application under section 17(4) may include provision—
    (a) that an application to a magistrates' court must be made to a particular magistrates' court;
    (b) that an application to the Crown Court must be made to the Crown Court sitting at a particular place;
    (c) requiring persons to be notified of an application.

(5) Rules made by virtue of this section may make different provision for different cases or classes of case.

References   See para 2.33.

20 Other statutory rules as to disclosure

(1) A duty under any of the disclosure provisions shall not affect or be affected by any duty arising under any other enactment with regard to material to be provided to or by the accused or a person representing him; but this is subject to subsection (2).

(2) In making an order under section 9 of the Criminal Justice Act 1987 or section 31 of this Act (preparatory hearings) the judge may take account of anything which—
    (a) has been done,
    (b) has been required to be done, or
    (c) will be required to be done,
in pursuance of any of the disclosure provisions.

(3) Without prejudice to the generality of section 144(1) of the Magistrates' Courts Act 1980 (magistrates' court rules) the power to make rules under that section includes power to make, with regard to any proceedings before a magistrates' court which relate to an alleged offence, provision for—
    (a) requiring any party to the proceedings to disclose to the other party or parties any expert evidence which he proposes to adduce in the proceedings;
    (b) prohibiting a party who fails to comply in respect of any evidence with any requirement imposed by virtue of paragraph (a) from adducing that evidence without the leave of the court.

(4) Rules made by virtue of subsection (3)—
    (a) may specify the kinds of expert evidence to which they apply;
    (b) may exempt facts or matters of any description specified in the rules.

(5) For the purposes of this section—
- (a) the disclosure provisions are sections 3 to 9;
- (b) "enactment" includes an enactment comprised in subordinate legislation (which here has the same meaning as in the Interpretation Act 1978).

Definitions For "the accused", see, by virtue of s 2(1), (6), s 1(1), (2), and note also s 2(2); for "material", see s 2(4), (6). Note as to "the disclosure provisions" and "enactment", sub-s (5) above.
References See para 2.34.

21 Common law rules as to disclosure

(1) Where this Part applies as regards things falling to be done after the relevant time in relation to an alleged offence, the rules of common law which—
- (a) were effective immediately before the appointed day, and
- (b) relate to the disclosure of material by the prosecutor,

do not apply as regards things falling to be done after that time in relation to the alleged offence.

(2) Subsection (1) does not affect the rules of common law as to whether disclosure is in the public interest.

(3) References in subsection (1) to the relevant time are to the time when—
- (a) the accused pleads not guilty (where this Part applies by virtue of section 1(1)),
- (b) the accused is committed for trial (where this Part applies by virtue of section 1(2)(a)),
- (c) the proceedings are transferred (where this Part applies by virtue of section 1(2)(b) or (c)),
- (d) the count is included in the indictment (where this Part applies by virtue of section 1(2)(d)), or
- (e) the bill of indictment is preferred (where this Part applies by virtue of section 1(2)(e)).

(4) The reference in subsection (1) to the appointed day is to the day appointed under section 1(5).

Definitions For "the accused", see, by virtue of s 2(1), (6), s 1(1), (2), and note also s 2(2); for "the prosecutor", see s 2(3), (6); for "material", see s 2(4), (6).
References See paras 3.13, 3.20.

PART II
CRIMINAL INVESTIGATIONS

22 Introduction

(1) For the purposes of this Part a criminal investigation is an investigation conducted by police officers with a view to it being ascertained—
- (a) whether a person should be charged with an offence, or
- (b) whether a person charged with an offence is guilty of it.

(2) In this Part references to material are to material of all kinds, and in particular include references to—
- (a) information, and
- (b) objects of all descriptions.

(3) In this Part references to recording information are to putting it in a durable or retrievable form (such as writing or tape).

References See para 3.3.

23 Code of practice

(1) The Secretary of State shall prepare a code of practice containing provisions designed to secure—

- (a) that where a criminal investigation is conducted all reasonable steps are taken for the purposes of the investigation and, in particular, all reasonable lines of inquiry are pursued;
- (b) that information which is obtained in the course of a criminal investigation and may be relevant to the investigation is recorded;
- (c) that any record of such information is retained;
- (d) that any other material which is obtained in the course of a criminal investigation and may be relevant to the investigation is retained;
- (e) that information falling within paragraph (b) and material falling within paragraph (d) is revealed to a person who is involved in the prosecution of criminal proceedings arising out of or relating to the investigation and who is identified in accordance with prescribed provisions;
- (f) that where such a person inspects information or other material in pursuance of a requirement that it be revealed to him, and he requests that it be disclosed to the accused, the accused is allowed to inspect it or is given a copy of it;
- (g) that where such a person is given a document indicating the nature of information or other material in pursuance of a requirement that it be revealed to him, and he requests that it be disclosed to the accused, the accused is allowed to inspect it or is given a copy of it;
- (h) that the person who is to allow the accused to inspect information or other material or to give him a copy of it shall decide which of those (inspecting or giving a copy) is appropriate;
- (i) that where the accused is allowed to inspect material as mentioned in paragraph (f) or (g) and he requests a copy, he is given one unless the person allowing the inspection is of opinion that it is not practicable or not desirable to give him one;
- (j) that a person mentioned in paragraph (e) is given a written statement that prescribed activities which the code requires have been carried out.

(2) The code may include provision—

- (a) that a police officer identified in accordance with prescribed provisions must carry out a prescribed activity which the code requires;
- (b) that a police officer so identified must take steps to secure the carrying out by a person (whether or not a police officer) of a prescribed activity which the code requires;
- (c) that a duty must be discharged by different people in succession in prescribed circumstances (as where a person dies or retires).

(3) The code may include provision about the form in which information is to be recorded.

(4) The code may include provision about the manner in which and the period for which—

- (a) a record of information is to be retained, and
- (b) any other material is to be retained;

and if a person is charged with an offence the period may extend beyond a conviction or an acquittal.

(5) The code may include provision about the time when, the form in which, the way in which, and the extent to which, information or any other material is to be revealed to the person mentioned in subsection (1)(e).

Criminal Procedure and Investigations Act 1996, s 24

(6) The code must be so framed that it does not apply to material intercepted in obedience to a warrant issued under section 2 of the Interception of Communications Act 1985.

(7) The code may—
- (a) make different provision in relation to different cases or descriptions of case;
- (b) contain exceptions as regards prescribed cases or descriptions of case.

(8) In this section "prescribed" means prescribed by the code.

Definitions For "criminal investigation", see s 21(1); for "material", see s 21(2); as to the recording of information, see s 21(3). Note as to "prescribed", sub-s (8) above.
References See paras 3.4, 3.41.

24 Examples of disclosure provisions

(1) This section gives examples of the kinds of provision that may be included in the code by virtue of section 23(5).

(2) The code may provide that if the person required to reveal material has possession of material which he believes is sensitive he must give a document which—
- (a) indicates the nature of that material, and
- (b) states that he so believes.

(3) The code may provide that if the person required to reveal material has possession of material which is of a description prescribed under this subsection and which he does not believe is sensitive he must give a document which—
- (a) indicates the nature of that material, and
- (b) states that he does not so believe.

(4) The code may provide that if—
- (a) a document is given in pursuance of provision contained in the code by virtue of subsection (2), and
- (b) a person identified in accordance with prescribed provisions asks for any of the material,

the person giving the document must give a copy of the material asked for to the person asking for it or (depending on the circumstances) must allow him to inspect it.

(5) The code may provide that if—
- (a) a document is given in pursuance of provision contained in the code by virtue of subsection (3),
- (b) all or any of the material is of a description prescribed under this subsection, and
- (c) a person is identified in accordance with prescribed provisions as entitled to material of that description,

the person giving the document must give a copy of the material of that description to the person so identified or (depending on the circumstances) must allow him to inspect it.

(6) The code may provide that if—
- (a) a document is given in pursuance of provision contained in the code by virtue of subsection (3),
- (b) all or any of the material is not of a description prescribed under subsection (5), and
- (c) a person identified in accordance with prescribed provisions asks for any of the material not of that description,

the person giving the document must give a copy of the material asked for to the person asking for it or (depending on the circumstances) must allow him to inspect it.

(7) The code may provide that if the person required to reveal material has possession of material which he believes is sensitive and of such a nature that provision contained in the code by virtue of subsection (2) should not apply with regard to it—
    (a)   that provision shall not apply with regard to the material,
    (b)   he must notify a person identified in accordance with prescribed provisions of the existence of the material, and
    (c)   he must allow the person so notified to inspect the material.

(8) For the purposes of this section material is sensitive to the extent that its disclosure under Part I would be contrary to the public interest.

(9) In this section "prescribed" means prescribed by the code.

Definitions   For "material", see s 21(2). Note as to "sensitive", sub-s (8) above, and as to "prescribed", sub-s (9) above.
References   See paras 2.31, 3.4.

25 Operation and revision of code

(1) When the Secretary of State has prepared a code under section 23—
    (a)   he shall publish it in the form of a draft,
    (b)   he shall consider any representations made to him about the draft, and
    (c)   he may modify the draft accordingly.

(2) When the Secretary of State has acted under subsection (1) he shall lay the code before each House of Parliament, and when he has done so he may bring it into operation on such day as he may appoint by order.

(3) A code brought into operation under this section shall apply in relation to suspected or alleged offences into which no criminal investigation has begun before the day so appointed.

(4) The Secretary of State may from time to time revise a code previously brought into operation under this section; and the preceding provisions of this section shall apply to a revised code as they apply to the code as first prepared.

Definitions   For "criminal investigation", see s 21(1).
References   See paras 3.2, 3.41.

26 Effect of code

(1) A person other than a police officer who is charged with the duty of conducting an investigation with a view to it being ascertained—
    (a)   whether a person should be charged with an offence, or
    (b)   whether a person charged with an offence is guilty of it,
shall in discharging that duty have regard to any relevant provision of a code which would apply if the investigation were conducted by police officers.

(2) A failure—
    (a)   by a police officer to comply with any provision of a code for the time being in operation by virtue of an order under section 25, or
    (b)   by a person to comply with subsection (1),
shall not in itself render him liable to any criminal or civil proceedings.

(3) In all criminal and civil proceedings a code in operation at any time by virtue of an order under section 25 shall be admissible in evidence.

(4) If it appears to a court or tribunal conducting criminal or civil proceedings that—
  (a) any provision of a code in operation at any time by virtue of an order under section 25, or
  (b) any failure mentioned in subsection (2)(a) or (b),
is relevant to any question arising in the proceedings, the provision or failure shall be taken into account in deciding the question.

References See para 3.38, 3.40.

27 Common law rules as to criminal investigations

(1) Where a code prepared under section 23 and brought into operation under section 25 applies in relation to a suspected or alleged offence, the rules of common law which—
  (a) were effective immediately before the appointed day, and
  (b) relate to the matter mentioned in subsection (2),
shall not apply in relation to the suspected or alleged offence.

(2) The matter is the revealing of material—
  (a) by a police officer or other person charged with the duty of conducting an investigation with a view to it being ascertained whether a person should be charged with an offence or whether a person charged with an offence is guilty of it;
  (b) to a person involved in the prosecution of criminal proceedings.

(3) In subsection (1) "the appointed day" means the day appointed under section 25 with regard to the code as first prepared.

Definitions For "material", see s 21(2). Note as to "the appointed day" in sub-s (1), sub-s (3) above.
References See para 3.41.

PART III
PREPARATORY HEARINGS

Introduction

28 Introduction

(1) This Part applies in relation to an offence if—
  (a) on or after the appointed day the accused is committed for trial for the offence concerned,
  (b) proceedings for the trial on the charge concerned are transferred to the Crown Court on or after the appointed day, or
  (c) a bill of indictment relating to the offence is preferred on or after the appointed day under the authority of section 2(2)(b) of the Administration of Justice (Miscellaneous Provisions) Act 1933 (bill preferred by direction of Court of Appeal, or by direction or with consent of a judge).

(2) References in subsection (1) to the appointed day are to such day as is appointed for the purposes of this section by the Secretary of State by order.

(3) If an order under this section so provides, this Part applies only in relation to the Crown Court sitting at a place or places specified in the order.

(4) References in this Part to the prosecutor are to any person acting as prosecutor, whether an individual or a body.

Criminal Procedure and Investigations Act 1996, s 29

Preparatory hearings

29 Power to order preparatory hearing

(1) Where it appears to a judge of the Crown Court that an indictment reveals a case of such complexity, or a case whose trial is likely to be of such length, that substantial benefits are likely to accrue from a hearing—
    (a) before the jury are sworn, and
    (b) for any of the purposes mentioned in subsection (2),

he may order that such a hearing (in this Part referred to as a preparatory hearing) shall be held.

(2) The purposes are those of—
    (a) identifying issues which are likely to be material to the verdict of the jury;
    (b) assisting their comprehension of any such issues;
    (c) expediting the proceedings before the jury;
    (d) assisting the judge's management of the trial.

(3) No order may be made under subsection (1) where it appears to a judge of the Crown Court that the evidence on an indictment reveals a case of fraud of such seriousness or complexity as is mentioned in section 7(1) of the Criminal Justice Act 1987 (preparatory hearings in cases of serious or complex fraud).

(4) A judge may make an order under subsection (1)—
    (a) on the application of the prosecutor,
    (b) on the application of the accused or, if there is more than one, any of them, or
    (c) of the judge's own motion.

Definitions   For "the prosecutor", see s 28(4). Note as to "preparatory hearing", sub-s (1) above.
References   See paras 4.6, 4.7, 4.25.

30 Start of trial and arraignment

If a judge orders a preparatory hearing—
    (a) the trial shall start with that hearing, and
    (b) arraignment shall take place at the start of that hearing, unless it has taken place before then.

References   See para 4.10.

31 The preparatory hearing

(1) At the preparatory hearing the judge may exercise any of the powers specified in this section.

(2) The judge may adjourn a preparatory hearing from time to time.

(3) He may make a ruling as to—
    (a) any question as to the admissibility of evidence;
    (b) any other question of law relating to the case.

(4) He may order the prosecutor—
    (a) to give the court and the accused or, if there is more than one, each of them a written statement (a case statement) of the matters falling within subsection (5);

- (b) to prepare the prosecution evidence and any explanatory material in such a form as appears to the judge to be likely to aid comprehension by the jury and to give it in that form to the court and to the accused or, if there is more than one, to each of them;
- (c) to give the court and the accused or, if there is more than one, each of them written notice of documents the truth of the contents of which ought in the prosecutor's view to be admitted and of any other matters which in his view ought to be agreed;
- (d) to make any amendments of any case statement given in pursuance of an order under paragraph (a) that appear to the judge to be appropriate, having regard to objections made by the accused or, if there is more than one, by any of them.

(5) The matters referred to in subsection (4)(a) are—
- (a) the principal facts of the case for the prosecution;
- (b) the witnesses who will speak to those facts;
- (c) any exhibits relevant to those facts;
- (d) any proposition of law on which the prosecutor proposes to rely;
- (e) the consequences in relation to any of the counts in the indictment that appear to the prosecutor to flow from the matters falling within paragraphs (a) to (d).

(6) Where a judge has ordered the prosecutor to give a case statement and the prosecutor has complied with the order, the judge may order the accused or, if there is more than one, each of them—
- (a) to give the court and the prosecutor a written statement setting out in general terms the nature of his defence and indicating the principal matters on which he takes issue with the prosecution;
- (b) to give the court and the prosecutor written notice of any objections that he has to the case statement;
- (c) to give the court and the prosecutor written notice of any point of law (including any point as to the admissibility of evidence) which he wishes to take, and any authority on which he intends to rely for that purpose.

(7) Where a judge has ordered the prosecutor to give notice under subsection (4)(c) and the prosecutor has complied with the order, the judge may order the accused or, if there is more than one, each of them to give the court and the prosecutor a written notice stating—
- (a) the extent to which he agrees with the prosecutor as to documents and other matters to which the notice under subsection (4)(c) relates, and
- (b) the reason for any disagreement.

(8) A judge making an order under subsection (6) or (7) shall warn the accused or, if there is more than one, each of them of the possible consequence under section 34 of not complying with it.

(9) If it appears to a judge that reasons given in pursuance of subsection (7) are inadequate, he shall so inform the person giving them and may require him to give further or better reasons.

(10) An order under this section may specify the time within which any specified requirement contained in it is to be complied with.

(11) An order or ruling made under this section shall have effect throughout the trial, unless it appears to the judge on application made to him that the interests of justice require him to vary or discharge it.

Definitions For "the prosecutor", see s 28(4); for "preparatory hearing", see s 29(1). Note as to "a case statement", sub-s (4)(a) above.
References See paras 4.11, 4.12, 4.18, 4.21.

32 Orders before preparatory hearing

(1) This section applies where—
    (a) a judge orders a preparatory hearing, and
    (b) he decides that any order which could be made under section 31(4) to (7) at the hearing should be made before the hearing.

(2) In such a case—
    (a) he may make any such order before the hearing (or at the hearing), and
    (b) section 31(4) to (11) shall apply accordingly.

References   See para 4.13.

33 Crown Court Rules

(1) Crown Court Rules may provide that except to the extent that disclosure is required—
    (a) by rules under section 81 of the Police and Criminal Evidence Act 1984 (expert evidence), or
    (b) by section 5(7) of this Act,

anything required to be given by an accused in pursuance of a requirement imposed under section 31 need not disclose who will give evidence.

(2) Crown Court Rules may make provision as to the minimum or maximum time that may be specified under section 31(10).

34 Later stages of trial

(1) Any party may depart from the case he disclosed in pursuance of a requirement imposed under section 31.

(2) Where—
    (a) a party departs from the case he disclosed in pursuance of a requirement imposed under section 31, or
    (b) a party fails to comply with such a requirement,

the judge or, with the leave of the judge, any other party may make such comment as appears to the judge or the other party (as the case may be) to be appropriate and the jury may draw such inference as appears proper.

(3) In deciding whether to give leave the judge shall have regard—
    (a) to the extent of the departure or failure, and
    (b) to whether there is any justification for it.

(4) Except as provided by this section no part—
    (a) of a statement given under section 31(6)(a), or
    (b) of any other information relating to the case for the accused or, if there is more than one, the case for any of them, which was given in pursuance of a requirement imposed under section 31,

may be disclosed at a stage in the trial after the jury have been sworn without the consent of the accused concerned.

References   See para 4.14.

Appeals

35 Appeals to Court of Appeal

(1) An appeal shall lie to the Court of Appeal from any ruling of a judge under section 31(3), but only with the leave of the judge or of the Court of Appeal.

(2) The judge may continue a preparatory hearing notwithstanding that leave to appeal has been granted under subsection (1), but no jury shall be sworn until after the appeal has been determined or abandoned.

(3) On the termination of the hearing of an appeal, the Court of Appeal may confirm, reverse or vary the decision appealed against.

(4) Subject to rules of court made under section 53(1) of the Supreme Court Act 1981 (power by rules to distribute business of Court of Appeal between its civil and criminal divisions)—
  (a) the jurisdiction of the Court of Appeal under subsection (1) above shall be exercised by the criminal division of the court;
  (b) references in this Part to the Court of Appeal shall be construed as references to that division.

Definitions For "preparatory hearing", see s 29(1). Note as to "Court of Appeal", sub-s (4) above.
References See para 4.22.

36 Appeals to House of Lords

(1) In the Criminal Appeal Act 1968, in—
  (a) section 33(1) (right of appeal to House of Lords), and
  (b) section 36 (bail),

after "1987" there shall be inserted "or section 35 of the Criminal Procedure and Investigations Act 1996".

(2) The judge may continue a preparatory hearing notwithstanding that leave to appeal has been granted under Part II of the Criminal Appeal Act 1968, but no jury shall be sworn until after the appeal has been determined or abandoned.

References See paras 4.19, 4.23.

Reporting restrictions

37 Restrictions on reporting

(1) Except as provided by this section—
  (a) no written report of proceedings falling within subsection (2) shall be published in Great Britain;
  (b) no report of proceedings falling within subsection (2) shall be included in a relevant programme for reception in Great Britain.

(2) The following proceedings fall within this subsection—
  (a) a preparatory hearing;
  (b) an application for leave to appeal in relation to such a hearing;
  (c) an appeal in relation to such a hearing.

(3) The judge dealing with a preparatory hearing may order that subsection (1) shall not apply, or shall not apply to a specified extent, to a report of—

(a) the preparatory hearing, or
(b) an application to the judge for leave to appeal to the Court of Appeal under section 35(1) in relation to the preparatory hearing.

(4) The Court of Appeal may order that subsection (1) shall not apply, or shall not apply to a specified extent, to a report of—
(a) an appeal to the Court of Appeal under section 35(1) in relation to a preparatory hearing,
(b) an application to that Court for leave to appeal to it under section 35(1) in relation to a preparatory hearing, or
(c) an application to that Court for leave to appeal to the House of Lords under Part II of the Criminal Appeal Act 1968 in relation to a preparatory hearing.

(5) The House of Lords may order that subsection (1) shall not apply, or shall not apply to a specified extent, to a report of—
(a) an appeal to that House under Part II of the Criminal Appeal Act 1968 in relation to a preparatory hearing, or
(b) an application to that House for leave to appeal to it under Part II of the Criminal Appeal Act 1968 in relation to a preparatory hearing.

(6) Where there is only one accused and he objects to the making of an order under subsection (3), (4) or (5) the judge or the Court of Appeal or the House of Lords shall make the order if (and only if) satisfied after hearing the representations of the accused that it is in the interests of justice to do so; and if the order is made it shall not apply to the extent that a report deals with any such objection or representations.

(7) Where there are two or more accused and one or more of them objects to the making of an order under subsection (3), (4) or (5) the judge or the Court of Appeal or the House of Lords shall make the order if (and only if) satisfied after hearing the representations of each of the accused that it is in the interests of justice to do so; and if the order is made it shall not apply to the extent that a report deals with any such objection or representations.

(8) Subsection (1) does not apply to—
(a) the publication of a report of a preparatory hearing,
(b) the publication of a report of an appeal in relation to a preparatory hearing or of an application for leave to appeal in relation to such a hearing,
(c) the inclusion in a relevant programme of a report of a preparatory hearing, or
(d) the inclusion in a relevant programme of a report of an appeal in relation to a preparatory hearing or of an application for leave to appeal in relation to such a hearing,

at the conclusion of the trial of the accused or of the last of the accused to be tried.

(9) Subsection (1) does not apply to a report which contains only one or more of the following matters—
(a) the identity of the court and the name of the judge;
(b) the names, ages, home addresses and occupations of the accused and witnesses;
(c) the offence or offences, or a summary of them, with which the accused is or are charged;
(d) the names of counsel and solicitors in the proceedings;
(e) where the proceedings are adjourned, the date and place to which they are adjourned;
(f) any arrangements as to bail;
(g) whether legal aid was granted to the accused or any of the accused.

(10) The addresses that may be published or included in a relevant programme under subsection (9) are addresses—
    (a)   at any relevant time, and
    (b)   at the time of their publication or inclusion in a relevant programme;
and "relevant time" here means a time when events giving rise to the charges to which the proceedings relate occurred.

(11) Nothing in this section affects any prohibition or restriction imposed by virtue of any other enactment on a publication or on matter included in a programme.

(12) In this section—
    (a)   "publish", in relation to a report, means publish the report, either by itself or as part of a newspaper or periodical, for distribution to the public;
    (b)   expressions cognate with "publish" shall be construed accordingly;
    (c)   "relevant programme" means a programme included in a programme service, within the meaning of the Broadcasting Act 1990.

Definitions   For "preparatory hearing", see s 29(1); for "Court of Appeal", see s 35(4) (and the note thereto). Note as to "publish" (and cognate expressions) and "relevant programme", sub-s (12) above.
References   See paras 4.19, 4.27, 4.28.

38 Offences in connection with reporting

(1) If a report is published or included in a relevant programme in contravention of section 37 each of the following persons is guilty of an offence—
    (a)   in the case of a publication of a written report as part of a newspaper or periodical, any proprietor, editor or publisher of the newspaper or periodical;
    (b)   in the case of a publication of a written report otherwise than as part of a newspaper or periodical, the person who publishes it;
    (c)   in the case of the inclusion of a report in a relevant programme, any body corporate which is engaged in providing the service in which the programme is included and any person having functions in relation to the programme corresponding to those of an editor of a newspaper.

(2) A person guilty of an offence under this section is liable on summary conviction to a fine of an amount not exceeding level 5 on the standard scale

(3) Proceedings for an offence under this section shall not be instituted in England and Wales otherwise than by or with the consent of the Attorney General.

(4) Subsection (12) of section 37 applies for the purposes of this section as it applies for the purposes of that.

Definitions   For "publish" (and cognate expressions) and "relevant programme", see, by virtue of sub-s (4) above, s 37(12).
References   See para 4.29.

PART IV
RULINGS

39 Meaning of pre-trial hearing

(1) For the purposes of this Part a hearing is a pre-trial hearing if it relates to a trial on indictment and it takes place—

(a) after the accused has been committed for trial for the offence concerned or after the proceedings for the trial have been transferred to the Crown Court, and
(b) before the start of the trial.

(2) For the purposes of this Part a hearing is also a pre-trial hearing if—
(a) it relates to a trial on indictment to be held in pursuance of a bill of indictment preferred under the authority of section 2(2)(b) of the Administration of Justice (Miscellaneous Provisions) Act 1933 (bill preferred by direction of Court of Appeal, or by direction or with consent of a judge), and
(b) it takes place after the bill of indictment has been preferred and before the start of the trial.

(3) For the purposes of this section the start of a trial on indictment occurs when a jury is sworn to consider the issue of guilt or fitness to plead or, if the court accepts a plea of guilty before a jury is sworn, when that plea is accepted; but this is subject to section 8 of the Criminal Justice Act 1987 and section 30 of this Act (preparatory hearings).

References   See paras 5.8, 5.11.

40 Power to make rulings

(1) A judge may make at a pre-trial hearing a ruling as to—
(a) any question as to the admissibility of evidence;
(b) any other question of law relating to the case concerned.

(2) A ruling may be made under this section—
(a) on an application by a party to the case, or
(b) of the judge's own motion.

(3) Subject to subsection (4), a ruling made under this section has binding effect from the time it is made until the case against the accused or, if there is more than one, against each of them is disposed of; and the case against an accused is disposed of if—
(a) he is acquitted or convicted, or
(b) the prosecutor decides not to proceed with the case against him.

(4) A judge may discharge or vary (or further vary) a ruling made under this section if it appears to him that it is in the interests of justice to do so; and a judge may act under this subsection—
(a) on an application by a party to the case, or
(b) of the judge's own motion.

(5) No application may be made under subsection (4)(a) unless there has been a material change of circumstances since the ruling was made or, if a previous application has been made, since the application (or last application) was made.

(6) The judge referred to in subsection (4) need not be the judge who made the ruling or, if it has been varied, the judge (or any of the judges) who varied it.

(7) For the purposes of this section the prosecutor is any person acting as prosecutor, whether an individual or a body.

Definitions   For "pre-trial hearing", see s 39. Note as to "the prosecutor", sub-s (7) above.
References   See paras 5.8, 5.11, 5.12.

41 Restrictions on reporting

(1) Except as provided by this section—
- (a) no written report of matters falling within subsection (2) shall be published in Great Britain;
- (b) no report of matters falling within subsection (2) shall be included in a relevant programme for reception in Great Britain.

(2) The following matters fall within this subsection—
- (a) a ruling made under section 40;
- (b) proceedings on an application for a ruling to be made under section 40;
- (c) an order that a ruling made under section 40 be discharged or varied or further varied;
- (d) proceedings on an application for a ruling made under section 40 to be discharged or varied or further varied.

(3) The judge dealing with any matter falling within subsection (2) may order that subsection (1) shall not apply, or shall not apply to a specified extent, to a report of the matter.

(4) Where there is only one accused and he objects to the making of an order under subsection (3) the judge shall make the order if (and only if) satisfied after hearing the representations of the accused that it is in the interests of justice to do so; and if the order is made it shall not apply to the extent that a report deals with any such objection or representations.

(5) Where there are two or more accused and one or more of them objects to the making of an order under subsection (3) the judge shall make the order if (and only if) satisfied after hearing the representations of each of the accused that it is in the interests of justice to do so; and if the order is made it shall not apply to the extent that a report deals with any such objection or representations.

(6) Subsection (1) does not apply to—
- (a) the publication of a report of matters, or
- (b) the inclusion in a relevant programme of a report of matters,

at the conclusion of the trial of the accused or of the last of the accused to be tried.

(7) Nothing in this section affects any prohibition or restriction imposed by virtue of any other enactment on a publication or on matter included in a programme.

(8) In this section—
- (a) "publish", in relation to a report, means publish the report, either by itself or as part of a newspaper or periodical, for distribution to the public;
- (b) expressions cognate with "publish" shall be construed accordingly;
- (c) "relevant programme" means a programme included in a programme service, within the meaning of the Broadcasting Act 1990.

References See para 5.13.

42 Offences in connection with reporting

(1) If a report is published or included in a relevant programme in contravention of section 41 each of the following persons is guilty of an offence—
- (a) in the case of a publication of a written report as part of a newspaper or periodical, any proprietor, editor or publisher of the newspaper or periodical;
- (b) in the case of a publication of a written report otherwise than as part of a newspaper or periodical, the person who publishes it;

(c) in the case of the inclusion of a report in a relevant programme, any body corporate which is engaged in providing the service in which the programme is included and any person having functions in relation to the programme corresponding to those of an editor of a newspaper.

(2) A person guilty of an offence under this section is liable on summary conviction to a fine of an amount not exceeding level 5 on the standard scale.

(3) Proceedings for an offence under this section shall not be instituted in England and Wales otherwise than by or with the consent of the Attorney General.

(4) Subsection (8) of section 41 applies for the purposes of this section as it applies for the purposes of that.

Definitions For "publish" (and cognate expressions) and "relevant programme" see, by virtue of sub-s (4) above, s 41(8).
References See para 5.13.

43 Application of this Part

(1) This Part applies in relation to pre-trial hearings beginning on or after the appointed day.

(2) The reference in subsection (1) to the appointed day is to such day as is appointed for the purposes of this section by the Secretary of State by order.

Definitions For "pre-trial hearing", see s 39.

PART V
COMMITTAL, TRANSFER, ETC

44 Reinstatement of certain provisions

(1) The Criminal Justice and Public Order Act 1994 shall be amended as follows.

(2) Section 44 and Schedule 4 (which provide for transfer for trial instead of committal proceedings) shall be omitted.

(3) In each of sections 34, 36 and 37 for paragraph (a) of subsection (2) (magistrates' court proceeding with a view to transfer) there shall be substituted—

"(a) a magistrates' court inquiring into the offence as examining justices;".

(4) Sections 34(7), 36(8) and 37(7) (transitional) shall be omitted.

(5) In Schedule 11 (repeals) the entries relating to the following (which concern committal, transfer and other matters) shall be omitted—
(a) sections 13(3) and 49(2) of the Criminal Justice Act 1925;
(b) section 1 of the Criminal Procedure (Attendance of Witnesses) Act 1965;
(c) section 7 of the Criminal Justice Act 1967 and in section 36(1) of that Act the definition of "committal proceedings";
(d) in paragraph 1 of Schedule 2 to the Criminal Appeal Act 1968 the words from "section 13(3)" to "but";
(e) in section 46(1) of the Criminal Justice Act 1972 the words "Section 102 of the Magistrates' Courts Act 1980 and", "which respectively allow", "committal proceedings and in other", "and section 106 of the said Act of 1980", "which punish the making of", "102 or" and ", as the case may be", and section 46(2) of that Act;

(f) in section 32(1)(b) of the Powers of Criminal Courts Act 1973 the words "tried or";
(g) in Schedule 1 to the Interpretation Act 1978, paragraph (a) of the definition of "Committed for trial";
(h) in section 97(1) of the Magistrates' Courts Act 1980 the words from "at an inquiry" to "be) or", sections 102, 103, 105, 106 and 145(1)(e) of that Act, in section 150(1) of that Act the definition of "committal proceedings", and paragraph 2 of Schedule 5 to that Act;
(i) in section 2(2)(g) of the Criminal Attempts Act 1981 the words "or committed for trial";
(j) in section 1(2) of the Criminal Justice Act 1982 the words "trial or";
(k) paragraphs 10 and 11 of Schedule 2 to the Criminal Justice Act 1987;
(l) in section 20(4)(a) of the Legal Aid Act 1988 the words "trial or", and section 20(4)(bb) and (5) of that Act;
(m) in section 1(4) of the War Crimes Act 1991 the words "England, Wales or", and Part I of the Schedule to that Act.

(6) The 1994 Act shall be treated as having been enacted with the amendments made by subsections (2) and (5).

(7) Subsections (3) and (4) apply where a magistrates' court begins to inquire into an offence as examining justices after the day on which this Act is passed.

References See paras 6.3, 6.7.

45 Notices of transfer

(1) Section 5 of the Criminal Justice Act 1987 (notices of transfer in cases of serious or complex fraud) shall be amended as mentioned in subsections (2) and (3).

(2) In subsection (9)(a) (regulations) for the words "a statement of the evidence" there shall be substituted "copies of the documents containing the evidence (including oral evidence)".

(3) The following subsection shall be inserted after subsection (9)—

"(9A) Regulations under subsection (9)(a) above may provide that there shall be no requirement for copies of documents to accompany the copy of the notice of transfer if they are referred to, in documents sent with the notice of transfer, as having already been supplied."

(4) In Schedule 6 to the Criminal Justice Act 1991 (notices of transfer in certain cases involving children) paragraph 4 (regulations) shall be amended as mentioned in subsections (5) and (6).

(5) In sub-paragraph (1)(a) for the words "a statement of the evidence" there shall be substituted "copies of the documents containing the evidence (including oral evidence)".

(6) The following sub-paragraph shall be inserted after sub-paragraph (1)—

"(1A) Regulations under sub-paragraph (1)(a) above may provide that there shall be no requirement for copies of documents to accompany the copy of the notice of transfer if they are referred to, in documents sent with the notice of transfer, as having already been supplied."

(7) In paragraph 6 of Schedule 6 to the 1991 Act (reporting restrictions) in sub-paragraph (8) for the words "sub-paragraphs (5) and (6)" there shall be substituted "sub-paragraphs (5) and (7)".

(8) This section applies where a notice of transfer is given under section 4 of the 1987 Act or served under section 53 of the 1991 Act (as the case may be) on or after the appointed day.

(9) The reference in subsection (8) to the appointed day is to such day as is appointed for the purposes of this section by the Secretary of State by order.

References See paras 6.3, 6.8.

46 War crimes: abolition of transfer procedure

(1) In the War Crimes Act 1991—
  (a) in section 1(4) (which introduces the Schedule providing a procedure for use instead of committal proceedings for certain war crimes) the words "England, Wales or" shall be omitted, and
  (b) Part I of the Schedule (procedure for use in England and Wales instead of committal proceedings) shall be omitted.

(2) In section 20(4) of the Legal Aid Act 1988 (power of magistrates' court to grant legal aid for Crown Court proceedings)—
  (a) the word "or" shall be inserted at the end of paragraph (b), and
  (b) paragraph (bb) (which relates to a notice of transfer under Part I of the Schedule to the War Crimes Act 1991) shall be omitted.

References See paras 6.3, 6.9.

47 Committal proceedings

Schedule 1 to this Act (which contains provisions about committal proceedings and related matters) shall have effect.

References See paras 6.3, 6.10.

PART VI
MAGISTRATES' COURTS

48 Non-appearance of accused: issue of warrant

(1) Section 13 of the Magistrates' Courts Act 1980 (non-appearance of accused: issue of warrant) shall be amended as follows.

(2) In subsection (2) (no warrant where summons has been issued unless certain conditions fulfilled) for the words from "unless" to the end of the subsection there shall be substituted "unless the condition in subsection (2A) below or that in subsection (2B) below is fulfilled".

(3) The following subsections shall be inserted after subsection (2)—

"(2A) The condition in this subsection is that it is proved to the satisfaction of the court, on oath or in such other manner as may be prescribed, that the summons was served on the accused within what appears to the court to be a reasonable time before the trial or adjourned trial.

(2B) The condition in this subsection is that—
  (a) the adjournment now being made is a second or subsequent adjournment of the trial,

(b) the accused was present on the last (or only) occasion when the trial was adjourned, and
(c) on that occasion the court determined the time for the hearing at which the adjournment is now being made."

(4) This section applies where the court proposes to issue a warrant under section 13 on or after the appointed day.

(5) The reference in subsection (4) to the appointed day is to such day as is appointed for the purposes of this section by the Secretary of State by order.

References See paras 7.2, 7.3.

49 Either way offences: accused's intention as to plea

(1) The Magistrates' Courts Act 1980 shall be amended as follows.

(2) The following sections shall be inserted after section 17 (offences triable on indictment or summarily)—

"17A Initial procedure: accused to indicate intention as to plea

(1) This section shall have effect where a person who has attained the age of 18 years appears or is brought before a magistrates' court on an information charging him with an offence triable either way.

(2) Everything that the court is required to do under the following provisions of this section must be done with the accused present in court.

(3) The court shall cause the charge to be written down, if this has not already been done, and to be read to the accused.

(4) The court shall then explain to the accused in ordinary language that he may indicate whether (if the offence were to proceed to trial) he would plead guilty or not guilty, and that if he indicates that he would plead guilty—
(a) the court must proceed as mentioned in subsection (6) below; and
(b) he may be committed for sentence to the Crown Court under section 38 below if the court is of such opinion as is mentioned in subsection (2) of that section.

(5) The court shall then ask the accused whether (if the offence were to proceed to trial) he would plead guilty or not guilty.

(6) If the accused indicates that he would plead guilty the court shall proceed as if—
(a) the proceedings constituted from the beginning the summary trial of the information; and
(b) section 9(1) above was complied with and he pleaded guilty under it.

(7) If the accused indicates that he would plead not guilty section 18(1) below shall apply.

(8) If the accused in fact fails to indicate how he would plead, for the purposes of this section and section 18(1) below he shall be taken to indicate that he would plead not guilty.

(9) Subject to subsection (6) above, the following shall not for any purpose be taken to constitute the taking of a plea—
(a) asking the accused under this section whether (if the offence were to proceed to trial) he would plead guilty or not guilty;
(b) an indication by the accused under this section of how he would plead.

17B Intention as to plea: absence of accused

(1) This section shall have effect where—
   (a) a person who has attained the age of 18 years appears or is brought before a magistrates' court on an information charging him with an offence triable either way,
   (b) the accused is represented by a legal representative,
   (c) the court considers that by reason of the accused's disorderly conduct before the court it is not practicable for proceedings under section 17A above to be conducted in his presence, and
   (d) the court considers that it should proceed in the absence of the accused.

(2) In such a case—
   (a) the court shall cause the charge to be written down, if this has not already been done, and to be read to the representative;
   (b) the court shall ask the representative whether (if the offence were to proceed to trial) the accused would plead guilty or not guilty;
   (c) if the representative indicates that the accused would plead guilty the court shall proceed as if the proceedings constituted from the beginning the summary trial of the information, and as if section 9(1) above was complied with and the accused pleaded guilty under it;
   (d) if the representative indicates that the accused would plead not guilty section 18(1) below shall apply.

(3) If the representative in fact fails to indicate how the accused would plead, for the purposes of this section and section 18(1) below he shall be taken to indicate that the accused would plead not guilty.

(4) Subject to subsection (2)(c) above, the following shall not for any purpose be taken to constitute the taking of a plea—
   (a) asking the representative under this section whether (if the offence were to proceed to trial) the accused would plead guilty or not guilty;
   (b) an indication by the representative under this section of how the accused would plead.

17C Intention as to plea: adjournment

A magistrates' court proceeding under section 17A or 17B above may adjourn the proceedings at any time, and on doing so on any occasion when the accused is present may remand the accused, and shall remand him if—
   (a) on the occasion on which he first appeared, or was brought, before the court to answer to the information he was in custody or, having been released on bail, surrendered to the custody of the court; or
   (b) he has been remanded at any time in the course of proceedings on the information;

and where the court remands the accused, the time fixed for the resumption of proceedings shall be that at which he is required to appear or be brought before the court in pursuance of the remand or would be required to be brought before the court but for section 128(3A) below."

(3) In section 18(1) (initial procedure) after "either way" there shall be inserted

"and—
   (a) he indicates under section 17A above that (if the offence were to proceed to trial) he would plead not guilty, or
   (b) his representative indicates under section 17B above that (if the offence were to proceed to trial) he would plead not guilty".

(4) In section 19 (court to consider which mode of trial appears more suitable) paragraph (a) of subsection (2) (charge to be read to accused) shall be omitted.

(5) In—
(a) subsections (1A), (3A), (3C) and (3E) of section 128 (remand), and
(b) subsection (1) of section 130 (transfer of remand hearings),
after "10(1)" there shall be inserted ", 17C".

(6) This section applies where a person appears or is brought before a magistrates' court on or after the appointed day, unless he has appeared or been brought before such a court in respect of the same offence on a previous occasion falling before that day.

(7) The reference in subsection (6) to the appointed day is to such day as is appointed for the purposes of this section by the Secretary of State by order.

Definitions For "magistrates' court", see the Magistrates' Courts Act 1980, s 148.
References See paras 7.1, 7.4.

50 Enforcement of payment of fines

(1) In section 87 of the Magistrates' Courts Act 1980 (enforcement of fines) in subsection (3) (no proceedings unless court authorises it after inquiry into means) for the words from "authorised" to the end of the subsection there shall be substituted "there has been an inquiry under section 82 above into that person's means and he appeared to the court to have sufficient means to pay the sum forthwith."

(2) This section applies where the clerk of a magistrates' court proposes to take proceedings by virtue of section 87(1) on or after the appointed day.

(3) The reference in subsection (2) to the appointed day is to such day as is appointed for the purposes of this section by the Secretary of State by order.

References See paras 7.2, 7.15.

51 Summons to witness and warrant for his arrest

(1) In section 97 of the Magistrates' Courts Act 1980 (summons to witness and warrant for his arrest) the following subsections shall be inserted after subsection (2A)—

"(2B) A justice may refuse to issue a summons under subsection (1) above in relation to the summary trial of an information if he is not satisfied that an application for the summons was made by a party to the case as soon as reasonably practicable after the accused pleaded not guilty.

(2C) In relation to the summary trial of an information, subsection (2) above shall have effect as if the reference to the matters mentioned in subsection (1) above included a reference to the matter mentioned in subsection (2B) above."

(2) This section applies in relation to any proceedings for the purpose of which no summons has been issued under section 97(1), and no warrant has been issued under section 97(2), before the appointed day.

(3) The reference in subsection (2) to the appointed day is to such day as is appointed for the purposes of this section by the Secretary of State by order.

References See paras 7.2, 7.17.

52 Remand

(1) In section 128 of the Magistrates' Courts Act 1980 (remand in custody or on bail) paragraph (c) of subsection (1A) and paragraph (c) of subsection (3A) (which restrict certain provisions about remand to persons who have attained the age of 17) shall be omitted.

(2) In section 128A(1) of that Act (power to make order allowing remand in custody for more than 8 clear days if accused has attained the age of 17) the words "who has attained the age of 17" shall be omitted.

(3) Subsection (1) applies where the offence with which the person concerned is charged is alleged to be committed on or after the appointed day.

(4) The reference in subsection (3) to the appointed day is to such day as is appointed for the purposes of this section by the Secretary of State by order.

References See paras 7.1, 7.20.

53 Attachment of earnings

(1) In section 3 of the Attachment of Earnings Act 1971 (court's power to make order) the following subsections shall be inserted after subsection (3A)—

"(3B) Where—
  (a) a magistrates' court imposes a fine on a person in respect of an offence, and
  (b) that person consents to an order being made under this subsection,

the court may at the time it imposes the fine, and without the need for an application, make an attachment of earnings order to secure the payment of the fine.

(3C) Where—
  (a) a magistrates' court makes in the case of a person convicted of an offence an order under section 35 of the Powers of Criminal Courts Act 1973 (a compensation order) requiring him to pay compensation or to make other payments, and
  (b) that person consents to an order being made under this subsection,

the court may at the time it makes the compensation order, and without the need for an application, make an attachment of earnings order to secure the payment of the compensation or other payments."

(2) This section applies in relation to—
  (a) fines imposed in respect of offences committed on or after the appointed day;
  (b) compensation orders made on convictions for offences committed on or after that day.

(3) The reference in subsection (2) to the appointed day is to such day as is appointed for the purposes of this section by the Secretary of State by order.

Definitions For "earnings", see the Attachment of Earnings Act 1971, s 24; for "the court", see s 25(1) thereof; by virtue of s 25(6) of the 1971 Act, for "magistrates' court", see the Magistrates' Courts Act 1980, s 148, for "fine", see s 150(1) of the 1980 Act, and for "offence", see s 150(5) thereof.
References See para 7.2.

PART VII
MISCELLANEOUS AND GENERAL

Tainted acquittals

54 Acquittals tainted by intimidation etc

(1) This section applies where—
   (a) a person has been acquitted of an offence, and
   (b) a person has been convicted of an administration of justice offence involving interference with or intimidation of a juror or a witness (or potential witness) in any proceedings which led to the acquittal.

(2) Where it appears to the court before which the person was convicted that—
   (a) there is a real possibility that, but for the interference or intimidation, the acquitted person would not have been acquitted, and
   (b) subsection (5) does not apply,
the court shall certify that it so appears.

(3) Where a court certifies under subsection (2) an application may be made to the High Court for an order quashing the acquittal, and the Court shall make the order if (but shall not do so unless) the four conditions in section 55 are satisfied.

(4) Where an order is made under subsection (3) proceedings may be taken against the acquitted person for the offence of which he was acquitted.

(5) This subsection applies if, because of lapse of time or for any other reason, it would be contrary to the interests of justice to take proceedings against the acquitted person for the offence of which he was acquitted.

(6) For the purposes of this section the following offences are administration of justice offences—
   (a) the offence of perverting the course of justice;
   (b) the offence under section 51(1) of the Criminal Justice and Public Order Act 1994 (intimidation etc of witnesses, jurors and others);
   (c) an offence of aiding, abetting, counselling, procuring, suborning or inciting another person to commit an offence under section 1 of the Perjury Act 1911.

(7) This section applies in relation to acquittals in respect of offences alleged to be committed on or after the appointed day.

(8) The reference in subsection (7) to the appointed day is to such day as is appointed for the purposes of this section by the Secretary of State by order.

References See paras 8.2, 8.3, 8.5, 8.6.

55 Conditions for making order

(1) The first condition is that it appears to the High Court likely that, but for the interference or intimidation, the acquitted person would not have been acquitted.

(2) The second condition is that it does not appear to the Court that, because of lapse of time or for any other reason, it would be contrary to the interests of justice to take proceedings against the acquitted person for the offence of which he was acquitted.

(3) The third condition is that it appears to the Court that the acquitted person has been given a reasonable opportunity to make written representations to the Court.

(4) The fourth condition is that it appears to the Court that the conviction for the administration of justice offence will stand.

(5) In applying subsection (4) the Court shall—
- (a) take into account all the information before it, but
- (b) ignore the possibility of new factors coming to light.

(6) Accordingly, the fourth condition has the effect that the Court shall not make an order under section 54(3) if (for instance) it appears to the Court that any time allowed for giving notice of appeal has not expired or that an appeal is pending.

References   See paras 8.2, 8.5, 8.6.

56   Time limits for proceedings

(1) Where—
- (a) an order is made under section 54(3) quashing an acquittal,
- (b) by virtue of section 54(4) it is proposed to take proceedings against the acquitted person for the offence of which he was acquitted, and
- (c) apart from this subsection, the effect of an enactment would be that the proceedings must be commenced before a specified period calculated by reference to the commission of the offence,

in relation to the proceedings the enactment shall have effect as if the period were instead one calculated by reference to the time the order is made under section 54(3).

(2) Subsection (1)(c) applies however the enactment is expressed so that (for instance) it applies in the case of—
- (a) paragraph 10 of Schedule 2 to the Sexual Offences Act 1956 (prosecution for certain offences may not be commenced more than 12 months after offence);
- (b) section 127(1) of the Magistrates' Courts Act 1980 (magistrates' court not to try information unless it is laid within 6 months from time when offence committed);
- (c) an enactment that imposes a time limit only in certain circumstances (as where proceedings are not instituted by or with the consent of the Director of Public Prosecutions).

References   See paras 8.2, 8.5, 8.6.

57   Tainted acquittals: supplementary

(1) Section 45 of the Offences Against the Person Act 1861 (which releases a person from criminal proceedings in certain circumstances) shall have effect subject to section 54(4) of this Act.

(2) The Contempt of Court Act 1981 shall be amended as mentioned in subsections (3) and (4).

(3) In section 4 (contemporary reports of proceedings) after subsection (2) there shall be inserted—

"(2A) Where in proceedings for any offence which is an administration of justice offence for the purposes of section 54 of the Criminal Procedure and Investigations Act 1996 (acquittal tainted by an administration of justice offence) it appears to the court that there is a possibility that (by virtue of that section) proceedings may be taken against a person for an offence of which he has been acquitted, subsection (2) of this section shall apply as if those proceedings were pending or imminent."

(4) In Schedule 1 (time when proceedings are active for purposes of section 2) in paragraph 3 (period for which criminal proceedings are active) after "4" there shall be inserted "or 4A", and after paragraph 4 there shall be inserted—

> "4A.—Where as a result of an order under section 54 of the Criminal Procedure and Investigations Act 1996 (acquittal tainted by an administration of justice offence) proceedings are brought against a person for an offence of which he has previously been acquitted, the initial step of the proceedings is a certification under subsection (2) of that section; and paragraph 4 has effect subject to this."

Definitions In the Contempt of Court Act 1981, for "the court" and "proceedings", see s 19 thereof, (and as to "proceedings" in Sch 1 to that Act, see para 1 thereof).
References See paras 8.2, 8.5, 8.7.

Derogatory assertions

58 Orders in respect of certain assertions

(1) This section applies where a person has been convicted of an offence and a speech in mitigation is made by him or on his behalf before—
    (a) a court determining what sentence should be passed on him in respect of the offence, or
    (b) a magistrates' court determining whether he should be committed to the Crown Court for sentence.

(2) This section also applies where a sentence has been passed on a person in respect of an offence and a submission relating to the sentence is made by him or on his behalf before—
    (a) a court hearing an appeal against or reviewing the sentence, or
    (b) a court determining whether to grant leave to appeal against the sentence.

(3) Where it appears to the court that there is a real possibility that an order under subsection (8) will be made in relation to the assertion, the court may make an order under subsection (7) in relation to the assertion.

(4) Where there are substantial grounds for believing—
    (a) that an assertion forming part of the speech or submission is derogatory to a person's character (for instance, because it suggests that his conduct is or has been criminal, immoral or improper), and
    (b) that the assertion is false or that the facts asserted are irrelevant to the sentence,
the court may make an order under subsection (8) in relation to the assertion.

(5) An order under subsection (7) or (8) must not be made in relation to an assertion if it appears to the court that the assertion was previously made—
    (a) at the trial at which the person was convicted of the offence, or
    (b) during any other proceedings relating to the offence.

(6) Section 59 has effect where a court makes an order under subsection (7) or (8).

(7) An order under this subsection—
    (a) may be made at any time before the court has made a determination with regard to sentencing;
    (b) may be revoked at any time by the court;
    (c) subject to paragraph (b), shall cease to have effect when the court makes a determination with regard to sentencing.

Criminal Procedure and Investigations Act 1996, s 58

(8) An order under this subsection—
- (a) may be made after the court has made a determination with regard to sentencing, but only if it is made as soon as is reasonably practicable after the making of the determination;
- (b) may be revoked at any time by the court;
- (c) subject to paragraph (b), shall cease to have effect at the end of the period of 12 months beginning with the day on which it is made;
- (d) may be made whether or not an order has been made under subsection (7) with regard to the case concerned.

(9) For the purposes of subsections (7) and (8) the court makes a determination with regard to sentencing—
- (a) when it determines what sentence should be passed (where this section applies by virtue of subsection (1)(a));
- (b) when it determines whether the person should be committed to the Crown Court for sentence (where this section applies by virtue of subsection (1)(b));
- (c) when it determines what the sentence should be (where this section applies by virtue of subsection (2)(a));
- (d) when it determines whether to grant leave to appeal (where this section applies by virtue of subsection (2)(b)).

References See paras 8.8–8.10, 8.13.

59 Restriction on reporting of assertions

(1) Where a court makes an order under section 58(7) or (8) in relation to any assertion, at any time when the order has effect the assertion must not—
- (a) be published in Great Britain in a written publication available to the public, or
- (b) be included in a relevant programme for reception in Great Britain.

(2) In this section—
"relevant programme" means a programme included in a programme service, within the meaning of the Broadcasting Act 1990;
"written publication" includes a film, a soundtrack and any other record in permanent form but does not include an indictment or other document prepared for use in particular legal proceedings.

(3) For the purposes of this section an assertion is published or included in a programme if the material published or included—
- (a) names the person about whom the assertion is made or, without naming him, contains enough to make it likely that members of the public will identify him as the person about whom it is made, and
- (b) reproduces the actual wording of the matter asserted or contains its substance.

References See paras 8.11, 8.13.

60 Reporting of assertions: offences

(1) If an assertion is published or included in a relevant programme in contravention of section 59, each of the following persons is guilty of an offence—
- (a) in the case of publication in a newspaper or periodical, any proprietor, any editor and any publisher of the newspaper or periodical;

(b) in the case of publication in any other form, the person publishing the assertion;

(c) in the case of an assertion included in a relevant programme, any body corporate engaged in providing the service in which the programme is included and any person having functions in relation to the programme corresponding to those of an editor of a newspaper.

(2) A person guilty of an offence under this section is liable on summary conviction to a fine of an amount not exceeding level 5 on the standard scale.

(3) Where a person is charged with an offence under this section it is a defence to prove that at the time of the alleged offence—

(a) he was not aware, and neither suspected nor had reason to suspect, that an order under section 58(7) or (8) had effect at that time, or

(b) he was not aware, and neither suspected nor had reason to suspect, that the publication or programme in question was of, or (as the case may be) included, the assertion in question.

(4) Where an offence under this section committed by a body corporate is proved to have been committed with the consent or connivance of, or to be attributable to any neglect on the part of—

(a) a director, manager, secretary or other similar officer of the body corporate, or

(b) a person purporting to act in any such capacity,

he as well as the body corporate is guilty of the offence and liable to be proceeded against and punished accordingly.

(5) In relation to a body corporate whose affairs are managed by its members "director" in subsection (4) means a member of the body corporate.

(6) Subsections (2) and (3) of section 59 apply for the purposes of this section as they apply for the purposes of that.

Definitions By virtue of sub-s (6) above, for "relevant programme", see s 59(2), and for "published" and "included in a ... programme", see s 59(3).
References See paras 8.12, 8.13.

61 Reporting of assertions: commencement and supplementary

(1) Section 58 applies where the offence mentioned in subsection (1) or (2) of that section is committed on or after the appointed day.

(2) The reference in subsection (1) to the appointed day is to such day as is appointed for the purposes of this section by the Secretary of State by order.

(3) Nothing in section 58 or 59 affects any prohibition or restriction imposed by virtue of any other enactment on a publication or on matter included in a programme.

(4) Nothing in section 58 or 59 affects section 3 of the Law of Libel Amendment Act 1888 (privilege of newspaper reports of court proceedings).

(5) Section 8 of the Law of Libel Amendment Act 1888 (order of judge required for prosecution for libel published in a newspaper) does not apply to a prosecution for an offence under section 60.

Criminal Procedure and Investigations Act 1996, s 61

(6) In section 159 of the Criminal Justice Act 1988 (appeal to Court of Appeal against orders restricting reports etc) in subsection (1) the following paragraph shall be inserted after paragraph (a)—

"(aa) an order made by the Crown Court under section 58(7) or (8) of the Criminal Procedure and Investigations Act 1996 in a case where the Court has convicted a person on a trial on indictment;".

References   See para 8.13.

Evidence: special provisions

62 Television links and video recordings

(1) In section 32 of the Criminal Justice Act 1988 (evidence through television links) the following subsections shall be inserted after subsection (3B)—

"(3C) Where—
(a) the court gives leave for a person to give evidence through a live television link, and
(b) the leave is given by virtue of subsection (1)(b) above,

then, subject to subsection (3D) below, the person concerned may not give evidence otherwise than through a live television link.

(3D) In a case falling within subsection (3C) above the court may give permission for the person to give evidence otherwise than through a live television link if it appears to the court to be in the interests of justice to give such permission.

(3E) Permission may be given under subsection (3D) above—
(a) on an application by a party to the case, or
(b) of the court's own motion;

but no application may be made under paragraph (a) above unless there has been a material change of circumstances since the leave was given by virtue of subsection (1)(b) above."

(2) In section 32A of the Criminal Justice Act 1988 (video recordings of testimony from child witnesses) the following subsections shall be inserted after subsection (6)—

"(6A) Where the court gives leave under subsection (2) above the child witness shall not give relevant evidence (within the meaning given by subsection (6D) below) otherwise than by means of the video recording; but this is subject to subsection (6B) below.

(6B) In a case falling within subsection (6A) above the court may give permission for the child witness to give relevant evidence (within the meaning given by subsection (6D) below) otherwise than by means of the video recording if it appears to the court to be in the interests of justice to give such permission.

(6C) Permission may be given under subsection (6B) above—
(a) on an application by a party to the case, or
(b) of the court's own motion;

but no application may be made under paragraph (a) above unless there has been a material change of circumstances since the leave was given under subsection (2) above.

(6D) For the purposes of subsections (6A) and (6B) above evidence is relevant evidence if—

(a) it is evidence in chief on behalf of the party who tendered the video recording, and
(b) it relates to matter which, in the opinion of the court, is dealt with in the recording and which the court has not directed to be excluded under subsection (3) above."

(3) This section applies where the leave concerned is given on or after the appointed day.

(4) The reference in subsection (3) to the appointed day is to such day as is appointed for the purposes of this section by the Secretary of State by order.

References See para 8.14.

63 Road traffic and transport: provision of specimens

(1) In section 7(3) of the Road Traffic Act 1988 (provision of blood or urine in course of investigating whether certain road traffic offences have been committed) after paragraph (b) there shall be inserted—

"(bb) a device of the type mentioned in subsection (1)(a) above has been used at the police station but the constable who required the specimens of breath has reasonable cause to believe that the device has not produced a reliable indication of the proportion of alcohol in the breath of the person concerned, or".

(2) In section 31(4) of the Transport and Works Act 1992 (provision of blood or urine in course of investigating whether certain offences have been committed by persons working on transport systems) the word "or" at the end of paragraph (b) shall be omitted and after that paragraph there shall be inserted—

"(bb) a device of the type mentioned in subsection (1)(a) above has been used at the police station but the constable who required the specimens of breath has reasonable cause to believe that the device has not produced a reliable indication of the proportion of alcohol in the breath of the person concerned, or".

(3) This section applies where it is proposed to make a requirement mentioned in section 7(3) of the 1988 Act or section 31(3) of the 1992 Act after the appointed day.

(4) The reference in subsection (3) to the appointed day is to such day as is appointed for the purposes of this section by the Secretary of State by order.

References See para 8.15.

64 Checks against fingerprints etc

(1) In section 63A of the Police and Criminal Evidence Act 1984 the following subsections shall be substituted for subsection (1) (checks against fingerprints etc where a person has been arrested on suspicion of being involved in a recordable offence)—

"(1) Where a person has been arrested on suspicion of being involved in a recordable offence or has been charged with such an offence or has been informed that he will be reported for such an offence, fingerprints or samples or the information derived from samples taken under any power conferred by this Part of this Act from the person may be checked against—
(a) other fingerprints or samples to which the person seeking to check has access and which are held by or on behalf of a police force (or police forces) falling within subsection (1A) below or are held in connection with or as a result of an investigation of an offence;

Criminal Procedure and Investigations Act 1996, s 64

(b) information derived from other samples if the information is contained in records to which the person seeking to check has access and which are held as mentioned in paragraph (a) above.

(1A) Each of the following police forces falls within this subsection—
- (a) a police force within the meaning given by section 62 of the Police Act 1964 (which relates to England and Wales);
- (b) a police force within the meaning given by section 50 of the Police (Scotland) Act 1967;
- (c) the Royal Ulster Constabulary and the Royal Ulster Constabulary Reserve;
- (d) the States of Jersey Police Force;
- (e) the salaried police force of the Island of Guernsey;
- (f) the Isle of Man Constabulary."

(2) This section applies where a person—
- (a) is arrested on suspicion of being involved in a recordable offence,
- (b) is charged with a recordable offence, or
- (c) is informed that he will be reported for a recordable offence,

after the day on which this Act is passed.

Definitions For "fingerprints", see the Police and Criminal Evidence Act 1984, s 65; for "recordable offence", see s 118(1) of that Act.
References See para 8.16.

Witness orders and summonses

65 Abolition of witness orders

(1) Section 1 of the Criminal Procedure (Attendance of Witnesses) Act 1965 (examining justices to order witness to attend and give evidence before Crown Court) shall be omitted.

(2) In that Act the following words shall be omitted—
- (a) in section 3(1) the words "witness order or";
- (b) in section 4(1) the words "witness order or" and (where they next occur) "order or";
- (c) in the proviso to section 4(1) the words from "in the case" (where they first occur) to "witness summons";
- (d) in section 4(2) the words "a witness order or" and (where they next occur) "order or".

(3) In section 145 of the Magistrates' Courts Act 1980 (rules) subsection (1)(e) (which relates to witness orders) shall be omitted.

(4) This section shall have effect in accordance with provision made by the Secretary of State by order.

References See para 8.19.

66 Summons to witness to attend Crown Court

(1) The Criminal Procedure (Attendance of Witnesses) Act 1965 shall be amended as follows.

(2) The following shall be substituted for section 2 (summons to witness to attend Crown Court)—

Criminal Procedure and Investigations Act 1996, s 66

"*Issue of witness summons on application*

2 Issue of witness summons on application to Crown Court

(1) This section applies where the Crown Court is satisfied that—
   (a) a person is likely to be able to give evidence likely to be material evidence, or produce any document or thing likely to be material evidence, for the purpose of any criminal proceedings before the Crown Court, and
   (b) the person will not voluntarily attend as a witness or will not voluntarily produce the document or thing.

(2) In such a case the Crown Court shall, subject to the following provisions of this section, issue a summons (a witness summons) directed to the person concerned and requiring him to—
   (a) attend before the Crown Court at the time and place stated in the summons, and
   (b) give the evidence or produce the document or thing.

(3) A witness summons may only be issued under this section on an application; and the Crown Court may refuse to issue the summons if any requirement relating to the application is not fulfilled.

(4) Where a person has been committed for trial for any offence to which the proceedings concerned relate, an application must be made as soon as is reasonably practicable after the committal.

(5) Where the proceedings concerned have been transferred to the Crown Court, an application must be made as soon as is reasonably practicable after the transfer.

(6) Where the proceedings concerned relate to an offence in relation to which a bill of indictment has been preferred under the authority of section 2(2)(b) of the Administration of Justice (Miscellaneous Provisions) Act 1933 (bill preferred by direction of Court of Appeal, or by direction or with consent of judge) an application must be made as soon as is reasonably practicable after the bill was preferred.

(7) An application must be made in accordance with Crown Court rules; and different provision may be made for different cases or descriptions of case.

(8) Crown Court rules—
   (a) may, in such cases as the rules may specify, require an application to be made by a party to the case;
   (b) may, in such cases as the rules may specify, require the service of notice of an application on the person to whom the witness summons is proposed to be directed;
   (c) may, in such cases as the rules may specify, require an application to be supported by an affidavit containing such matters as the rules may stipulate;
   (d) may, in such cases as the rules may specify, make provision for enabling the person to whom the witness summons is proposed to be directed to be present or represented at the hearing of the application for the witness summons.

(9) Provision contained in Crown Court rules by virtue of subsection (8)(c) above may in particular require an affidavit to—
   (a) set out any charge on which the proceedings concerned are based;
   (b) specify any stipulated evidence, document or thing in such a way as to enable the directed person to identify it;

(c) specify grounds for believing that the directed person is likely to be able to give any stipulated evidence or produce any stipulated document or thing;
(d) specify grounds for believing that any stipulated evidence is likely to be material evidence;
(e) specify grounds for believing that any stipulated document or thing is likely to be material evidence.

(10) In subsection (9) above—
(a) references to any stipulated evidence, document or thing are to any evidence, document or thing whose giving or production is proposed to be required by the witness summons;
(b) references to the directed person are to the person to whom the witness summons is proposed to be directed.

2A Power to require advance production

A witness summons which is issued under section 2 above and which requires a person to produce a document or thing as mentioned in section 2(2) above may also require him to produce the document or thing—
(a) at a place stated in the summons, and
(b) at a time which is so stated and precedes that stated under section 2(2) above,

for inspection by the person applying for the summons.

2B Summons no longer needed

(1) If—
(a) a document or thing is produced in pursuance of a requirement imposed by a witness summons under section 2A above,
(b) the person applying for the summons concludes that a requirement imposed by the summons under section 2(2) above is no longer needed, and
(c) he accordingly applies to the Crown Court for a direction that the summons shall be of no further effect,

the court may direct accordingly.

(2) An application under this section must be made in accordance with Crown Court rules; and different provision may be made for different cases or descriptions of case.

(3) Crown Court rules may, in such cases as the rules may specify, require the effect of a direction under this section to be notified to the person to whom the summons is directed.

2C Application to make summons ineffective

(1) If a witness summons issued under section 2 above is directed to a person who—
(a) applies to the Crown Court,
(b) satisfies the court that he was not served with notice of the application to issue the summons and that he was neither present nor represented at the hearing of the application, and
(c) satisfies the court that he cannot give any evidence likely to be material evidence or, as the case may be, produce any document or thing likely to be material evidence,

the court may direct that the summons shall be of no effect.

(2) For the purposes of subsection (1) above it is immaterial—
(a) whether or not Crown Court rules require the person to be served with notice of the application to issue the summons;

(b) whether or not Crown Court rules enable the person to be present or represented at the hearing of the application.

(3) In subsection (1)(b) above "served" means—
   (a) served in accordance with Crown Court rules, in a case where such rules require the person to be served with notice of the application to issue the summons;
   (b) served in such way as appears reasonable to the court to which the application is made under this section, in any other case.

(4) The Crown Court may refuse to make a direction under this section if any requirement relating to the application under this section is not fulfilled.

(5) An application under this section must be made in accordance with Crown Court rules; and different provision may be made for different cases or descriptions of case.

(6) Crown Court rules may, in such cases as the rules may specify, require the service of notice of an application under this section on the person on whose application the witness summons was issued.

(7) Crown Court rules may, in such cases as the rules may specify, require that where—
   (a) a person applying under this section can produce a particular document or thing, but
   (b) he seeks to satisfy the court that the document or thing is not likely to be material evidence,

he must arrange for the document or thing to be available at the hearing of the application.

(8) Where a direction is made under this section that a witness summons shall be of no effect, the person on whose application the summons was issued may be ordered to pay the whole or any part of the costs of the application under this section.

(9) Any costs payable under an order made under subsection (8) above shall be taxed by the proper officer of the court, and payment of those costs shall be enforceable in the same manner as an order for payment of costs made by the High Court in a civil case or as a sum adjudged summarily to be paid as a civil debt.

Issue of witness summons of court's own motion

2D Issue of witness summons of Crown Court's own motion

For the purpose of any criminal proceedings before it, the Crown Court may of its own motion issue a summons (a witness summons) directed to a person and requiring him to—
   (a) attend before the court at the time and place stated in the summons, and
   (b) give evidence, or produce any document or thing specified in the summons.

2E Application to make summons ineffective

(1) If a witness summons issued under section 2D above is directed to a person who—
   (a) applies to the Crown Court, and
   (b) satisfies the court that he cannot give any evidence likely to be material evidence or, as the case may be, produce any document or thing likely to be material evidence,

the court may direct that the summons shall be of no effect.

Criminal Procedure and Investigations Act 1996, s 66

(2) The Crown Court may refuse to make a direction under this section if any requirement relating to the application under this section is not fulfilled.

(3) An application under this section must be made in accordance with Crown Court rules; and different provision may be made for different cases or descriptions of case.

(4) Crown Court rules may, in such cases as the rules may specify, require that where—
  (a) a person applying under this section can produce a particular document or thing, but
  (b) he seeks to satisfy the court that the document or thing is not likely to be material evidence,

he must arrange for the document or thing to be available at the hearing of the application.

Other provisions".

(3) In section 3 (punishment for disobedience to witness summons) after subsection (1) there shall be inserted—

"(1A) Any person who without just excuse disobeys a requirement made by any court under section 2A above shall be guilty of contempt of that court and may be punished summarily by that court as if his contempt had been committed in the face of the court."

(4) In section 3, in subsection (2) for the words "such disobedience" there shall be substituted "any disobedience mentioned in subsection (1) or (1A) above".

(5) In section 4 (further process to secure attendance of witness) in the proviso to subsection (1) after the word "give" there shall be inserted "evidence likely to be".

(6) Schedule 1 (application for direction that witness summons shall be of no effect) shall be omitted.

(7) This section applies in relation to any proceedings for the purpose of which no witness summons has been issued under section 2 of the 1965 Act before the appointed day.

(8) The reference in subsection (7) to the appointed day is to such day as is appointed for the purposes of this section by the Secretary of State by order.

References   See paras 8.20, 8.25.

67 Witness summons: securing attendance of witness

(1) In section 4(1) of the Criminal Procedure (Attendance of Witnesses) Act 1965 (judge of High Court may issue warrant to arrest witness in respect of whom witness summons is in force) for the words "High Court" there shall be substituted "Crown Court".

(2) This section shall have effect in accordance with provision made by the Secretary of State by order.

References   See para 8.25.

Other miscellaneous provisions

68 Use of written statements and depositions at trial

Schedule 2 to this Act (which relates to the use at the trial of written statements and depositions admitted in evidence in committal proceedings) shall have effect.

References   See paras 6.49, 8.26.

69 Proof by written statement

(1) In section 9 of the Criminal Justice Act 1967 (proof by written statement) in subsection (3)(a) (statement by person under 21 must give his age) for "twenty-one" there shall be substituted "eighteen".

(2) This section applies in relation to statements tendered in evidence on or after the appointed day.

(3) The reference in subsection (2) to the appointed day is to such day as is appointed for the purposes of this section by the Secretary of State by order.

References   See para 8.27.

70 Indemnification of justices and justices' clerks

(1) In section 53 of the Justices of the Peace Act 1979 (indemnification of justices and justices' clerks) the following subsection shall be inserted after subsection (1)—

> "(1A) So far as the duty mentioned in subsection (1) above relates to criminal matters, that subsection shall have effect as if—
> (a)   for the word "may" there were substituted "shall", and
> (b)   for the words following paragraph (c) there were substituted "unless it is proved, in respect of the matters giving rise to the proceedings or claim, that he acted in bad faith".

(2) This section applies in relation to things done or omitted on or after the appointed day.

(3) The reference in subsection (2) to the appointed day is to such day as is appointed for the purposes of this section by the Secretary of State by order.

References   See para 8.28.

71 Meaning of preliminary stage of criminal proceedings

(1) Section 22 of the Prosecution of Offences Act 1985 (power of Secretary of State to set time limits in relation to preliminary stages of criminal proceedings) shall be amended as mentioned in subsections (2) and (3).

(2) In subsection (11) the following shall be substituted for the definition of "preliminary stage"—

> ""preliminary stage", in relation to any proceedings, does not include any stage after the start of the trial (within the meaning given by subsections (11A) and (11B) below);".

(3) The following subsections shall be inserted after subsection (11)—

> "(11A) For the purposes of this section, the start of a trial on indictment shall be taken to occur when a jury is sworn to consider the issue of guilt or

fitness to plead or, if the court accepts a plea of guilty before a jury is sworn, when that plea is accepted; but this is subject to section 8 of the Criminal Justice Act 1987 and section 30 of the Criminal Procedure and Investigations Act 1996 (preparatory hearings).

(11B) For the purposes of this section, the start of a summary trial shall be taken to occur—
- (a) when the court begins to hear evidence for the prosecution at the trial or to consider whether to exercise its power under section 37(3) of the Mental Health Act 1983 (power to make hospital order without convicting the accused), or
- (b) if the court accepts a plea of guilty without proceeding as mentioned above, when that plea is accepted."

(4) The Prosecution of Offences (Custody Time Limits) Regulations 1987 shall be amended as follows, but without prejudice to the power to make further regulations amending or revoking the provisions amended—
- (a) in regulation 2 (interpretation) for paragraph (3) there shall be substituted—

  "(3)In these Regulations any reference to the start of the trial shall be construed in accordance with section 22(11A) and (11B) of the 1985 Act.";
- (b) in regulation 4 (custody time limits in magistrates' courts) in paragraphs (2) and (3) for "commencement" there shall be substituted "start";
- (c) in regulation 5 (custody time limits in Crown Court) for "his arraignment" in paragraphs (3)(a) and (b) and (6)(a) and (b), and for "the accused's arraignment" in paragraph (5), there shall be substituted "the start of the trial";
- (d) regulation 5(7) (when arraignment occurs) shall be omitted.

(5) This section applies in relation to—
- (a) any time limit which begins to run on or after the appointed day, and
- (b) any time limit which has begun to run and has not expired before that day,

except that it does not apply in relation to proceedings for an offence for which the accused has been duly arraigned in the Crown Court before that day.

(6) The reference in subsection (5) to the appointed day is to such day as is appointed for the purposes of this section by the Secretary of State by order.

References See paras 5.16, 8.29, 8.30.

72 Fraud

Schedule 3 (which amends provisions relating to serious or complex fraud) shall have effect.

References See para 8.31.

73 Amendments to the Criminal Procedure (Scotland) Act 1995

(1) The Criminal Procedure (Scotland) Act 1995 shall be amended as follows.

(2) In section 27 (breach of bail conditions: offences) the following subsection shall be inserted after subsection (4)—

"(4A) The fact that the subsequent offence was committed while the accused was on bail shall, unless challenged—
  (a) in the case of proceedings on indictment, by giving notice of a preliminary objection under paragraph (b) of section 72(1) of this Act or under that paragraph as applied by section 71(2) of this Act; or
  (b) in summary proceedings, by preliminary objection before his plea is recorded,
be held as admitted.".

(3) In subsection (1) of section 65 (prevention of delay in trials), for the words from "shall be discharged forthwith" to the end of the subsection there shall be substituted—

"(a) shall be discharged forthwith from any indictment as respects the offence; and
(b) shall not at any time be proceeded against on indictment as respects the offence".

(4) In Schedule 9 (certificates as to proof of certain routine matters), in the entry relating to the Social Security Administration Act 1992, for "Section 114(4)" in column 1 there shall be substituted "Section 112(1)".

References   See para 8.32.

74   Alibi

(1) Section 11 of the Criminal Justice Act 1967 (notice of alibi) shall cease to have effect, but subject to the following provisions of this section.

(2) Subsection (1) does not affect the application of section 11 of the Criminal Justice Act 1967 to proceedings before courts martial by virtue of section 12 of that Act.

(3) The reference in section 12 of the Criminal Justice Act 1967 to section 11 as it applies to proceedings on indictment shall be construed as a reference to it as it would apply to proceedings on indictment apart from subsection (1) of this section.

(4) In section 9(6) of the Criminal Justice Act 1987 (disclosure in cases involving fraud) in paragraph (a) for the words "section 11 of the Criminal Justice Act 1967" there shall be substituted "section 5(7) of the Criminal Procedure and Investigations Act 1996".

(5) This section applies in relation to alleged offences into which no criminal investigation, within the meaning given by section 1(4), has begun before the day appointed under section 1(5).

References   See para 8.33.

General

75   Time when alleged offence committed

(1) Subsection (2) applies for the purposes of sections 52(3) and 54(7).

(2) Where an offence is alleged to be committed over a period of more than one day, or at some time during a period of more than one day, it must be taken to be alleged to be committed on the last of the days in the period.

(3) Subsection (2) applies for the purposes of section 61(1) as if "alleged to be" (in each place) were omitted.

References   See para 8.34.

Criminal Procedure and Investigations Act 1996, s 76

76 Power of magistrates' courts

In section 148(2) of the Magistrates' Courts Act 1980 (power of court to act where another may act) the reference to that Act includes a reference to this Act.

References See para 8.35.

77 Orders and regulations

(1) This section concerns the powers of the Secretary of State to make orders or regulations under this Act.

(2) Any power to make an order or regulations may be exercised differently in relation to different areas or in relation to other different cases or descriptions of case.

(3) Any order or regulations may include such supplementary, incidental, consequential or transitional provisions as appear to the Secretary of State to be necessary or expedient.

(4) Any power to make an order or regulations shall be exercisable by statutory instrument.

(5) No order under section 25 shall have effect unless approved by a resolution of each House of Parliament.

(6) A statutory instrument containing—
   (a) an order under section 78, or
   (b) regulations,

shall be subject to annulment in pursuance of a resolution of either House of Parliament.

References See para 8.36.

78 Application to armed forces

(1) Subject to subsection (2) and to section 74(2) and (3), nothing in this Act applies to—
   (a) proceedings before a court martial constituted under the Army Act 1955, the Air Force Act 1955 or the Naval Discipline Act 1957;
   (b) proceedings before a Standing Civilian Court;
   (c) any investigation conducted with a view to it being ascertained whether a person should be charged with an offence under any of those Acts or whether a person charged with such an offence is guilty of it.

(2) The Secretary of State may by order—
   (a) make as regards any proceedings falling within subsection (3) provision which is equivalent to the provisions contained in or made under Part I, subject to such modifications as he thinks fit and specifies in the order;
   (b) make as regards any investigation falling within subsection (4) provision which is equivalent to the provisions contained in or made under Part II, subject to such modifications as he thinks fit and specifies in the order.

(3) The proceedings falling within this subsection are—
   (a) proceedings before a court martial constituted under the Army Act 1955;
   (b) proceedings before a court martial constituted under the Air Force Act 1955;

(c) proceedings before a court martial constituted under the Naval Discipline Act 1957;
(d) proceedings before a Standing Civilian Court.

(4) An investigation falls within this subsection if it is conducted with a view to it being ascertained whether a person should be charged with an offence under any of the Acts mentioned in subsection (3) or whether a person charged with such an offence is guilty of it.

(5) An order under this section may make provision in such way as the Secretary of State thinks fit, and may in particular apply any of the provisions concerned subject to such modifications as he thinks fit and specifies in the order.

(6) Without prejudice to the generality of section 77(3), an order under this section may include provision—
(a) repealing section 11 of the Criminal Justice Act 1967 (alibi) as it applies to proceedings before courts martial;
(b) amending or repealing any provision of section 12 of that Act or of section 74 above.

References See para 8.37.

79 Extent

(1) This Act does not extend to Scotland, with the exception of—
(a) sections 37, 38, 41, 42, 59, 60, 61(3), 63, 72, 73, 74(2) and (3) and 78, this section and section 81;
(b) paragraphs 6 and 7 of Schedule 3, and paragraph 8 of that Schedule so far as it relates to paragraphs 6 and 7;
(c) paragraph 5 of Schedule 5;
(d) paragraph 12 of Schedule 5 so far as it relates to provisions amending section 11 of the Criminal Justice Act 1987.

(2) Section 73 extends only to Scotland.

(3) Parts III and VI and sections 44, 47, 65, 67, 68 and 71 do not extend to Northern Ireland.

(4) In its application to Northern Ireland, this Act has effect subject to the modifications set out in Schedule 4.

(5) Section 74(2) and (3) extend to any place where proceedings before courts martial may be held.

(6) Section 78 extends as follows—
(a) so far as it relates to proceedings, it extends to any place where such proceedings may be held;
(b) so far as it relates to investigations, it extends to any place where such investigations may be conducted.

References See para 8.38.

80 Repeals

The provisions mentioned in Schedule 5 are repealed (or revoked) to the extent specified in column 3, but subject to any provision of that Schedule.

81 Citation

This Act may be cited as the Criminal Procedure and Investigations Act 1996.

SCHEDULES

SCHEDULE 1

Section 47

COMMITTAL PROCEEDINGS

PART I

MAGISTRATES' COURTS ACT 1980

Introduction

1. The Magistrates' Courts Act 1980 shall be amended as mentioned in this Part of this Schedule.

Amendments

2.—(1) Section 4 (general nature of committal proceedings) shall be amended as follows.

(2) The following subsection shall be substituted for subsection (3)—

"(3) Subject to subsection (4) below, evidence tendered before examining justices shall be tendered in the presence of the accused."

(3) In subsection (4) for the word "given" (in each place) there shall be substituted "tendered".

3. The following sections shall be inserted after section 5—

"5A Evidence which is admissible

(1) Evidence falling within subsection (2) below, and only that evidence, shall be admissible by a magistrates' court inquiring into an offence as examining justices.

(2) Evidence falls within this subsection if it—
  (a) is tendered by or on behalf of the prosecutor, and
  (b) falls within subsection (3) below.

(3) The following evidence falls within this subsection—
  (a) written statements complying with section 5B below;
  (b) the documents or other exhibits (if any) referred to in such statements;
  (c) depositions complying with section 5C below;
  (d) the documents or other exhibits (if any) referred to in such depositions;
  (e) statements complying with section 5D below;
  (f) documents falling within section 5E below.

(4) In this section "document" means anything in which information of any description is recorded.

5B Written statements

(1) For the purposes of section 5A above a written statement complies with this section if—
  (a) the conditions falling within subsection (2) below are met, and
  (b) such of the conditions falling within subsection (3) below as apply are met.

(2) The conditions falling within this subsection are that—
  (a) the statement purports to be signed by the person who made it;
  (b) the statement contains a declaration by that person to the effect that it is true to the best of his knowledge and belief and that he made the statement knowing that, if it were tendered in evidence, he would be liable to

prosecution if he wilfully stated in it anything which he knew to be false or did not believe to be true;
(c) before the statement is tendered in evidence a copy of the statement is given, by or on behalf of the prosecutor, to each of the other parties to the proceedings.

(3) The conditions falling within this subsection are that—
(a) if the statement is made by a person under 18 years old, it gives his age;
(b) if it is made by a person who cannot read it, it is read to him before he signs it and is accompanied by a declaration by the person who so read the statement to the effect that it was so read;
(c) if it refers to any other document as an exhibit, the copy given to any other party to the proceedings under subsection (2)(c) above is accompanied by a copy of that document or by such information as may be necessary to enable the party to whom it is given to inspect that document or a copy of it.

(4) So much of any statement as is admitted in evidence by virtue of this section shall, unless the court commits the accused for trial by virtue of section 6(2) below or the court otherwise directs, be read aloud at the hearing; and where the court so directs an account shall be given orally of so much of any statement as is not read aloud.

(5) Any document or other object referred to as an exhibit and identified in a statement admitted in evidence by virtue of this section shall be treated as if it had been produced as an exhibit and identified in court by the maker of the statement.

(6) In this section "document" means anything in which information of any description is recorded.

5C Depositions

(1) For the purposes of section 5A above a deposition complies with this section if—
(a) a copy of it is sent to the prosecutor under section 97A(9) below,
(b) the condition falling within subsection (2) below is met, and
(c) the condition falling within subsection (3) below is met, in a case where it applies.

(2) The condition falling within this subsection is that before the magistrates' court begins to inquire into the offence concerned as examining justices a copy of the deposition is given, by or on behalf of the prosecutor, to each of the other parties to the proceedings.

(3) The condition falling within this subsection is that, if the deposition refers to any other document as an exhibit, the copy given to any other party to the proceedings under subsection (2) above is accompanied by a copy of that document or by such information as may be necessary to enable the party to whom it is given to inspect that document or a copy of it.

(4) So much of any deposition as is admitted in evidence by virtue of this section shall, unless the court commits the accused for trial by virtue of section 6(2) below or the court otherwise directs, be read aloud at the hearing; and where the court so directs an account shall be given orally of so much of any deposition as is not read aloud.

(5) Any document or other object referred to as an exhibit and identified in a deposition admitted in evidence by virtue of this section shall be treated as if it had been produced as an exhibit and identified in court by the person whose evidence is taken as the deposition.

(6) In this section "document" means anything in which information of any description is recorded.

5D Statements

(1) For the purposes of section 5A above a statement complies with this section if the conditions falling within subsections (2) to (4) below are met.

(2) The condition falling within this subsection is that, before the committal proceedings begin, the prosecutor notifies the magistrates' court and each of the other parties to the proceedings that he believes—

Criminal Procedure and Investigations Act 1996, Sch 1

      (a) that the statement might by virtue of section 23 or 24 of the Criminal Justice Act 1988 (statements in certain documents) be admissible as evidence if the case came to trial, and

      (b) that the statement would not be admissible as evidence otherwise than by virtue of section 23 or 24 of that Act if the case came to trial.

  (3) The condition falling within this subsection is that—

      (a) the prosecutor's belief is based on information available to him at the time he makes the notification,

      (b) he has reasonable grounds for his belief, and

      (c) he gives the reasons for his belief when he makes the notification.

  (4) The condition falling within this subsection is that when the court or a party is notified as mentioned in subsection (2) above a copy of the statement is given, by or on behalf of the prosecutor, to the court or the party concerned.

  (5) So much of any statement as is in writing and is admitted in evidence by virtue of this section shall, unless the court commits the accused for trial by virtue of section 6(2) below or the court otherwise directs, be read aloud at the hearing; and where the court so directs an account shall be given orally of so much of any statement as is not read aloud.

5E Other documents

  (1) The following documents fall within this section—

      (a) any document which by virtue of any enactment is evidence in proceedings before a magistrates' court inquiring into an offence as examining justices;

      (b) any document which by virtue of any enactment is admissible, or may be used, or is to be admitted or received, in or as evidence in such proceedings;

      (c) any document which by virtue of any enactment may be considered in such proceedings;

      (d) any document whose production constitutes proof in such proceedings by virtue of any enactment;

      (e) any document by the production of which evidence may be given in such proceedings by virtue of any enactment.

  (2) In subsection (1) above—

      (a) references to evidence include references to prima facie evidence;

      (b) references to any enactment include references to any provision of this Act.

  (3) So much of any document as is admitted in evidence by virtue of this section shall, unless the court commits the accused for trial by virtue of section 6(2) below or the court otherwise directs, be read aloud at the hearing; and where the court so directs an account shall be given orally of so much of any document as is not read aloud.

  (4) In this section "document" means anything in which information of any description is recorded.

5F Proof by production of copy

  (1) Where a statement, deposition or document is admissible in evidence by virtue of section 5B, 5C, 5D or 5E above it may be proved by the production of—

      (a) the statement, deposition or document, or

      (b) a copy of it or the material part of it.

  (2) Subsection (1)(b) above applies whether or not the statement, deposition or document is still in existence.

  (3) It is immaterial for the purposes of this section how many removes there are between a copy and the original.

  (4) In this section "copy", in relation to a statement, deposition or document, means anything onto which information recorded in the statement, deposition or document has been copied, by whatever means and whether directly or indirectly."

  4. In section 6 (discharge or committal for trial) the following subsections shall be substituted for subsections (1) and (2)—

"(1) A magistrates' court inquiring into an offence as examining justices shall on consideration of the evidence—
  (a) commit the accused for trial if it is of opinion that there is sufficient evidence to put him on trial by jury for any indictable offence;
  (b) discharge him if it is not of that opinion and he is in custody for no other cause than the offence under inquiry;
but the preceding provisions of this subsection have effect subject to the provisions of this and any other Act relating to the summary trial of indictable offences.

(2) If a magistrates' court inquiring into an offence as examining justices is satisfied that all the evidence tendered by or on behalf of the prosecutor falls within section 5A(3) above, it may commit the accused for trial for the offence without consideration of the contents of any statements, depositions or other documents, and without consideration of any exhibits which are not documents, unless—
  (a) the accused or one of the accused has no legal representative acting for him in the case, or
  (b) a legal representative for the accused or one of the accused, as the case may be, has requested the court to consider a submission that there is insufficient evidence to put that accused on trial by jury for the offence;
and subsection (1) above shall not apply to a committal for trial under this subsection."

5.—(1) Section 25 (change from summary trial to committal proceedings) shall be amended as follows.

(2) In subsections (2) and (6) for the words "may adjourn the hearing without remanding the accused" there shall be substituted "shall adjourn the hearing."

(3) The following subsection shall be inserted after subsection (7)—

"(8) If the court adjourns the hearing under subsection (2) or (6) above it may (if it thinks fit) do so without remanding the accused."

6. Section 28 (using in summary trial evidence given in committal proceedings) shall be omitted.

7. In section 97 (summons to witness and warrant for his arrest) in subsection (1)—
  (a) the words "at an inquiry into an indictable offence by a magistrates' court for that commission area or" shall be omitted;
  (b) for the words "such a court" there shall be substituted "a magistrates' court for that commission area".

8. The following section shall be inserted after section 97—

"97A Summons or warrant as to committal proceedings

(1) Subsection (2) below applies where a justice of the peace for any commission area is satisfied that—
  (a) any person in England or Wales is likely to be able to make on behalf of the prosecutor a written statement containing material evidence, or produce on behalf of the prosecutor a document or other exhibit likely to be material evidence, for the purposes of proceedings before a magistrates' court inquiring into an offence as examining justices,
  (b) the person will not voluntarily make the statement or produce the document or other exhibit, and
  (c) the magistrates' court mentioned in paragraph (a) above is a court for the commission area concerned.

(2) In such a case the justice shall issue a summons directed to that person requiring him to attend before a justice at the time and place appointed in the summons to have his evidence taken as a deposition or to produce the document or other exhibit.

(3) If a justice of the peace is satisfied by evidence on oath of the matters mentioned in subsection (1) above, and also that it is probable that a summons under subsection (2) above would not procure the result required by it, the justice may instead of issuing a summons issue a warrant to arrest the person concerned and bring him before a justice at the time and place specified in the warrant.

(4) A summons may also be issued under subsection (2) above if the justice is satisfied that the person concerned is outside the British Islands, but no warrant may be issued under subsection (3) above unless the justice is satisfied by evidence on oath that the person concerned is in England or Wales.

(5) If—
   (a) a person fails to attend before a justice in answer to a summons under this section,
   (b) the justice is satisfied by evidence on oath that he is likely to be able to make a statement or produce a document or other exhibit as mentioned in subsection (1)(a) above,
   (c) it is proved on oath, or in such other manner as may be prescribed, that he has been duly served with the summons and that a reasonable sum has been paid or tendered to him for costs and expenses, and
   (d) it appears to the justice that there is no just excuse for the failure,

the justice may issue a warrant to arrest him and bring him before a justice at a time and place specified in the warrant.

(6) Where—
   (a) a summons is issued under subsection (2) above or a warrant is issued under subsection (3) or (5) above, and
   (b) the summons or warrant is issued with a view to securing that a person has his evidence taken as a deposition,

the time appointed in the summons or specified in the warrant shall be such as to enable the evidence to be taken as a deposition before a magistrates' court begins to inquire into the offence concerned as examining justices.

(7) If any person attending or brought before a justice in pursuance of this section refuses without just excuse to have his evidence taken as a deposition, or to produce the document or other exhibit, the justice may do one or both of the following—
   (a) commit him to custody until the expiration of such period not exceeding one month as may be specified in the summons or warrant or until he sooner has his evidence taken as a deposition or produces the document or other exhibit;
   (b) impose on him a fine not exceeding £2,500.

(8) A fine imposed under subsection (7) above shall be deemed, for the purposes of any enactment, to be a sum adjudged to be paid by a conviction.

(9) If in pursuance of this section a person has his evidence taken as a deposition, the clerk of the justice concerned shall as soon as is reasonably practicable send a copy of the deposition to the prosecutor.

(10) If in pursuance of this section a person produces an exhibit which is a document, the clerk of the justice concerned shall as soon as is reasonably practicable send a copy of the document to the prosecutor.

(11) If in pursuance of this section a person produces an exhibit which is not a document, the clerk of the justice concerned shall as soon as is reasonably practicable inform the prosecutor of the fact and of the nature of the exhibit."

9. Section 102 (written statements before examining justices) shall be omitted.

10.—(1) Section 103 (evidence of children in certain committal proceedings) shall be amended as follows.

(2) The following subsection shall be substituted for subsection (1)—

"(1) In any proceedings before a magistrates' court inquiring as examining justices into an offence to which this section applies, a statement made in writing by or taken in writing from a child shall be admissible in evidence of any matter."

(3) Subsections (3) and (4) (exclusion of subsection (1) and of section 28) shall be omitted.

11. Section 105 (deposition of person dangerously ill may be given in evidence before examining justices) shall be omitted.

12. In section 106 (false written statements tendered in evidence) in subsection (1) for "tendered" there shall be substituted "admitted" and for "section 102" there shall be substituted "section 5B".

13. In Schedule 3 the following shall be substituted for paragraph 2(a) (representative may make statement on behalf of corporation before examining justices)—

> "(a) make before examining justices such representations as could be made by an accused who is not a corporation;".

Definitions For "magistrates' court", see the Magistrates' Courts Act 1980, s 148; for "enactment", see s 150(1) of that Act, (and note s 5A(5)(b) thereof, as inserted above); for "offence", see s 150(5) thereof.
References See paras 6.11–6.17, 6.19–6.27.

PART II

OTHER PROVISIONS

Criminal Law Amendment Act 1867

14. Sections 6 and 7 of the Criminal Law Amendment Act 1867 (statements taken under section 105 of the Magistrates' Courts Act 1980) shall be omitted.

Bankers' Books Evidence Act 1879

15. The following shall be inserted at the end of section 4 of the Bankers' Books Evidence Act 1879—

> "Where the proceedings concerned are proceedings before a magistrates' court inquiring into an offence as examining justices, this section shall have effect with the omission of the words "orally or"."

16. The following shall be inserted at the end of section 5 of the Bankers' Books Evidence Act 1879—

> "Where the proceedings concerned are proceedings before a magistrates' court inquiring into an offence as examining justices, this section shall have effect with the omission of the words "either orally or"."

Administration of Justice (Miscellaneous Provisions) Act 1933

17. In section 2 of the Administration of Justice (Miscellaneous Provisions) Act 1933 (procedure for indictment of offenders) in proviso (i) to subsection (2) for the words "in any examination or deposition taken before a justice in his presence" there shall be substituted "to the magistrates' court inquiring into that offence as examining justices".

Criminal Justice Act 1948

18. In section 41 of the Criminal Justice Act 1948 (evidence by certificate) the following subsection shall be inserted after subsection (5)—

> "(5A) Where the proceedings mentioned in subsection (1) above are proceedings before a magistrates' court inquiring into an offence as examining justices this section shall have effect with the omission of—
> (a) subsection (4), and
> (b) in subsection (5), paragraph (b) and the word "or" immediately preceding it."

Theft Act 1968

19. In section 27 of the Theft Act 1968 (evidence on charge of theft or handling stolen goods) the following subsection shall be inserted after subsection (4)—

> "(4A) Where the proceedings mentioned in subsection (4) above are proceedings before a magistrates' court inquiring into an offence as examining justices that subsection shall have effect with the omission of the words from "subject to the following conditions" to the end of the subsection."

20. In section 28 of the Theft Act 1968 (orders for restitution) in subsection (4) for the words from "the depositions" to the end of the subsection there shall be substituted "and such written statements, depositions and other documents as were tendered by or on behalf of the prosecutor at any committal proceedings".

Criminal Procedure and Investigations Act 1996, Sch 1

Children and Young Persons Act 1969

21. In Schedule 5 to the Children and Young Persons Act 1969, in paragraph 55 for the words "section 102" there shall be substituted "section 5B".

Criminal Justice Act 1972

22.—(1) Section 46 of the Criminal Justice Act 1972 (written statements made outside England and Wales) shall be amended as follows.

(2) In subsection (1) the following words shall be omitted—
   (a) "Section 102 of the Magistrates' Courts Act 1980 and";
   (b) "which respectively allow";
   (c) "committal proceedings and in other";
   (d) "and section 106 of the said Act of 1980";
   (e) "which punish the making of";
   (f) "102 or";
   (g) ", as the case may be".

(3) The following subsections shall be inserted after subsection (1)—

   "(1A) The following provisions, namely—
      (a) so much of section 5A of the Magistrates' Courts Act 1980 as relates to written statements and to documents or other exhibits referred to in them,
      (b) section 5B of that Act, and
      (c) section 106 of that Act,
   shall apply where written statements are made in Scotland or Northern Ireland as well as where written statements are made in England and Wales.

   (1B) The following provisions, namely—
      (a) so much of section 5A of the Magistrates' Courts Act 1980 as relates to written statements and to documents or other exhibits referred to in them, and
      (b) section 5B of that Act,
   shall (subject to subsection (1C) below) apply where written statements are made outside the United Kingdom.

   (1C) Where written statements are made outside the United Kingdom—
      (a) section 5B of the Magistrates' Courts Act 1980 shall apply with the omission of subsections (2)(b) and (3A);
      (b) paragraph 1 of Schedule 2 to the Criminal Procedure and Investigations Act 1996 (use of written statements at trial) shall not apply."

(4) Subsection (2) shall be omitted.

Sexual Offences (Amendment) Act 1976

23.—(1) Section 3 of the Sexual Offences (Amendment) Act 1976 (application of restrictions on evidence at certain trials to committal proceedings etc) shall be amended as follows.

(2) The following subsection shall be substituted for subsection (1)—

   "(1) Where a magistrates' court inquires into a rape offence as examining justices, then, except with the consent of the court, no restricted matter shall be raised; and for this purpose a restricted matter is a matter as regards which evidence could not be adduced and a question could not be asked without leave in pursuance of section 2 of this Act if—
      (a) the inquiry were a trial at which a person is charged as mentioned in section 2(1) of this Act, and
      (b) each of the accused at the inquiry were charged at the trial with the offence or offences of which he is accused at the inquiry."

(3) In subsection (2) for the words "evidence or question" (in each place) there shall be substituted "matter".

Police and Criminal Evidence Act 1984

24. The following shall be inserted at the end of section 71 of the Police and Criminal Evidence Act 1984 (microfilm copies)—

"Where the proceedings concerned are proceedings before a magistrates' court inquiring into an offence as examining justices this section shall have effect with the omission of the words "authenticated in such manner as the court may approve."

25. In section 76 of the Police and Criminal Evidence Act 1984 (confessions) the following subsection shall be inserted after subsection (8)—

"(9) Where the proceedings mentioned in subsection (1) above are proceedings before a magistrates' court inquiring into an offence as examining justices this section shall have effect with the omission of—
  (a) in subsection (1) the words "and is not excluded by the court in pursuance of this section", and
  (b) subsections (2) to (6) and (8)."

26. In section 78 of the Police and Criminal Evidence Act 1984 (exclusion of unfair evidence) the following subsection shall be inserted after subsection (2)—

"(3) This section shall not apply in the case of proceedings before a magistrates' court inquiring into an offence as examining justices."

27. In Schedule 3 to the Police and Criminal Evidence Act 1984 (computer records) at the end of paragraph 9 there shall be inserted the words "; but the preceding provisions of this paragraph shall not apply where the court is a magistrates' court inquiring into an offence as examining justices."

Criminal Justice Act 1988

28. In section 23 of the Criminal Justice Act 1988 (first-hand hearsay) the following subsection shall be inserted after subsection (4)—

"(5) This section shall not apply to proceedings before a magistrates' court inquiring into an offence as examining justices."

29. In section 24 of the Criminal Justice Act 1988 (business etc documents) the following subsection shall be inserted after subsection (4)—

"(5) This section shall not apply to proceedings before a magistrates' court inquiring into an offence as examining justices."

30. The following shall be inserted at the end of section 26 of the Criminal Justice Act 1988 (statements in certain documents)—

"This section shall not apply to proceedings before a magistrates' court inquiring into an offence as examining justices."

31. The following shall be inserted at the end of section 27 of the Criminal Justice Act 1988 (proof of statements contained in documents)—

"This section shall not apply to proceedings before a magistrates' court inquiring into an offence as examining justices."

32. In section 30 of the Criminal Justice Act 1988 (expert reports) the following subsection shall be inserted after subsection (4)—

"(4A) Where the proceedings mentioned in subsection (1) above are proceedings before a magistrates' court inquiring into an offence as examining justices this section shall have effect with the omission of—
  (a) in subsection (1) the words "whether or not the person making it attends to give oral evidence in those proceedings", and
  (b) subsections (2) to (4)."

33. In section 32A(10) of the Criminal Justice Act 1988 (video recordings) the words "notwithstanding that the child witness is not called at the committal proceedings" shall be omitted.

34. In section 40 of the Criminal Justice Act 1988 (power to join in indictment count for common assault etc) in subsection (1) for the words from "in an examination" to the end of the subsection there shall be substituted "to a magistrates' court inquiring into the offence as examining justices".

Road Traffic Offenders Act 1988

35. In section 11 of the Road Traffic Offenders Act 1988 (evidence by certificate as to driver, user or owner) the following subsection shall be inserted after subsection (3)—

"(3A) Where the proceedings mentioned in subsection (1) above are proceedings before a magistrates' court inquiring into an offence as examining justices this section shall have effect with the omission of—
  (a) subsection (2), and
  (b) in subsection (3), paragraph (b) and the word "or" immediately preceding it."

36. In section 13 of the Road Traffic Offenders Act 1988 (admissibility of records as evidence) the following subsection shall be inserted after subsection (6)—

"(7) Where the proceedings mentioned in subsection (2) above are proceedings before a magistrates' court inquiring into an offence as examining justices this section shall have effect as if—
  (a) in subsection (2) the words "to the same extent as oral evidence of that fact is admissible in those proceedings" were omitted;
  (b) in subsection (4) the word "and" were inserted at the end of paragraph (a);
  (c) in subsection (4), paragraphs (c) and (d) and the words "as if the accused had appeared and admitted it" were omitted."

37. In section 16 of the Road Traffic Offenders Act 1988 (specimens) the following subsection shall be inserted after subsection (6)—

"(6A) Where the proceedings mentioned in section 15(1) of this Act are proceedings before a magistrates' court inquiring into an offence as examining justices this section shall have effect with the omission of subsection (4)."

38. In section 20 of the Road Traffic Offenders Act 1988 (speeding etc) the following subsection shall be inserted after subsection (8)—

"(8A) Where the proceedings for an offence to which this section applies are proceedings before a magistrates' court inquiring into an offence as examining justices this section shall have effect as if in subsection (8) the words from "and nothing" to the end of the subsection were omitted."

Definitions In the Sexual Offences (Amendment) Act 1976, for "rape offence", see s 7(2) thereof.
In the Police and Criminal Evidence Act 1984, for "proceedings", see s 82(1) thereof.
References See paras 6.28–6.47.

PART III

COMMENCEMENT

39. Parts I and II of this Schedule shall have effect in accordance with provision made by the Secretary of State by order.

References See para 6.48.

SCHEDULE 2

Section 68

STATEMENTS AND DEPOSITIONS

Statements

1.—(1) Sub-paragraph (2) applies if—
  (a) a written statement has been admitted in evidence in proceedings before a magistrates' court inquiring into an offence as examining justices,
  (b) in those proceedings a person has been committed for trial,
  (c) for the purposes of section 5A of the Magistrates' Courts Act 1980 the statement complied with section 5B of that Act prior to the committal for trial,
  (d) the statement purports to be signed by a justice of the peace, and
  (e) sub-paragraph (3) does not prevent sub-paragraph (2) applying.

(2) Where this sub-paragraph applies the statement may without further proof be read as evidence on the trial of the accused, whether for the offence for which he was committed for trial or for any other offence arising out of the same transaction or set of circumstances.

(3) Sub-paragraph (2) does not apply if—
  (a) it is proved that the statement was not signed by the justice by whom it purports to have been signed,
  (b) the court of trial at its discretion orders that sub-paragraph (2) shall not apply, or
  (c) a party to the proceedings objects to sub-paragraph (2) applying.

(4) If a party to the proceedings objects to sub-paragraph (2) applying the court of trial may order that the objection shall have no effect if the court considers it to be in the interests of justice so to order.

Depositions

2.—(1) Sub-paragraph (2) applies if—
  (a) in pursuance of section 97A of the Magistrates' Courts Act 1980 (summons or warrant to have evidence taken as a deposition etc) a person has had his evidence taken as a deposition for the purposes of proceedings before a magistrates' court inquiring into an offence as examining justices,
  (b) the deposition has been admitted in evidence in those proceedings,
  (c) in those proceedings a person has been committed for trial,
  (d) for the purposes of section 5A of the Magistrates' Courts Act 1980 the deposition complied with section 5C of that Act prior to the committal for trial,
  (e) the deposition purports to be signed by the justice before whom it purports to have been taken, and
  (f) sub-paragraph (3) does not prevent sub-paragraph (2) applying.

(2) Where this sub-paragraph applies the deposition may without further proof be read as evidence on the trial of the accused, whether for the offence for which he was committed for trial or for any other offence arising out of the same transaction or set of circumstances.

(3) Sub-paragraph (2) does not apply if—
  (a) it is proved that the deposition was not signed by the justice by whom it purports to have been signed,
  (b) the court of trial at its discretion orders that sub-paragraph (2) shall not apply, or
  (c) a party to the proceedings objects to sub-paragraph (2) applying.

(4) If a party to the proceedings objects to sub-paragraph (2) applying the court of trial may order that the objection shall have no effect if the court considers it to be in the interests of justice so to order.

Signatures

3.—(1) A justice who signs a certificate authenticating one or more relevant statements or depositions shall be treated for the purposes of paragraphs 1 and 2 as signing the statement or deposition or (as the case may be) each of them.

(2) For this purpose—
  (a) a relevant statement is a written statement made by a person for the purposes of proceedings before a magistrates' court inquiring into an offence as examining justices;
  (b) a relevant deposition is a deposition made in pursuance of section 97A of the Magistrates' Courts Act 1980 for the purposes of such proceedings.

Time limit for objection

4. Without prejudice to section 84 of the Supreme Court Act 1981 (rules of court) the power to make rules under that section includes power to make provision—
  (a) requiring an objection under paragraph 1(3)(c) or 2(3)(c) to be made within a period prescribed in the rules;
  (b) allowing the court of trial at its discretion to permit such an objection to be made outside any such period.

Criminal Procedure and Investigations Act 1996, Sch 2

Retrial

5. In Schedule 2 to the Criminal Appeal Act 1968 (procedural and other provisions applicable on order for retrial) in paragraph 1 for the words from "section 13(3)" to "before the original trial" there shall be substituted "paragraphs 1 and 2 of Schedule 2 to the Criminal Procedure and Investigations Act 1996 (use of written statements and depositions) shall not apply to any written statement or deposition read as evidence at the original trial".

Repeals

6.—(1) Section 13(3) of the Criminal Justice Act 1925 (which relates to depositions taken before examining justices and is superseded by paragraph 2 above) shall be omitted.

(2) Section 7 of the Criminal Justice Act 1967 (which is superseded by paragraph 3 above) shall be omitted.

Commencement

7. This Schedule shall have effect in accordance with provision made by the Secretary of State by order.

References   See paras 6.49, 8.26.

SCHEDULE 3

Section 72

FRAUD

Introduction

1. The Criminal Justice Act 1987 shall be amended as provided by this Schedule.

Preparatory hearings

2. In section 7 (power to order preparatory hearing) subsections (3) to (5) (power to make order that could be made at the hearing) shall be omitted.

3.—(1) Section 9 (the preparatory hearing) shall be amended as follows.

(2) In subsection (7) (warning of possible consequence under section 10(1)) the word "(1)" shall be omitted.

(3) In subsection (10) for the words "at or for the purposes of a preparatory hearing" there shall be substituted "under this section".

4. The following section shall be inserted after section 9—

"**9A Orders before preparatory hearing**

(1) Subsection (2) below applies where—
 (a) a judge orders a preparatory hearing, and
 (b) he decides that any order which could be made under section 9(4) or (5) above at the hearing should be made before the hearing.

(2) In such a case—
 (a) he may make any such order before the hearing (or at the hearing), and
 (b) subsections (4) to (10) of section 9 above shall apply accordingly."

5. The following section shall be substituted for section 10 (later stages of trial)—

"**10 Later stages of trial**

(1) Any party may depart from the case he disclosed in pursuance of a requirement imposed under section 9 above.

(2) Where—
 (a) a party departs from the case he disclosed in pursuance of a requirement imposed under section 9 above, or
 (b) a party fails to comply with such a requirement,
the judge or, with the leave of the judge, any other party may make such comment as appears to the judge or the other party (as the case may be) to be appropriate and the jury may draw such inference as appears proper.

(3) In deciding whether to give leave the judge shall have regard—
   (a) to the extent of the departure or failure, and
   (b) to whether there is any justification for it.

(4) Except as provided by this section no part—
   (a) of a statement given under section 9(5) above, or
   (b) of any other information relating to the case for the accused or, if there is more than one, the case for any of them, which was given in pursuance of a requirement imposed under section 9 above,
may be disclosed at a stage in the trial after the jury have been sworn without the consent of the accused concerned."

Reporting restrictions

6. The following sections shall be substituted for section 11 (reporting restrictions)—

   "11 Restrictions on reporting

   (1) Except as provided by this section—
      (a) no written report of proceedings falling within subsection (2) below shall be published in Great Britain;
      (b) no report of proceedings falling within subsection (2) below shall be included in a relevant programme for reception in Great Britain.

   (2) The following proceedings fall within this subsection—
      (a) an application under section 6(1) above;
      (b) a preparatory hearing;
      (c) an application for leave to appeal in relation to such a hearing;
      (d) an appeal in relation to such a hearing.

   (3) The judge dealing with an application under section 6(1) above may order that subsection (1) above shall not apply, or shall not apply to a specified extent, to a report of the application.

   (4) The judge dealing with a preparatory hearing may order that subsection (1) above shall not apply, or shall not apply to a specified extent, to a report of—
      (a) the preparatory hearing, or
      (b) an application to the judge for leave to appeal to the Court of Appeal under section 9(11) above in relation to the preparatory hearing.

   (5) The Court of Appeal may order that subsection (1) above shall not apply, or shall not apply to a specified extent, to a report of—
      (a) an appeal to the Court of Appeal under section 9(11) above in relation to a preparatory hearing,
      (b) an application to that Court for leave to appeal to it under section 9(11) above in relation to a preparatory hearing, or
      (c) an application to that Court for leave to appeal to the House of Lords under Part II of the Criminal Appeal Act 1968 in relation to a preparatory hearing.

   (6) The House of Lords may order that subsection (1) above shall not apply, or shall not apply to a specified extent, to a report of—
      (a) an appeal to that House under Part II of the Criminal Appeal Act 1968 in relation to a preparatory hearing, or
      (b) an application to that House for leave to appeal to it under Part II of the Criminal Appeal Act 1968 in relation to a preparatory hearing.

   (7) Where there is only one accused and he objects to the making of an order under subsection (3), (4), (5) or (6) above the judge or the Court of Appeal or the House of Lords shall make the order if (and only if) satisfied after hearing the representations of the accused that it is in the interests of justice to do so; and if the order is made it shall not apply to the extent that a report deals with any such objection or representations.

   (8) Where there are two or more accused and one or more of them objects to the making of an order under subsection (3), (4), (5) or (6) above the judge or the Court of Appeal or the House of Lords shall make the order if (and only if) satisfied after hearing the representations of each of the accused that it is in the interests of justice to do so; and if the order is made it shall not apply to the extent that a report deals with any such objection or representations.

(9) Subsection (1) above does not apply to—
  (a) the publication of a report of an application under section 6(1) above, or
  (b) the inclusion in a relevant programme of a report of an application under section 6(1) above,
where the application is successful.

(10) Where—
  (a) two or more persons are jointly charged, and
  (b) applications under section 6(1) above are made by more than one of them,
subsection (9) above shall have effect as if for the words "the application is" there were substituted "all the applications are".

(11) Subsection (1) above does not apply to—
  (a) the publication of a report of an unsuccessful application made under section 6(1) above,
  (b) the publication of a report of a preparatory hearing,
  (c) the publication of a report of an appeal in relation to a preparatory hearing or of an application for leave to appeal in relation to such a hearing,
  (d) the inclusion in a relevant programme of a report of an unsuccessful application made under section 6(1) above,
  (e) the inclusion in a relevant programme of a report of a preparatory hearing, or
  (f) the inclusion in a relevant programme of a report of an appeal in relation to a preparatory hearing or of an application for leave to appeal in relation to such a hearing,
at the conclusion of the trial of the accused or of the last of the accused to be tried.

(12) Subsection (1) above does not apply to a report which contains only one or more of the following matters—
  (a) the identity of the court and the name of the judge;
  (b) the names, ages, home addresses and occupations of the accused and witnesses;
  (c) any relevant business information;
  (d) the offence or offences, or a summary of them, with which the accused is or are charged;
  (e) the names of counsel and solicitors in the proceedings;
  (f) where the proceedings are adjourned, the date and place to which they are adjourned;
  (g) any arrangements as to bail;
  (h) whether legal aid was granted to the accused or any of the accused.

(13) The addresses that may be published or included in a relevant programme under subsection (12) above are addresses—
  (a) at any relevant time, and
  (b) at the time of their publication or inclusion in a relevant programme;
and "relevant time" here means a time when events giving rise to the charges to which the proceedings relate occurred.

(14) The following is relevant business information for the purposes of subsection (12) above—
  (a) any address used by the accused for carrying on a business on his own account;
  (b) the name of any business which he was carrying on on his own account at any relevant time;
  (c) the name of any firm in which he was a partner at any relevant time or by which he was engaged at any such time;
  (d) the address of any such firm;
  (e) the name of any company of which he was a director at any relevant time or by which he was otherwise engaged at any such time;
  (f) the address of the registered or principal office of any such company;
  (g) any working address of the accused in his capacity as a person engaged by any such company;
and here "engaged" means engaged under a contract of service or a contract for services, and "relevant time" has the same meaning as in subsection (13) above.

(15) Nothing in this section affects any prohibition or restriction imposed by virtue of any other enactment on a publication or on matter included in a programme.

(16) In this section—
    (a) "publish", in relation to a report, means publish the report, either by itself or as part of a newspaper or periodical, for distribution to the public;
    (b) expressions cognate with "publish" shall be construed accordingly;
    (c) "relevant programme" means a programme included in a programme service, within the meaning of the Broadcasting Act 1990.

11A Offences in connection with reporting

(1) If a report is published or included in a relevant programme in contravention of section 11 above each of the following persons is guilty of an offence—
    (a) in the case of a publication of a written report as part of a newspaper or periodical, any proprietor, editor or publisher of the newspaper or periodical;
    (b) in the case of a publication of a written report otherwise than as part of a newspaper or periodical, the person who publishes it;
    (c) in the case of the inclusion of a report in a relevant programme, any body corporate which is engaged in providing the service in which the programme is included and any person having functions in relation to the programme corresponding to those of an editor of a newspaper.

(2) A person guilty of an offence under this section is liable on summary conviction to a fine of an amount not exceeding level 5 on the standard scale.

(3) Proceedings for an offence under this section shall not be instituted in England and Wales otherwise than by or with the consent of the Attorney General.

(4) Subsection (16) of section 11 above applies for the purposes of this section as it applies for the purposes of that."

7. In the list in section 17(2) (provisions extending to Scotland) after the entry relating to section 11 there shall be inserted "section 11A;".

General

8.—(1) This Schedule applies in relation to an offence if—
    (a) on or after the appointed day the accused is committed for trial for the offence,
    (b) proceedings for the trial on the charge concerned are transferred to the Crown Court on or after the appointed day, or
    (c) a bill of indictment relating to the offence is preferred on or after the appointed day under the authority of section 2(2)(b) of the Administration of Justice (Miscellaneous Provisions) Act 1933 (bill preferred by direction of Court of Appeal, or by direction or with consent of a judge).

(2) References in this paragraph to the appointed day are to such day as is appointed for the purposes of this Schedule by the Secretary of State by order.

References   See para 8.31.

SCHEDULE 4

Section 79

MODIFICATIONS FOR NORTHERN IRELAND

General

1. In their application to Northern Ireland the provisions of this Act mentioned in the following paragraphs of this Schedule shall have effect subject to the modifications set out in those paragraphs.

2. Where a provision of this Act which extends to Northern Ireland confers power on the Secretary of State to prepare a code of practice, that power may be so exercised as to prepare a code of practice having effect only in Northern Ireland and containing provisions different to those contained in any code of practice prepared under that provision and having effect in England and Wales.

3. In any provision of this Act which extends to Northern Ireland—
    (a) reference to an enactment includes reference to an enactment comprised in Northern Ireland legislation;
    (b) reference to a police officer is a reference to a member of the Royal Ulster Constabulary or of the Royal Ulster Constabulary Reserve.

Criminal Procedure and Investigations Act 1996, Sch 4

Part I of this Act

4. In section 1 for subsections (1) and (2) substitute—

"(1) This Part applies where a person is charged with an offence, the court proceeds to deal summarily with the charge and that person pleads not guilty.

(2) This Part also applies where—
- (a) a person is charged with an indictable offence and he is committed for trial for the offence concerned,
- (b) a person is charged with an indictable offence and proceedings for the trial of the person on the charge concerned are transferred to the Crown Court by virtue of a notice of transfer given under Article 3 of the Criminal Justice (Serious Fraud) (Northern Ireland) Order 1988 (serious or complex fraud),
- (c) a person is charged with an indictable offence and proceedings for the trial of the person on the charge concerned are transferred to the Crown Court by virtue of a notice of transfer given under Article 4 of the Children's Evidence (Northern Ireland) Order 1995 (certain cases involving children),
- (d) a count charging a person with a summary offence is included in an indictment under the authority of Article 193A of the Road Traffic (Northern Ireland) Order 1981 (offences relating to drink or drugs), or
- (e) an indictment charging a person with an indictable offence is presented under the authority of section 2(2)(c), (d), (e) or (f) of the Grand Jury (Abolition) Act (Northern Ireland) 1969.

(2A) In subsection (2)—

"indictable offence" means an offence which is triable on indictment, whether it is exclusively so triable or not;

"summary offence" has the same meaning as in Article 193A of the Road Traffic (Northern Ireland) Order 1981."

5.—(1) In section 5(2) for "section 5(9) of the Criminal Justice Act 1987" substitute "Article 4(7) of the Criminal Justice (Serious Fraud) (Northern Ireland) Order 1988".

(2) In section 5(3) for "paragraph 4 of Schedule 6 to the Criminal Justice Act 1991" substitute "paragraph 3 of Schedule 1 to the Children's Evidence (Northern Ireland) Order 1995".

6. In section 13(1) for "the bill of indictment is preferred" substitute "the indictment is presented".

7. After section 14 there shall be inserted—

"**14A Public interest: review for scheduled offences**

(1) This section applies where this Part applies by virtue of section 1(2) and the offence charged is a scheduled offence within the meaning of section 1 of the Northern Ireland (Emergency Provisions) Act 1996.

(2) At any time—
- (a) after a court makes an order under section 3(6), 7(5), 8(5) or 9(8), and
- (b) before the accused is acquitted or convicted or the prosecutor decides not to proceed with the case concerned,

the accused may apply to the court for a review of the question whether it is still not in the public interest to disclose material affected by its order.

(3) In such a case the court must review that question, and if it concludes that it is in the public interest to disclose material to any extent—
- (a) it shall so order; and
- (b) it shall take such steps as are reasonable to inform the prosecutor of its order.

(4) Where the prosecutor is informed of an order made under subsection (3) he must act accordingly having regard to the provisions of this Part (unless he decides not to proceed with the case concerned)."

8. In section 15(1) at the end add "and section 14A does not apply".

9. In section 16 after "14(2)" insert ", 14A(2)" and after "14(3)" insert ", 14A(3)".

10. In section 17(1)(a) after "14" insert ", 14A".

11. In section 18 at the end add—

"(11) In section 13 (legal aid) of the Contempt of Court Act 1981 (as set out in Schedule 4 to that Act) in subsection (1)(a) after sub-paragraph (ii) there shall be inserted—

"(iia) by a magistrates' court or the Crown Court under section 18 of the Criminal Procedure and Investigations Act 1996; or"."

12.—(1) In section 19(1) for the words from the beginning to "includes" substitute—

"Without prejudice to the generality of—
(a) Article 13 of the Magistrates' Courts (Northern Ireland) Order 1981 (magistrates' courts rules), and
(b) section 52 of the Judicature (Northern Ireland) Act 1978 (Crown Court rules),
the power to make rules under each of those provisions includes".

(2) In section 19(2)(b) after "14(2)" insert ", 14A(2)".

(3) In section 19(2)(d) after "14(3)" insert ", 14A(3)".

(4) In section 19 omit subsection (3).

13.—(1) In section 20(2) for "section 9 of the Criminal Justice Act 1987 or section 31 of this Act" substitute "Article 8 of the Criminal Justice (Serious Fraud) (Northern Ireland) Order 1988".

(2) In section 20(3) for the words from the beginning to "that section" substitute "Without prejudice to the generality of Article 13 of the Magistrates' Courts (Northern Ireland) Order 1981 (magistrates' courts rules) the power to make rules under that Article."

(3) In section 20(5) for paragraph (b) substitute—

"(b) "enactment" includes a statutory instrument within the meaning of section 1(d) of the Interpretation Act (Northern Ireland) 1954."

14. In section 21(3) for paragraph (e) substitute—

"(e) the indictment is presented (where this Part applies by virtue of section 1(2)(e))".

Part IV of this Act

15. In section 39 for subsections (2) and (3) substitute—

"(2) For the purposes of this Part a hearing is also a pre-trial hearing if—
(a) it relates to a trial on indictment to be held in pursuance of an indictment presented under the authority of section 2(2)(c), (d), (e) or (f) of the Grand Jury (Abolition) Act (Northern Ireland) 1969, and
(b) it takes place after the indictment has been presented and before the start of the trial.

(3) For the purposes of this section the start of a trial on indictment occurs—
(a) in the case of a trial to which section 11 of the Northern Ireland (Emergency Provisions) Act 1996 applies (trial by court without a jury), at the opening of the case for the prosecution or, if the court accepts a plea of guilty before that time, when that plea is accepted,
(b) in any other case, when a jury is sworn to consider the issue of guilt or fitness to be tried or, if the court accepts a plea of guilty before a jury is sworn, when that plea is accepted,
but this is subject to Article 7 of the Criminal Justice (Serious Fraud) (Northern Ireland) Order 1988."

16. In section 41(1) for "Great Britain" where it twice occurs substitute "Northern Ireland".

17. In section 42(3) omit "in England and Wales", and after "Attorney General" insert "for Northern Ireland".

Criminal Procedure and Investigations Act 1996, Sch 4

Part V of this Act

18. In section 45 for subsections (1) to (8) substitute—

"(1) Article 4 of the Criminal Justice (Serious Fraud) (Northern Ireland) Order 1988 (notices of transfer in cases of serious or complex fraud) shall be amended as mentioned in subsections (2) and (3).

(2) In paragraph (7)(a) (regulations) for the words "a statement of the evidence" there shall be substituted "copies of the documents containing the evidence (including oral evidence)".

(3) The following paragraph shall be inserted after paragraph (7)—

"(7A) Regulations under paragraph (7)(a) may provide that there shall be no requirement for copies of documents to accompany the copy of the notice of transfer if they are referred to, in documents sent with the notice of transfer, as having already been supplied."

(4) In Schedule 1 to the Children's Evidence (Northern Ireland) Order 1995 (notices of transfer in certain cases involving children) paragraph 3 (regulations) shall be amended as mentioned in subsections (5) and (6).

(5) In sub-paragraph (1)(a) for the words "a statement of the evidence" there shall be substituted "copies of the documents containing the evidence (including oral evidence)".

(6) The following sub-paragraph shall be inserted after sub-paragraph (1)—

"(1A) Regulations under sub-paragraph (1)(a) may provide that there shall be no requirement for copies of documents to accompany the copy of the notice of transfer if they are referred to, in documents sent with the notice of transfer, as having already been supplied."

(7) In paragraph 5 of Schedule 1 to the 1995 Order (reporting restrictions) in sub-paragraph (8) for the words "sub-paragraphs (5) and (6)" there shall be substituted "sub-paragraphs (5) and (7)".

(8) This section applies where a notice of transfer is given under Article 3 of the 1988 Order or Article 4 of the 1995 Order (as the case may be) on or after the appointed day".

19. In section 46 for subsections (1) and (2) substitute—

"(1) Part II of the Schedule to the War Crimes Act 1991 and section 1(4) of that Act so far as relating thereto (transfer procedure in Northern Ireland in cases of war crimes) shall cease to have effect.

(2) In Article 29(2) of the Legal Aid, Advice and Assistance (Northern Ireland) Order 1981 (free legal aid in Crown Court) sub-paragraph (d) (which relates to a notice of transfer under Part II of the Schedule to the War Crimes Act 1991) shall cease to have effect."

Part VII of this Act

20. In section 54(6) omit paragraph (b) and in paragraph (c) for "section 1 of the Perjury Act 1911" substitute "Article 3 of the Perjury (Northern Ireland) Order 1979".

21. In section 56(2) for paragraphs (a) to (c) substitute—

"(a) section 5 of the Criminal Law Amendment Act 1885 (no prosecution for offence under that section more than 12 months after the commission of the offence);
(b) Article 19(1)(a) of the Magistrates' Courts (Northern Ireland) Order 1981 (magistrates' court not to hear and determine certain complaints unless made within 6 months of time when offence committed);
(c) an enactment that imposes a time limit only in certain circumstances (as where proceedings are not instituted by or with the consent of the Director of Public Prosecutions for Northern Ireland)."

22. In section 57 omit subsection (1).

23.—(1) In section 58(1) omit paragraph (b) and the word "or" immediately before it.

(2) In section 58(9) omit paragraph (b).

24. In section 59(1) for "Great Britain" where it twice occurs substitute "Northern Ireland".

25. In section 62 for subsections (1) and (2) substitute—

"(1) In Article 81 of the Police and Criminal Evidence (Northern Ireland) Order 1989 (evidence through television links) the following paragraphs shall be inserted after paragraph (3)—

"(3A) Where the court gives leave under paragraph (2) for a witness falling within paragraph (1)(b)(ii) to give evidence through a live television link, then, subject to paragraph (3B), the witness concerned may not give evidence otherwise than through a live television link.

(3B) In a case falling within paragraph (3A) the court may give permission for the witness to give evidence otherwise than through a live television link if it appears to the court to be in the interests of justice to give such permission.

(3C) Permission may be given under paragraph (3B)—
    (a) on an application by a party to the case, or
    (b) of the court's own motion;
but no application may be made under sub-paragraph (a) unless there has been a material change of circumstances since the leave was given under paragraph (2)."

(2) In Article 81A of the Police and Criminal Evidence (Northern Ireland) Order 1989 (video recordings of testimony from child witnesses) the following paragraphs shall be inserted after paragraph (6)—

"(6A) Where the court gives leave under paragraph (2) the child witness shall not give relevant evidence (within the meaning given by paragraph (6D)) otherwise than by means of the video recording; but this is subject to paragraph (6B).

(6B) In a case falling within paragraph (6A) the court may give permission for the child witness to give relevant evidence (within the meaning given by paragraph (6D)) otherwise than by means of the video recording if it appears to the court to be in the interests of justice to give such permission.

(6C) Permission may be given under paragraph (6B)—
    (a) on an application by a party to the case, or
    (b) of the court's own motion;
but no application may be made under sub-paragraph (a) unless there has been a material change of circumstances since the leave was given under paragraph (2).

(6D) For the purposes of paragraphs (6A) and (6B) evidence is relevant evidence if—
    (a) it is evidence in chief on behalf of the party who tendered the video recording, and
    (b) it relates to matter which, in the opinion of the court, is dealt with in the recording and which the court has not directed to be excluded under paragraph (3).".".

26. For section 63 substitute—

"63 Road traffic: provision of specimens

(1) In Article 18(4) of the Road Traffic (Northern Ireland) Order 1995 (provision of blood or urine in course of investigating whether certain road traffic offences have been committed) after sub-paragraph (b) there shall be inserted—

"(bb) a device of the type mentioned in paragraph (1)(a) has been used in the circumstances described in paragraph (2) but the constable who required the specimens of breath has reasonable cause to believe that the device has not produced a reliable indication of the proportion of alcohol in the breath of the person concerned, or".

(2) This section applies where it is proposed to make a requirement mentioned in Article 18(4) of the 1995 Order after the appointed day.

(3) The reference in subsection (2) to the appointed day is to such day as is appointed for the purposes of this section by the Department of the Environment for Northern Ireland by order.

(4) The power of the Department of the Environment for Northern Ireland to make an order under subsection (3) shall be exercisable by statutory rule for the purposes of the Statutory Rules (Northern Ireland) Order 1979."

27. In section 64 for subsection (1) substitute—

"(1) In Article 63A of the Police and Criminal Evidence (Northern Ireland) Order 1989 the following paragraphs shall be substituted for paragraph (1) (checks against fingerprints etc where a person has been arrested on suspicion of being involved in a recordable offence)—

"(1) Where a person has been arrested on suspicion of being involved in a recordable offence or has been charged with such an offence or has been informed that he will be reported for such an offence, fingerprints or samples or the information derived from samples taken under any power conferred by this Part from the person may be checked against—
  (a) other fingerprints or samples to which the person seeking to check has access and which are held by or on behalf of a police force (or police forces) falling within paragraph (1A) or are held in connection with or as the result of an investigation of an offence;
  (b) information derived from other samples if the information is contained in records to which the person seeking to check has access and which are held as mentioned in sub-paragraph (a).

(1A) Each of the following police forces falls within this paragraph—
  (a) the Royal Ulster Constabulary and the Royal Ulster Constabulary Reserve;
  (b) a police force within the meaning given by section 62 of the Police Act 1964;
  (c) a police force within the meaning given by section 50 of the Police (Scotland) Act 1967;
  (d) the States of Jersey Police Force;
  (e) the salaried police force of the Island of Guernsey;
  (f) the Isle of Man Constabulary."."

28. For section 66 substitute—

"**66.**—(1) After section 51 of the Judicature (Northern Ireland) Act 1978 there shall be inserted—

"51A Issue of witness summons on application to Crown Court

(1) This section applies where the Crown Court is satisfied that—
  (a) a person is likely to be able to give evidence likely to be material evidence, or produce any document or thing likely to be material evidence, for the purpose of any criminal proceedings before the Crown Court, and
  (b) the person will not voluntarily attend as a witness or will not voluntarily produce the document or thing.

(2) In such a case the Crown Court shall, subject to the following provisions of this section, issue a summons (a witness summons) directed to the person concerned and requiring him to—
  (a) attend before the Crown Court at the time and place stated in the summons, and
  (b) give the evidence or produce the document or thing.

(3) A witness summons may only be issued under this section on an application; and the Crown Court may refuse to issue the summons if any requirement relating to the application is not fulfilled.

(4) Where a person has been committed for trial for any offence to which the proceedings concerned relate, an application must be made as soon as is reasonably practicable after the committal.

(5) Where the proceedings concerned have been transferred to the Crown Court, an application must be made as soon as is reasonably practicable after the transfer.

(6) Where the proceedings concerned relate to an offence in relation to which an indictment has been presented under the authority of section 2(2)(c), (d), (e) or (f) of the Grand Jury (Abolition) Act (Northern Ireland) 1969, an application must be made as soon as is reasonably practicable after the indictment is presented.

(7) An application must be made in accordance with Crown Court rules; and different provision may be made for different cases or descriptions of case.

(8) Crown Court rules—
  (a) may, in such cases as the rules may specify, require an application to be made by a party to the case;
  (b) may, in such cases as the rules may specify, require the service of notice of an application on the person to whom the witness summons is proposed to be directed;
  (c) may, in such cases as the rules may specify, require an application to be supported by an affidavit containing such matters as the rules may stipulate;
  (d) may, in such cases as the rules may specify, make provision for enabling the person to whom the witness summons is proposed to be directed to be present or represented at the hearing of the application for the witness summons.

(9) Provision contained in Crown Court rules by virtue of subsection (8)(c) may in particular require an affidavit to—
  (a) set out any charge on which the proceedings concerned are based;
  (b) specify any stipulated evidence, document or thing in such a way as to enable the directed person to identify it;
  (c) specify grounds for believing that the directed person is likely to be able to give any stipulated evidence or produce any stipulated document or thing;
  (d) specify grounds for believing that any stipulated evidence is likely to be material evidence;
  (e) specify grounds for believing that any stipulated document or thing is likely to be material evidence.

(10) In subsection (9)—
  (a) references to any stipulated evidence, document or thing are to any evidence, document or thing whose giving or production is proposed to be required by the witness summons;
  (b) references to the directed person are to the person to whom the witness summons is proposed to be directed.

51B Power to require advance production

A witness summons which is issued under section 51A and which requires a person to produce a document or thing as mentioned in section 51A(2) may also require him to produce the document or thing—
  (a) at a place stated in the summons, and
  (b) at a time which is so stated and precedes that stated under section 51A(2),
for inspection by the person applying for the summons.

51C Summons no longer needed

(1) If—
  (a) a document or thing is produced in pursuance of a requirement imposed by a witness summons under section 51B,
  (b) the person applying for the summons concludes that a requirement imposed by the summons under section 51A(2) is no longer needed, and
  (c) he accordingly applies to the Crown Court for a direction that the summons shall be of no further effect,
the court may direct accordingly.

(2) An application under this section must be made in accordance with Crown Court rules; and different provision may be made for different cases or descriptions of case.

(3) Crown Court rules may, in such cases as the rules may specify, require the effect of a direction under this section to be notified to the person to whom the summons is directed.

51D Application to make summons ineffective

(1) If a witness summons issued under section 51A is directed to a person who—
- (a) applies to the Crown Court,
- (b) satisfies the court that he was not served with notice of the application to issue the summons and that he was neither present nor represented at the hearing of the application, and
- (c) satisfies the court that he cannot give any evidence likely to be material evidence or, as the case may be, produce any document or thing likely to be material evidence,

the court may direct that the summons shall be of no effect.

(2) For the purposes of subsection (1) it is immaterial—
- (a) whether or not Crown Court rules require the person to be served with notice of the application to issue the summons;
- (b) whether or not Crown Court rules enable the person to be present or represented at the hearing of the application.

(3) In subsection (1)(b) "served" means—
- (a) served in accordance with Crown Court rules, in a case where such rules require the person to be served with notice of the application to issue the summons;
- (b) served in such way as appears reasonable to the Crown Court, in any other case.

(4) The Crown Court may refuse to make a direction under this section if any requirement relating to the application under this section is not fulfilled.

(5) An application under this section must be made in accordance with Crown Court rules; and different provision may be made for different cases or descriptions of case.

(6) Crown Court rules may, in such cases as the rules may specify, require the service of notice of an application under this section on the person on whose application the witness summons was issued.

(7) Crown Court rules may, in such cases as the rules may specify, require that where—
- (a) a person applying under this section can produce a particular document or thing, but
- (b) he seeks to satisfy the court that the document or thing is not likely to be material evidence,

he must arrange for the document or thing to be available at the hearing of the application.

(8) Where a direction is made under this section that a witness summons shall be of no effect, the person on whose application the summons was issued may be ordered to pay the whole or any part of the costs of the application under this section.

(9) Any costs payable under an order made under subsection (8) shall be taxed by the Master (Taxing Office), and payment of those costs shall be enforceable in the same manner as an order for payment of costs made by the High Court in a civil case or as a sum adjudged summarily to be paid as a civil debt.

51E Issue of witness summons of Crown Court's own motion

For the purpose of any criminal proceedings before it, the Crown Court may of its own motion issue a summons (a witness summons) directed to a person and requiring him to—
> (a) attend before the court at the time and place stated in the summons; and
> (b) give evidence or produce any document or thing specified in the summons.

51F Application to make summons ineffective

(1)   If a witness summons issued under section 51E is directed to a person who—
> (a) applies to the Crown Court, and
> (b) satisfies the court that he cannot give any evidence likely to be material evidence or, as the case may be, produce any document or thing likely to be material evidence,

the court may direct that the summons shall be of no effect.

(2)   The Crown Court may refuse to make a direction under this section if any requirement relating to the application under this section is not fulfilled.

(3)   An application under this section must be made in accordance with Crown Court rules; and different provision may be made for different cases or descriptions of case.

(4)   Crown Court rules may, in such cases as the rules may specify, require that where—
> (a) a person applying under this section can produce a particular document or thing, but
> (b) he seeks to satisfy the court that the document or thing is not likely to be material evidence,

he must arrange for the document or thing to be available at the hearing of the application.

51G Punishment for disobedience to witness summons

(1)   Any person who without just excuse—
> (a) disobeys a witness summons requiring him to attend before the Crown Court; or
> (b) disobeys a requirement made by the Crown Court under section 51B,

shall be guilty of contempt of that court and may be punished summarily by that court as if his contempt were in the face of the court.

(2)   A person shall not be committed to prison by reason of any disobedience mentioned in subsection (1) for a period exceeding three months.

51H Further process to secure attendance of witnesses

(1)   If the Crown Court is satisfied by evidence on oath that—
> (a) a witness in respect of whom a witness summons is in force is unlikely to comply with the summons; and
> (b) the witness is likely to be able to give evidence likely to be material evidence or produce any document or thing likely to be material evidence in the proceedings,

the Crown Court may issue a warrant to arrest the witness and bring him before the court.

(2)   Where a witness who is required to attend before the Crown Court by virtue of a witness summons fails to attend in compliance with the summons, the Crown Court may—
> (a) in any case, cause to be served on him a notice requiring him to attend the court forthwith or at such time as may be specified in the notice;
> (b) if the court is satisfied that there are reasonable grounds for believing that he has failed to attend without just excuse, or if he has failed to comply with a notice under paragraph (a), issue a warrant to arrest him and bring him before the court.

(3) A witness brought before the Crown Court in pursuance of a warrant under this section may be remanded by that court in custody or on bail (with or without sureties) until such time as the court may appoint for receiving his evidence or dealing with him under section 51G.

(4) Where a witness attends the Crown Court in pursuance of a notice under this section, the court may direct that the notice shall have effect as if it required him to attend at any later time appointed by the court for receiving his evidence or dealing with him under section 51G."

(2) No subpoena ad testificandum or subpoena duces tecum shall issue after the appointed day in respect of any criminal proceedings for the purposes of which—

(a) a witness summons may be issued under section 51A of the Judicature (Northern Ireland) Act 1978; or

(b) a summons may be issued under Article 118 of the Magistrates' Courts (Northern Ireland) Order 1981 (process for attendance of witnesses in magistrates' courts).

(3) In section 47(4) of the Judicature (Northern Ireland) Act 1978 after the words "Subject to" there shall be inserted the words "section 66(2) of the Criminal Procedure and Investigations Act 1996 (subpoenas not to issue in certain criminal cases) and to".

(4) This section applies in relation to any proceedings for the purposes of which no summons requiring the attendance of a witness has been issued before the appointed day.

(5) The references in subsections (2) and (4) to the appointed day are to such day as is appointed for the purposes of this section by the Secretary of State by order."

29. In section 69(1) for "section 9 of the Criminal Justice Act 1967" substitute "section 1 of the Criminal Justice (Miscellaneous Provisions) Act (Northern Ireland) 1968" and for "subsection (3)(a)" substitute "subsection (4)(a)".

30. In section 70 for subsection (1) substitute—

"(1) In Article 10 of the Magistrates' Courts (Northern Ireland) Order 1981—

(a) in paragraph (1) (power of Lord Chancellor to defray expenses in connection with proceedings) after the words "justice or clerk" (where they first occur) there shall be inserted "in relation to any matter other than a criminal matter", and

(b) after paragraph (1) there shall be inserted—

"(1A) The Lord Chancellor shall defray any expenses reasonably incurred by a resident magistrate or other justice of the peace or by a clerk of petty sessions in, or in connection with, any proceedings or claim brought as a result of the execution, or purported execution, of the office of that magistrate, justice or clerk in relation to any criminal matter, unless it is proved, in respect of the matters giving rise to the proceedings or claim, that he acted in bad faith."."

31.—(1) In section 74 for subsection (1) substitute—

"(1) The Evidence of Alibi Act (Northern Ireland) 1972 shall cease to have effect."

(2) In section 74 omit subsections (2) and (3).

(3) In section 74 for subsection (4) substitute—

"(4) In Article 8(6) of the Criminal Justice (Serious Fraud) (Northern Ireland) Order 1988 (disclosure in cases involving fraud) in sub-paragraph (a) for the words "section 1 of the Evidence of Alibi Act (Northern Ireland) 1972" there shall be substituted the words "section 5(7) of the Criminal Procedure and Investigations Act 1996"."

32. In section 75(1) for "sections 52(3) and 54(7)" substitute "section 54(7)".

33. For section 76 substitute—

"76 Power of magistrates' courts

Anything authorised or required by this Act to be done by, to or before the magistrates' court by, to or before which any other thing was done, or is to be done, may be done by, to or before any magistrates' court acting for the same county court division as that court."

34. In section 80 omit "(or revoked)".

35. For Schedule 3 substitute—

"SCHEDULE 3

FRAUD

Introduction

1. The Criminal Justice (Serious Fraud) (Northern Ireland) Order 1988 shall be amended as provided by this Schedule.

Notice of transfer

2. In Article 3 (transfer of certain fraud cases to the Crown Court) in paragraph (1)(b)(ii) for the words "seriousness and complexity" there shall be substituted the words "seriousness or complexity".

Preparatory hearings

3.—(1) Article 6 (power to order preparatory hearing) shall be amended as follows.

(2) In paragraph (1) for the words "seriousness and complexity" there shall be substituted the words "seriousness or complexity".

(3) Paragraphs (3) to (5) (power to make order that could be made at the hearing) shall be omitted.

4.—(1) Article 8 (the preparatory hearing) shall be amended as follows.

(2) In paragraph (7) (warning of possible consequence under Article 9(1)) the word "(1)" shall be omitted.

(3) In paragraph (10) for the words "at or for the purposes of a preparatory hearing" there shall be substituted "under this Article".

5. The following Article shall be inserted after Article 8—

"8A Orders before preparatory hearing

(1) Paragraph (2) applies where—
    (a) a judge orders a preparatory hearing, and
    (b) he decides that any order which could be made under Article 8(4) or (5) at the hearing should be made before the hearing.

(2) In such a case—
    (a) he may make any such order before the hearing (or at the hearing), and
    (b) paragraphs (4) to (10) of Article 8 shall apply accordingly."

6. The following Article shall be substituted for Article 9 (later stages of trial)—

"9 Later stages of trial

(1) Any party may depart from the case he disclosed in pursuance of a requirement imposed under Article 8.

(2) Where—
    (a) a party departs from the case he disclosed in pursuance of a requirement imposed under Article 8, or
    (b) a party fails to comply with such a requirement,
the judge or, with the leave of the judge, any other party may make such comment as appears to the judge or the other party (as the case may be) to be appropriate and the jury may draw such inference as appears proper.

(3) In deciding whether to give leave the judge shall have regard—
  (a) to the extent of the departure or failure, and
  (b) to whether there is any justification for it.

(4) Except as provided by this Article no part—
  (a) of a statement given under Article 8(5), or
  (b) of any other information relating to the case for the accused or, if there is more than one, the case for any of them, which was given in pursuance of a requirement imposed under Article 8,

may be disclosed at a stage in the trial after the jury have been sworn without the consent of the accused concerned."

Reporting restrictions

7. The following Articles shall be substituted for Article 10 (reporting restrictions)—

"**10 Restrictions on reporting**

(1) Except as provided by this Article—
  (a) no written report of proceedings falling within paragraph (2) shall be published in Northern Ireland;
  (b) no report of proceedings falling within paragraph (2) shall be included in a relevant programme for reception in Northern Ireland.

(2) The following proceedings fall within this paragraph—
  (a) an application under Article 5(1);
  (b) a preparatory hearing;
  (c) an application for leave to appeal in relation to such a hearing;
  (d) an appeal in relation to such a hearing.

(3) The judge dealing with an application under Article 5(1) may order that paragraph (1) shall not apply, or shall not apply to a specified extent, to a report of the application.

(4) The judge dealing with a preparatory hearing may order that paragraph (1) shall not apply, or shall not apply to a specified extent, to a report of—
  (a) the preparatory hearing, or
  (b) an application to the judge for leave to appeal to the Court of Appeal under Article 8(11) in relation to the preparatory hearing.

(5) The Court of Appeal may order that paragraph (1) shall not apply, or shall not apply to a specified extent, to a report of—
  (a) an appeal to the Court of Appeal under Article 8(11) in relation to a preparatory hearing,
  (b) an application to that Court for leave to appeal to it under Article 8(11) in relation to a preparatory hearing, or
  (c) an application to that Court for leave to appeal to the House of Lords under Part II of the Criminal Appeal (Northern Ireland) Act 1980 in relation to a preparatory hearing.

(6) The House of Lords may order that paragraph (1) shall not apply, or shall not apply to a specified extent, to a report of—
  (a) an appeal to that House under Part II of the Criminal Appeal (Northern Ireland) Act 1980 in relation to a preparatory hearing, or
  (b) an application to that House for leave to appeal to it under Part II of the Criminal Appeal (Northern Ireland) Act 1980 in relation to a preparatory hearing.

(7) Where there is only one accused and he objects to the making of an order under paragraph (3), (4), (5) or (6) the judge or the Court of Appeal or the House of Lords shall make the order if (and only if) satisfied after hearing the representations of the accused that it is in the interests of justice to do so; and if the order is made it shall not apply to the extent that a report deals with any such objection or representations.

(8) Where there are two or more accused and one or more of them objects to the making of an order under paragraph (3), (4), (5) or (6) the judge or the Court of Appeal or the House of Lords shall make the order if (and only if) satisfied after hearing the representations of each of the accused that it is in the interests of justice to do so; and if the order is made it shall not apply to the extent that a report deals with any such objection or representations.

(9) Paragraph (1) does not apply to—
- (a) the publication of a report of an application under Article 5(1), or
- (b) the inclusion in a relevant programme of a report of an application under Article 5(1),

where the application is successful.

(10) Where—
- (a) two or more persons are jointly charged, and
- (b) applications under Article 5(1) are made by more than one of them,

paragraph (9) shall have effect as if for the words "the application is" there were substituted "all the applications are".

(11) Paragraph (1) does not apply to—
- (a) the publication of a report of an unsuccessful application made under Article 5(1),
- (b) the publication of a report of a preparatory hearing,
- (c) the publication of a report of an appeal in relation to a preparatory hearing or of an application for leave to appeal in relation to such a hearing,
- (d) the inclusion in a relevant programme of a report of an unsuccessful application made under Article 5(1),
- (e) the inclusion in a relevant programme of a report of a preparatory hearing, or
- (f) the inclusion in a relevant programme of a report of an appeal in relation to a preparatory hearing or of an application for leave to appeal in relation to such a hearing,

at the conclusion of the trial of the accused or of the last of the accused to be tried.

(12) Paragraph (1) does not apply to a report which contains only one or more of the following matters—
- (a) the identity of the court and the name of the judge;
- (b) the names, ages, home addresses and occupations of the accused and witnesses;
- (c) any relevant business information;
- (d) the offence or offences, or a summary of them, with which the accused is or are charged;
- (e) the names of counsel and solicitors in the proceedings;
- (f) where the proceedings are adjourned, the date and place to which they are adjourned;
- (g) any arrangements as to bail;
- (h) whether legal aid was granted to the accused or any of the accused.

(13) The addresses that may be published or included in a relevant programme under paragraph (12) are addresses—
- (a) at any relevant time, and
- (b) at the time of their publication or inclusion in a relevant programme;

and "relevant time" here means a time when events giving rise to the charges to which the proceedings relate occurred.

(14) The following is relevant business information for the purposes of paragraph (12)—
- (a) any address used by the accused for carrying on a business on his own account;
- (b) the name of any business which he was carrying on on his own account at any relevant time;
- (c) the name of any firm in which he was a partner at any relevant time or by which he was engaged at any such time;

(d) the address of any such firm;

(e) the name of any company of which he was a director at any relevant time or by which he was otherwise engaged at any such time;

(f) the address of the registered or principal office of any such company;

(g) any working address of the accused in his capacity as a person engaged by any such company;

and here "engaged" means engaged under a contract of service or a contract for services, and "relevant time" has the same meaning as in paragraph (13).

(15) Nothing in this Article affects any prohibition or restriction imposed by virtue of any other enactment on a publication or on matter included in a programme.

(16) In this Article—

(a) "publish", in relation to a report, means publish the report, either by itself or as part of a newspaper or periodical, for distribution to the public;

(b) expressions cognate with "publish" shall be construed accordingly;

(c) "relevant programme" means a programme included in a programme service, within the meaning of the Broadcasting Act 1990.

10A Offences in connection with reporting

(1) If a report is published or included in a relevant programme in contravention of Article 10 each of the following persons is guilty of an offence—

(a) in the case of a publication of a written report as part of a newspaper or periodical, any proprietor, editor or publisher of the newspaper or periodical;

(b) in the case of a publication of a written report otherwise than as part of a newspaper or periodical, the person who publishes it;

(c) in the case of the inclusion of a report in a relevant programme, any body corporate which is engaged in providing the service in which the programme is included and any person having functions in relation to the programme corresponding to those of an editor of a newspaper.

(2) A person guilty of an offence under this Article is liable on summary conviction to a fine of an amount not exceeding level 5 on the standard scale.

(3) Proceedings for an offence under this Article shall not be instituted otherwise than by or with the consent of the Attorney General for Northern Ireland.

(4) Paragraph (16) of Article 10 applies for the purposes of this Article as it applies for the purposes of that."

General

8.—(1) This Schedule applies in relation to an offence if—

(a) the accused is committed for trial on the charge concerned, or proceedings for the trial on the charge concerned are transferred to the Crown Court, on or after the appointed day, or

(b) an indictment relating to the offence is presented on or after the appointed day under the authority of section 2(2)(c), (e) or (f) of the Grand Jury (Abolition) Act (Northern Ireland) 1969.

(2) References in this paragraph to the appointed day are to such day as is appointed for the purposes of this Schedule by the Secretary of State by order."

36. For Schedule 5 substitute—

"SCHEDULE 5
REPEALS

1. WAR CRIMES

Chapter or Number	Short title	Extent of repeal
1981 NI 18	The Legal Aid, Advice and Assistance (Northern Ireland) Order 1981	In Article 29(2), sub-paragraph (d) and the word "or" immediately before it.
1991 c 13	The War Crimes Act 1991	Section 1(4), so far as relating to Part II of the Schedule. Section 3(3). Part II of the Schedule.

2. SUMMONSES TO WITNESSES

Chapter	Short title	Extent of repeal
1831 c 44	The Tumultuous Risings (Ireland) Act 1831	Section 8.

This repeal has effect in accordance with section 66 of this Act.

3. ALIBI

Chapter or Number	Short title	Extent of repeal
1972 c 6 (NI)	The Evidence of Alibi Act (Northern Ireland) 1972	The whole Act.
1980 NI 6	The Criminal Justice (Northern Ireland) Order 1980	In Schedule 1, paragraph 61.
1988 NI 16	The Criminal Justice (Serious Fraud) (Northern Ireland) Order 1988	In the Schedule, paragraph 3.
1995 NI 3	The Children's Evidence (Northern Ireland) Order 1995	In Schedule 2, paragraph 6.

These repeals have effect in accordance with section 74 of this Act.

4. FRAUD

Chapter or Number	Short title	Extent of repeal
1988 NI 16	The Criminal Justice (Serious Fraud) (Northern Ireland) Order 1988	Article 6(3) to (5). In Article 8(7) the word "(1)".
1990 c 42	The Broadcasting Act 1990	In Schedule 20, paragraph 50.

These repeals have effect in accordance with Schedule 3 to this Act."

References   See para 8.38.

SCHEDULE 5

Section 80

REPEALS
1. REINSTATEMENT OF CERTAIN PROVISIONS

Chapter	Short title	Extent of repeal
1994 c 33	Criminal Justice and Public Order Act 1994	Section 34(7). Section 36(8). Section 37(7). Section 44. Schedule 4. In Schedule 11, the entries mentioned in note 1 below.

1. The entries in Schedule 11 to the 1994 Act are those relating to the following—
    (a) sections 13(3) and 49(2) of the Criminal Justice Act 1925;
    (b) section 1 of the Criminal Procedure (Attendance of Witnesses) Act 1965;
    (c) section 7 of the Criminal Justice Act 1967 and in section 36(1) of that Act the definition of "committal proceedings";
    (d) in paragraph 1 of Schedule 2 to the Criminal Appeal Act 1968 the words from "section 13(3)" to "but";
    (e) in section 46(1) of the Criminal Justice Act 1972 the words "Section 102 of the Magistrates' Courts Act 1980 and", "which respectively allow", "committal proceedings and in other", "and section 106 of the said Act of 1980", "which punish the making of", "102 or" and ", as the case may be", and section 46(2) of that Act;
    (f) in section 32(1)(b) of the Powers of Criminal Courts Act 1973 the words "tried or";
    (g) in Schedule 1 to the Interpretation Act 1978, paragraph (a) of the definition of "Committed for trial";

(h) in section 97(1) of the Magistrates' Courts Act 1980 the words from "at an inquiry" to "be) or", sections 102, 103, 105, 106 and 145(1)(e) of that Act, in section 150(1) of that Act the definition of "committal proceedings", and paragraph 2 of Schedule 5 to that Act;
(i) in section 2(2)(g) of the Criminal Attempts Act 1981 the words "or committed for trial";
(j) in section 1(2) of the Criminal Justice Act 1982 the words "trial or";
(k) paragraphs 10 and 11 of Schedule 2 to the Criminal Justice Act 1987;
(l) in section 20(4)(a) of the Legal Aid Act 1988 the words "trial or", and section 20(4)(bb) and (5) of that Act;
(m) in section 1(4) of the War Crimes Act 1991 the words "England, Wales or", and Part I of the Schedule to that Act.

2. The repeals under this paragraph (reinstatement of certain provisions) have effect in accordance with section 44 of this Act.

2. WAR CRIMES

Chapter	Short title	Extent of repeal
1988 c 34	Legal Aid Act 1988	Section 20(4)(bb).
1991 c 13	War Crimes Act 1991	In section 1(4) the words "England, Wales or".
		Section 3(2).
		Part I of the Schedule.

3. EITHER WAY OFFENCES

Chapter	Short title	Extent of repeal
1980 c 43	Magistrates' Courts Act 1980	Section 19(2)(a).

This repeal has effect in accordance with section 49 of this Act.

4. REMAND

Chapter	Short title	Extent of repeal
1980 c 43	Magistrates' Courts Act 1980	In section 128, subsections (1A)(c) and (3A)(c).
		In section 128A(1) the words "who has attained the age of 17".

These repeals have effect in accordance with section 52 of this Act.

5. SPECIMENS

Chapter	Short title	Extent of repeal
1992 c 42	Transport and Works Act 1992	In section 31(4) the word "or" at the end of paragraph (b).

This repeal has effect in accordance with section 63 of this Act.

6. WITNESS ORDERS

Chapter	Short title	Extent of repeal
1965 c 69	Criminal Procedure (Attendance of Witnesses) Act 1965	Section 1. In section 3(1) the words "witness order or". In section 4(1) the words "witness order or" and (where they next occur) "order or". In the proviso to section 4(1) the words from "in the case" (where they first occur) to "witness summons". In section 4(2) the words "a witness order or" and (where they next occur) "order or".
1971 c 23	Courts Act 1971	In Schedule 8, paragraph 45(1).
1980 c 43	Magistrates' Courts Act 1980	Section 145(1)(e).

These repeals have effect in accordance with provision made by the Secretary of State by order under section 65 of this Act.

7. SUMMONSES TO WITNESSES

Chapter	Short title	Extent of repeal
1965 c 69	Criminal Procedure (Attendance of Witnesses) Act 1965	Schedule 1.
1971 c 23	Courts Act 1971	In Schedule 8, paragraph 45(2) and (5).

These repeals have effect in accordance with section 66 of this Act.

8. PRELIMINARY STAGES

Number	Title	Extent of revocation
SI 1987/299	Prosecution of Offences (Custody Time Limits) Regulations 1987	Regulation 5(7).

This revocation has effect in accordance with section 71 of this Act.

9. ALIBI

Chapter	Short title	Extent of repeal
1967 c 80	Criminal Justice Act 1967	Section 11.
1980 c 43	Magistrates' Courts Act 1980	In Schedule 7, paragraph 64.
1987 c 38	Criminal Justice Act 1987	In Schedule 2, paragraph 2.
1994 c 33	Criminal Justice and Public Order Act 1994	In Schedule 4, paragraph 15(3).
		In Schedule 9, paragraphs 6(2) and 7.

These repeals have effect in accordance with section 74 of this Act.

10. COMMITTAL PROCEEDINGS

Chapter	Short title	Extent of repeal
1867 c 35	Criminal Law Amendment Act 1867	Section 6. Section 7.
1972 c 71	Criminal Justice Act 1972	In section 46(1) the following words— "Section 102 of the Magistrates' Courts Act 1980 and"; "which respectively allow"; "committal proceedings and in other"; "and section 106 of the said Act of 1980"; "which punish the making of";

Criminal Procedure and Investigations Act 1996, Sch 5

Chapter	Short title	Extent of repeal
1980 c 43	Magistrates' Courts Act 1980	"102 or"; ", as the case may be". Section 46(2). Section 28. In section 97(1) the words "at an inquiry into an indictable offence by a magistrates' court for that commission area or". Section 102. Section 103(3) and (4). Section 105. In Schedule 7, paragraph 2.
1988 c 33	Criminal Justice Act 1988	In section 32A(10) the words "notwithstanding that the child witness is not called at the committal proceedings". In Schedule 15, paragraph 68.

These repeals have effect in accordance with provision made by the Secretary of State by order under Schedule 1 to this Act.

11. STATEMENTS AND DEPOSITIONS

Chapter	Short title	Extent of repeal
1925 c 86	Criminal Justice Act 1925	Section 13(3).
1965 c 69	Criminal Procedure (Attendance of Witnesses) Act 1965	In Part I of Schedule 2, the entry relating to the Criminal Justice Act 1925.
1967 c 80	Criminal Justice Act 1967	Section 7.
1980 c 43	Magistrates' Courts Act 1980	In Schedule 7, paragraph 63.

These repeals have effect in accordance with provision made by the Secretary of State by order under Schedule 2 to this Act.

12. FRAUD

Chapter	Short title	Extent of repeal
1987 c 38	Criminal Justice Act 1987	In section 7, subsections (3) to (5). In section 9(7), the word "(1)".
1988 c 33	Criminal Justice Act 1988	In Schedule 15, paragraph 114.
1990 c 42	Broadcasting Act 1990	In Schedule 20, paragraph 47.

These repeals have effect in accordance with Schedule 3 to this Act.

Index

Accused
    compulsory disclosure by. *See under* DISCLOSURE
    faults in disclosure by. *See* DISCLOSURE
    voluntary disclosure by. *See* DISCLOSURE

Acquittal
    intimidation, tainted by, 8.2-8.7
    quashing–
        administration of justice offence as ground for, 8.3
        conditions to be satisfied, 8.6
        generally, 8.3
        procedure, 8.5-8.7
        re-trial following, 8.4

Alibi
    court martial, case tried by, 8.33
    disclosure in defence statement, 2.17
    fraud cases, in, 8.33
    notice of, abolition, 8.33
    persons able to support, duty to disclose details of, 2.17

Appeal
    'case management' decision, against, 4.25
    generally, 5.14-5.16
    interlocutory, 4.26, 5.14
    preparatory hearing ruling, against, 4.22-4.26, 5.16

Bail, offences by persons in Scotland, 8.32

Banker's book, copy of entry in, tendered as evidence, 6.29

Child
    committal proceedings–
        statements made by, 6.33
        video-recorded testimony by, 6.43, 8.14

Code of practice
    contents, 3.4, 3.5
    draft code–
        contents, 3.1
        modification, 3.2
        overview of contents, 3.6-3.37
        publication, 3.2

Code of practice—*contd*
    duty to prepare, 1.3, 3.1, 3.4
    effect, 1.4, 3.38-3.40

Committal proceedings
    abolition, 6.3
    admissibility of evidence generally, 6.46
    children's evidence, 6.33, 6.43
    computer evidence, 6.39
    contested committals, 6.4
    copy documents, admissibility, 6.41
    corporate representation at, 6.27
    depositions, 6.13, 6.49
    documentary evidence, admissibility, 6.15
    duress, confession obtained under, 6.37
    evidence, admissible, 6.11
    expert reports, 6.42
    false written statement, offence to tender, 6.26
    generally, 6.28-6.47
    hearsay evidence, 6.40
    limitation of evidence, 6.6
    magistrates' role, 6.6
    microfilm evidence, 6.36
    modification, 6.3, 6.17, 6.18
    new or additional counts, 6.30, 6.44
    oral evidence excluded from, 6.23-6.25
    orders for restitution, 6.32
    previous convictions, evidence of, 6.46
    proof by production of copy, 6.16
    rape offences, 6.35
    road traffic offences, documentary evidence relating to, 6.47
    statements–
        admissibility, 6.14
        written. *See* written statement *below*
    statutory amendments, 6.7-6.10, 6.28-6.47
    summons for, 6.21, 6.22
    switch of mode of hearing procedure, 6.19, 6.20

Index

Committal proceedings—*contd*
  transfer for trial–
    children, affecting, 6.3
    failure of attempt to reform, 6.3
    proposals for reform etc, 6.1-6.3
  uncontested committals, 6.5
  unfair evidence, exclusion, 6.38
  vehicle, evidence as to driver, owner or user, 6.45
  written statement–
    admissibility outside England and Wales, 6.34
    generally, 6.12, 6.49
Confession, duress, obtained under, 6.37
Confidential information
  contravention of confidentiality requirement, 2.32
  generally, 2.31
  unused material, 2.31
Court martial
  alibi evidence, 8.33
  Secretary of State's power to make orders in respect of proceedings before, 8.37
Criminal investigation
  meaning, 3.3
  code of practice. *See* CODE OF PRACTICE
  generally, 3.1-3.3
  supervision, code of practice provisions, 3.7
Criminal Procedure and Investigations Act
  committal provisions, amendments to, 6.7-6.10, 6.28-6.47
  extent, 8.38
  generally, 1.2-1.13
  interpretation, 3.3
  Northern Ireland, modification in relation to, 8.38
  orders and regulations, power to make, 8.36, 8.37
  purpose of Bill, 1.1
Crown Court
  compulsory disclosure by accused, 2.14-2.17
  preparatory hearing in. *See* PREPARATORY HEARING
Custody, time limits, 5.17, 5.18, 8.29, 8.30

Defence statement
  alibi, disclosing, 2.17
  differing from defence, 2.25, 2.26

Defence statement—*contd*
  duty to supply, 2.15
  failure to provide, 2.25
  nature and contents, 2.15
  subsequent disclosure by prosecutor following service of, 3.37
  voluntary disclosure by accused, 2.18
Deposition
  admissibility, 8.26
  committal proceedings, in, 6.13, 6.49
Derogatory assertion
  making, 8.8
  restriction order–
    appeal against, 8.13
    appointed day, offences after, 8.13
    assertion made previously, where, 8.10
    contravention of order, 8.11
    effect, 8.11
    full order, 8.9
    interim order, 8.9
    penalty for contravening, 8.12
    power to make, 8.8
Disclosure
  advance disclosure, 2.14-2.17
  application by accused for, 2.21, 2.22
  appointed day, investigation started on or after, 2.4
  binding ruling as to, application for, 5.19
  common law disclosure rules–
    applicability, 3.41
    non-applicability, 2.4, 3.41
    public interest, disclosure in, 2.5
  compulsory disclosure by accused–
    advance disclosure, 2.14
    alibi evidence, 2.14
    Crown Court, in, 2.14-2.17
    defence statement, of, 2.15
    secondary disclosure by prosecutor, 2.19, 2.20
  compulsory disclosure by prosecutor–
    inadvertent non-disclosure, 2.15
    material undermining prosecution case, 2.15
  confidential information. *See* CONFIDENTIAL INFORMATION
  defence statement. *See* DEFENCE STATEMENT

Index

Disclosure—*contd*
  duty to make, 1.2
  faults in disclosure by accused–
    defence differing from defence statement, 2.25, 2.26
    examples, 2.25
    inferences, right to draw, 2.25-2.27
    sanctions, 2.25
  generally, 2.1
  indictment, trial on, 2.3
  inspection of material deemed to be, 2.9
  intended prosecution witnesses, statements of, 2.8 fn[1]
  intercepted material, 2.11, 2.23
  magistrates' courts, rules affecting, 2.33, 2.34
  more than one accused, 2.7
  non-disclosure, procedure as to, 3.35
  non-sensitive material, schedule of, 2.13
  offence triable either way, 2.2
  persons under the age of 18, 2.2
  potentially non-disclosable material, 3.31
  prosecutor. *See* PROSECUTOR
  public interest, whether in, 2.5, 2.10, 2.11
  relevant material, of, 1.4
  rules of court, 2.33, 2.34
  Runciman Commission recommendations, 2.1
  secondary, by prosecutor, 2.19, 2.20
  sensitive material–
    exemption from disclosure, 3.13
    improvement of procedures, 3.15
    previous practice, 3.14
    schedule of. *See* SENSITIVE SCHEDULE
    See also PUBLIC INTEREST
  'staged approach to', 1.2
  statutory rules, 2.33, 2.34
  summary trial, 2.2
  time limits, 2.12, 2.13, 2.24
  'unused material', 2.1 fn[1]
  voluntary disclosure by accused–
    secondary disclosure by prosecutor, 2.19, 2.20
    summary trial, 2.18

Disclosure officer
  meaning, 3.6
  duties, 3.6, 3.12, 3.13

Evidence
  admissibility, judicial powers, 1.6
  certificate, given by, 6.31
  computer records, 6.39
  disclosure. *See* DISCLOSURE
  duty to collect, 2.6
  hearsay, admissibility, 6.40
  retention of material collected for purpose of prosecuting offenders, 3.5, 3.6, 3.11
  television link, via, 8.14
  vehicle, as to driver, owner or user, 6.45
  video-recording, via, 6.43, 8.14

Fingerprints
  checks against–
    former law, 8.17
    Scotland, in, 8.18
    speculative searches, 8.16

Fraud
  alibi evidence in, 8.33
  preparatory hearing in cases of, 8.31

Information
  recording–
    meaning, 3.3
    code of practice provisions, 3.6, 3.8-3.10

Informer, non-disclosure of identity, 2.5

Intercepted material
  non-disclosure, 2.11, 2.23
  warrant, issue of, 3.5

Investigation, officer in charge of: meaning and duties, 3.6

Investigator
  meaning, 3.6
  duties, 3.6

Justices, indemnification, 8.28
Justices' clerks, indemnification, 8.28
Juveniles, reform of remand procedures, 1.10

Magistrates' court
  adjournment of proceedings, 7.14
  attachment of earnings, 7.22
  either way offences, accused's intention as to plea, 7.4-7.13
  fines, enforcement of payment of, 7.15, 7.16
  generally, 7.1, 7.2
  non-appearance of accused, 7.3

157

Index

Magistrates' court—*contd*
powers of other courts in same petty sessional area, 8.35
procedural reforms generally, 1.9
remand, removal of age restrictions, 7.20, 7.21
remanding the accused, 7.14
rules of court, 2.33, 2.34
summons to witness, 7.17, 7.19
warrant for arrest of witness, 7.18
warrant, issue of, following non-appearance of accused, 7.3

Material, *meaning*, 3.3

Microfilm, evidence by, 6.36

Miscarriage of justice, prevention, duty to disclose information, 2.10

Offence, time of commission, determining, 8.34

Plea and directions hearing
binding rulings–
appeal, rights of, 5.14–5.16
making, 5.11
variation, 5.12
custody time limits, 5.18
generally, 5.5–5.7
reporting restrictions, 5.13
rulings, power to make, 5.8–5.10

Pre-trial review
generally, 5.2
history, nature and problems of, 5.3
Runciman Commission proposals, 5.4

Preparatory hearing
adjournment, 4.11
appeals against rulings, 4.22–4.26, 5.16
'case management' decision, appealing, 4.25
disclosure of evidence, judge ordering, 4.13
fraud cases, 8.31
generally, 4.1–4.4
interlocutory appeals, 4.26
judge's powers, 4.11–4.21
non-compliance with judge's directions etc, 4.18–4.21
power to order, 1.5, 4.7–4.10
procedure for holding, 4.15–4.17
purpose, 4.5, 4.6
reporting restrictions–
generally, 4.27, 4.28
offences, 4.29, 4.30
Scotland, in, 4.30

Preparatory hearing—*contd*
rulings on admissibility of evidence, 4.11
sanctions for non-compliance with judicial requirements, 1.5
scheme of, 1.5
written case statement, judge ordering, 4.11
written notice of objections etc by accused, 4.12
written reply, judge ordering accused to provide, 4.12

Prosecutor
compulsory disclosure by–
inadvertent non-disclosure, 2.15
material undermining prosecution case, 2.15, 2.23
time for, 2.23
continuing duty to disclose, 2.23, 3.37
defence statement, further disclosure following service of, 3.37
non-disclosure of material, procedure as to, 3.35
preparation of material for, 3.12
primary disclosure by, 2.8, 2.9, 2.24
public interest considerations. *See* PUBLIC INTEREST
revelation of material to, 3.6, 3.36
secondary disclosure by, 2.19, 2.20, 2.24, 3.6
statement of case, under no obligation to provide, 2.16
time limits for disclosure–
duty to adhere to, 2.12, 2.13
failure to observe, 2.24
unused materials, non-disclosure, 2.15

Public interest
common law rules, preservation of, 3.13
immunity–
application to court by disclosure officer, 3.17
child witness, material obtained in connection, 3.30
class-based, what may constitute, 3.20
confidence, material given in, 3.23
content-based, 3.18, 3.21
corporate investigations, material relating to, 3.29

Public interest—*contd*
immunity—*contd*
CPS, communications between police and, 3.27
financial investigations, material relating to, 3.29
informers etc, material given by, 3.24
intelligence and security agencies, material received by, 3.22
national security, material relating to, 3.22
no objection taken to evidence, where, 3.32
potentially non-disclosable material, 3.31
prima facie immunity, 3.33
prohibition on amendment of sensitive schedule, 3.19
search warrant, material on which obtained, 3.28
sensitive schedule, placing of material on, 3.16
social services' information regarding children, 3.30
surveillance, location etc of premises used for, 3.25
techniques and methods used by police, material revealing, 3.26
undercover officers etc, material given by, 3.24
material tending to establish innocence of accused, disclosure of, 2.10
miscarriage of justice, disclosure to prevent, 2.10
non-sensitive material, schedule of, 2.13
restrictions on disclosure of information, 2.5, 2.10, 2.11
review of non-disclosure ruling–
generally, 2.29, 2.30
indictment, trial on, 2.29
summary trials, in, 2.28
sensitive material. *See* SENSITIVE SCHEDULE
third party, material originating from, right to be heard on ruling, 2.30

Re-trial, provision for, 1.11, 1.12
Reporting restrictions
imposition, 1.13
penalties, 5.12

Reporting restrictions—*contd*
plea and directions hearing, at, 5.12
preparatory hearing, at. *See* PREPARATORY HEARING
representations against disclosure, making, 5.12
rulings hearing, at, 5.12
Road traffic offence
documentary evidence as to, provision of, 6.47
samples of breath, blood or urine, provision of, 8.15
Rulings
binding–
appeal, rights of, 5.14-5.16
application for, 5.19
generally, 5.11
variation, 5.12
generally, 5.1
plea and directions hearings. *See* PLEA AND DIRECTION HEARING
power to make, 5.8-5.10

Samples
blood, 6.47, 8.15
breath, 6.47, 8.15
material, as, 3.3
urine, 6.47, 8.15
Sensitive material. *See* PUBLIC INTEREST; SENSITIVE SCHEDULE
Sensitive schedule
amendment, prohibition on, 3.19
generally, 3.6, 3.13-3.15
inappropriate material for, 3.34
placing of material on, 3.16
revelation of material to prosecutor, 3.36
Specimen. *See* SAMPLES
Standing Civilian Court, Secretary of State's power to make orders in respect of proceedings before, 8.37
Summary trial
faults in disclosure by accused, 2.27
public interest material, review of non-disclosure ruling, 2.28
voluntary disclosure by accused, 2.18
Supervising ranks, job descriptions, drawing up, 3.7

Time limits
commencement of trials on indictment in Scotland, 8.32

Index

Time limits—*contd*
    custody time limits, 5.17, 5.18, 8.29, 8.30
    disclosure, for, 2.12, 2.13, 2.24

Transfer for trial. *See* COMMITTAL PROCEEDINGS

Video-recording, evidence given via, 6.43, 8.14

Witness
    order, abolition, 8.19
    summons—
        application for, 8.21
        costs, payment where summons rendered ineffective, 8.24
        Crown Court issuing summons of own motion, 8.25

Witness—*contd*
    summons–*contd*
        ineffective, application to have summons rendered, 8.23
        issue in respect of document or thing, 8.22
        power to issue, 8.20

Written statement
    admissibility–
        age restrictions, lowering of, 8.27
        England and Wales, outside, 6.34
        generally, 6.12, 6.49, 8.27